Job Satisfaction

Job Satisfaction

*How People Feel About Their Jobs
and How It Affects
Their Performance*

C. J. Cranny
Patricia Cain Smith

Bowling Green State University

Eugene F. Stone

The University at Albany, State University of New York

Lexington Books

An Imprint of Macmillan, Inc.
NEW YORK
Maxwell Macmillan Canada
TORONTO
Maxwell Macmillan International
NEW YORK • OXFORD • SINGAPORE • SYDNEY

This book is part of the Lexington Books Issues in Organization and Management Series, Arthur P. Brief and Benjamin Schneider, general editors.

Library of Congress Cataloging-in-Publication Data

Job satisfaction : how people feel about their jobs and how it affects
   their performance / [edited by] C. J. Cranny, Patricia Cain Smith,
   Eugene F. Stone.
              p.   cm.
   Includes bibliographical references.
   ISBN 0-669-21289-X
   1. Job satisfaction.   I. Cranny, C. J.   II. Smith, Patricia Cain.
   III. Stone, Eugene F.
   HF5549.5.J63J625   1992
   658.3'14'—dc20   91-44216
                                                          CIP

Lexington Books
An Imprint of Macmillan, Inc.
866 Third Avenue, New York, N. Y. 10022

Maxwell Macmillan Canada, Inc.
1200 Eglinton Avenue East
Suite 200
Don Mills, Ontario M3C 3N1

Macmillan, Inc. is part of the Maxwell Communication
Group of Companies.

Printed in the United States of America

printing number

1 2 3 4 5 6 7 8 9 10

Contents

PART THREE
Consequences of Job Satisfaction

PART FOUR
Job Satisfaction: The Way Forward

Foreword

Job satisfaction has probably received more attention from scholars in the organizational sciences than any other single topic. Scholars have conceptualized it as an independent, a mediating, and a dependent variable, and it has been seen as a panacea for the ills of working people as well as the foundation on which organizations can achieve bottom-line financial effectiveness.

What is job satisfaction? We feel very fortunate to have this book in our series to help provide some answers to the question. Cranny, Stone, and Smith present a series of challenging papers on the past, present, and (possibly) the future of job satisfaction research and theory. They have pulled together an impressive cross-section of scholars working on the topic who provide us with broad overviews of what we do and do not yet know about job satisfaction.

What came as the most pleasant surprise to us—and will, we hope, to readers—is the existence of numerous approaches to thinking about job satisfaction that have not received very much attention. The authors of the chapters in this book have identified new concepts and new procedures for pursuing the study of job satisfaction in new ways and from new vantage points.

It is a pleasure to welcome this volume on job satisfaction to the Series on Organization and Management.

—Benjamin Schneider
Arthur P. Brief

Preface

The depth and variety of approaches presented by the contributors to a conference on job satisfaction led us to collect the presentations in book form. This conference took place at Bowling Green State University in October of 1987. The contributors and most of those who participated were active researchers in the area of job satisfaction or related fields. In preparing their chapters for this book, the contributors updated and enlarged their original presentations with additional data.

These chapters provide not only a wealth of thoughtfully designed empirical research, much of it as yet unpublished, but also page after page of suggestions for further research—research that promises to be both theoretically meaningful and practically useful. The authors have much to say about the nature of job satisfaction, its antecedents and consequences, and the behaviors associated with it.

There are, therefore, at least two main audiences for the book. One comprises those concerned with establishing policy in their organizations, with the view to improving employees' feelings about their jobs and their job-related behavior. This group of readers will include human resource and personnel managers and specialists, general managers of labor-intensive organizations, and other policy makers and planners. The other audience will be researchers, including specialists in research organizations, graduate students, and advanced undergraduates in universities, who specialize in industrial-organizational psychology, social psychology, organizational management or development, human resource management, personnel management, and related fields. The book offers a gold mine of thesis and dissertation topics.

Although the contributors hold different viewpoints, a common theme runs through these chapters. The topic of job satisfaction, they agree, is now "on the cutting edge," as reviewers are wont to put it. This topic is important both because of its bearing on the physical and mental well-being of individual employees and because of its demonstrated implications for job-related behaviors and, hence, for the productivity and profitability of organizations.

Despite this consensus, the papers vary greatly in theoretical approach, in research design, in measures used, and in style. We have made no effort to gloss over these differences; rather, we have attempted to contrast and to highlight them in the brief introductions we have written to each part and in the main introduction to the book. We have assumed that the readers of this volume are too sophisticated to expect ready, canned, universally applicable solutions to their problems and thus will be stimulated by the diversity of approaches to think further for themselves.

In the final chapter, "Agenda for Research and Action," Guion provides an integration of the papers. There he presents, in a lively and stimulating manner, the principal implications, conclusions, and areas calling for research that have been raised in these chapters.

We encourage readers not only to attend to each of the chapters, but also to the introductions to parts, the introduction, and to the agenda. They constitute the mortar that holds the separate presentations together. We hope that considering this book as an assembled whole will prove as intellectually profitable for readers as building it was for the authors and editors.

We want to thank each of the authors for contributing their scholarship, insights, research skills, and clarity of expression to this volume. Further, we thank them for their patience in waiting for all the parts of the edifice to be assembled, for the logistics and mechanical details to be worked out, and for all the second—and third— guesses of their colleagues to be taken into account.

Gratitude is due to the assistants who helped to check the accuracy of the references, especially Heidi VandeKemp, who ran down some difficult sources for one of the authors who was temporarily disabled by a back injury. To the word processing artist, Cindy McNutt, goes a gold medal, awarded for carefulness, attention to detail, adherence to APA format (even when the authors forgot to do so) and, particularly, fortitude in the face of differing modes of input, differing systems, and the differing technical quality of incoming manuscripts.

It is our hope that this book will stimulate further advances in theory and research in the area of job satisfacion.

—C. J. Cranny
Patricia Cain Smith
Eugene F. Stone

Introduction

Job satisfaction is one of the most widely discussed and enthusiastically studied constructs in such related disciplines as industrial-organizational psychology, social psychology, organizational behavior, personnel and human resource management, and organizational management. It is also of pressing and recurring interest to managers in a variety of settings and, of course, to those who work with and for them.

Job satisfaction also plays a central role in the study of behavior at work. For the practitioner, knowledge of the determinants, the consequences, and other correlates of job satisfaction can be vital. Indeed, Roznowski and Hulin, in this volume, claim that, "Once an individual joins an organization, a vector of scores on a well-constructed, validated set of job satisfaction scales becomes the most informative data an organizational psychologist or manager can have." Effective management demands a concern with such questions as: What affects job satisfaction? What interventions are possible and effective? What are the results of changes in job satisfaction? What are the effects of satisfaction on productivity, turnover, absenteeism, goal setting, cooperative behavior, job involvement, and a host of other variables?

The study of the nature and correlates of job satisfaction has implications for theory as well as for policy. As Smith pointed out over thirty years ago, "The study of job satisfaction should be able to contribute to the general psychology of motivation, preferences, and attitudes."*

In view of the broad interest in the topic and of its importance, a conference on job satisfaction was held at Bowling Green State University in October of 1987. Its purpose was to assemble many of the

---

*Smith, P. C. (1957). Some applications of industrial psychology to general problems of human motivation. [Abstract] *Proceedings of the 15th International Congress of Psychology* (pp. 354–356). Amsterdam: North-Holland Publishing Company.

most influential and authoritative researchers and scholars of the topic to address the current "state of the art" in job satisfaction theory and research. The conference was quite successful, but many felt that the rather short time allowed for preparation, the very short time available for the presentations, and the limited size of the audience reduced the impact of the effort. Consequently, many of the presenters were eager to expand upon their ideas. This volume is the result. We believe that it not only meets the original goal of presenting the present state of thinking and research in the area of job satisfaction and related constructs, but also presents a number of new or revised models, and points the way to future advances in both theory and application.

The organization of the book is based on a construct validity approach to the consideration of job satisfaction. Thus, the successive parts deal in turn with the nature of the construct, its antecedents, and its theoretical and empirical consequences and correlates. This organization, although necessarily arbitrary, seems to us to reflect major themes arising from the conference and requiring elaboration here. The distinction made between antecedents and consequences is even more arbitrary, since little work has been done in this area with causal models (the James and James chapter is a notable exception); most of the research cited is correlational. In the final chapter of the volume, Guion deals with the problems associated with this distinction.

Other major themes that surfaced throughout the conference (and, we think, are clearly evident in the different sections of the book) are, first, pervasive concern with rigorous and appropriate methodology, and, second, insistence on a firm theoretical grounding for research. Other themes are highlighted by Guion in his concluding chapter, where his emphasis on the relationship between theory and managerial action is particularly notable. His four-part agenda contributes greatly to the coherence of this volume.

The first item, his "housecleaning" agenda, involves reorganizing cabinets and drawers to throw out useless words and concepts, group similar ones together, and clean the dust, crumbs, and cobwebs from around them. Next, placing job satisfaction in context involves considering antecedents and consequents and their somewhat blurred intersection. By making the necessary distinction between dissatisfaction and stress, it is hoped that the differences in their correlates will be clarified. Guion's third item, the methodological agenda, as usual, draws the interest of industrial-organizational psychologists, who are dedicated to the proposition that clean measurement precedes clear research and justifiable application. This stance pervades the entire book, perhaps more than any other theme or agenda. The last agenda, theory and management action, points to the trite phrase, "the bottom line." Many of the chapters are so tightly reasoned and concisely written that practitioners are well advised to read slowly, carefully—and twice. The potential payoff from "listening to the leaders" is great.

The notion of dealing with sets of behaviors, which involves the substitutability of specific variables, is explicitly addressed by Roznowski and Hulin and by Locke and Fisher and noted by Smith. This notion is also implied by the chapters in the part discussing antecedents, as well.

Not only may satisfaction (or dissatisfaction) be exhibited in any one or more behaviors, but also satisfaction (or dissatisfaction) has causes that are numerous and complex. Seeking one-to-one correspondences may lead to incomplete models and unimpressive results from managerial actions. At least five new models, including causal models (and one that involves no boxes, circles, or arrows!), are presented here. A theme common to many of the models and chapters is concern with behavioral taxonomies and the methodological difficulties involved in their creation.

We can find no evidence here of emphasis merely on the triumphs of the past. Nor is there any hint that job satisfaction is a stagnant area or one in which little of interest is left to learn. Instead, the picture is of a vital and growing area of research, with ties to other concepts and areas. It is clear that these authors are engaged in an important and central area in the psychology of work behavior. Their work is replete with exciting implications for both research and policy.

We hope that this book will help achieve some of the agenda explicated by Guion in his chapter. It should help to clarify and refine concepts, move toward a broader and more systematic understanding of the job satisfaction construct and its place in wider theoretical frameworks, and to identify directions for research and innovative applications. It may even make a contribution to improving the quality of life for all of us who work.

PART ONE

The Construct
of Job Satisfaction

The two chapters in this section are concerned with the construct of job satisfaction. Over the years, social science theorists and researchers in such fields as industrial and organizational psychology, organizational behavior, vocational psychology, organizational sociology, and human resources management have devoted a great deal of attention to this construct. Indicative of this, Locke (1976) estimated that, as of 1976, about 3,350 articles or dissertations had been written on the topic. Were a count of relevant articles and dissertations made today there would undoubtedly be more than 5,000 such works.

A sizable number of articles, dissertations, and books in the job satisfaction literature have been devoted primarily or secondarily to developing appropriate constitutive (that is, conceptual) and operational definitions of the job satisfaction construct, including overall or general job satisfaction and satisfaction with such facets of jobs as the work itself, coworkers, supervision, pay, working conditions, company policies and procedures, and opportunities for promotion. A sample of the measures that have resulted from this work are presented in books by Cook, Hepworth, Wall, and Warr (1981) and Robinson, Athanasiou, and Head (1969). As a review of these works clearly shows, considerable progress has been made in developing psychometrically sound and useful measures not only of overall job satisfaction, but also of satisfaction with specific job facets.

Considerable progress has also been made in defining the job satisfaction construct (see Herzberg, Mausner, Peterson, & Capwell, 1957; Locke, 1969, 1976). Although a review of published works shows that constitutive definitions of the construct vary somewhat from one work to the next, there appears to be general agreement that job satisfaction is an affective (that is, emotional) reaction to a job that results from the incumbent's comparison of actual outcomes with those that are desired (expected, deserved, and so on). Some definitions of the construct that are consistent with this view are as follows: Lofquist and Dawis (1969) noted that satisfaction is "a function of the correspondence between the reinforcer system of the work environment and the individual's needs" (p. 53); Locke (1976) stated that job satisfaction can be viewed as "*a pleasurable or positive emotional state resulting from the appraisal of one's job or job experiences*" (p. 1300); Locke and Henne (1986) wrote that "the achievement of one's job values in the work situation results in the pleasurable emotional state known as *job satisfaction*" (p. 21); and Porter, Lawler, and Hackman (1975) characterized satisfaction as a feeling about a job that "is determined by the difference between the amount of some valued outcome that a person receives and the amount of the outcome he feels he *should* receive" (pp. 53–54). These definitions are all consistent with related conceptions of satisfaction that can be found in the literature of other fields (for example, social psychology). For instance, Thibaut and Kelley (1959) noted that an individual is satisfied with a relationship and attracted to it to the extent that the actual outcomes exceed the level of outcomes that he or she feels are deserved (that is, the individual's comparison level). The current seemingly high level of agreement among social scientists as to the meaning of the construct of job satisfaction is the result of many decades of effort by psychologists, sociologists, psychiatrists, and other professionals.

Among the most commonly used measures of job satisfaction is the Job Descriptive Index (Smith, Kendall, & Hulin, 1969). In chapter 1, Patricia Cain Smith, a key figure in the development of this instrument, considers the importance of measuring general or overall job satisfaction. She views general job satisfaction to be a function of a variety of features of the work environment. In addition, she argues that this attitude is a critical determinant of a number of important outcomes, one of which is the way workers respond to management-backed changes in jobs or other features of the work environment. Although such changes are likely to have a greater immediate impact on various facets of satisfaction than on general satisfaction, eventually their cumulative effects will be reflected in general satisfaction. Moreover, she reasons that general satisfaction will influence the way in which workers subsequently evaluate specific aspects of their jobs or the work environment (for example, satisfaction with pay, working conditions, and supervision). Consistent with her continuing interest in the job satisfaction construct, Smith and her colleagues have recently developed a measure of overall satisfaction (Ironson, Smith, Brannick, Gibson, & Paul, 1989) that can be used to address the research questions presented in her chapter.

As noted above, a review of the relevant literature clearly demonstrates that many social scientists have devoted considerable effort to the development of sound constitutive and operational definitions of job satisfaction. In spite of this, the legitimacy of the job satisfaction construct and the need-satisfaction framework or model on which it is predicated have been harshly criticized by advocates of the social information processing (SIP) approach to job characteristics, job attitudes, and job behaviors. In chapter 2, Eugene Stone assesses the validity of a host of criticisms that proponents of the SIP approach have made of the theory and research associated with need satisfaction models. He asserts that most such criticisms have arisen because the SIP advocates have either: (a) made erroneous assumptions about the need satisfaction model, or (b) had a low level of familiarity with current model-related theory and research on need satisfaction. Moreover, he cites a number of threats to the validity of the research that has been used to argue for the legitimacy of the SIP approach. As a consequence, and in opposition to what has been advocated by SIP supporters, Stone's analysis leads him to conclude that there is no sound basis for either stopping work on the need-satisfaction model or for the SIP model supplanting the need-satisfaction model.

References

Cook, J. D., Hepworth, S. J., Wall, T. D., & Warr, P. B. (1981). *The experience of work*. London: Academic Press.

Herzberg, F., Mausner, B., Peterson, R. O., & Capwell, D. F. (1957). *Job attitudes: Review of research and opinions*. Pittsburgh: Psychological Service of Pittsburgh.

Ironson, G. H., Smith, P. C., Brannick, M. T., Gibson, W. M., & Paul, K. B. (1989). Construction of a job in general scale: A comparison of global, composite, and specific measures. *Journal of Applied Psychology, 74,* 193–200.

Locke, E. A. (1969). What is job satisfaction? *Organizational Behavior and Human Performance, 4,* 309–336.

Locke, E. A. (1976). The nature and causes of job satisfaction. In M. D. Dunnette (Ed.), *Handbook of industrial and organizational psychology* (pp. 1297–1349). Chicago: Rand McNally.

Locke, E. A., & Henne, D. (1986). Work motivation theories. In C. L. Cooper & I. Robertson (Eds.), *International review of industrial and organizational psychology* (pp. 1–35). London: Wiley.

Lofquist, L. H., & Dawis, R. V. (1969). *Adjustment to work: A psychological view of man's problems in a work-oriented society*. New York: Appleton-Century-Crofts.

Porter, L. W., Lawler, E. E., & Hackman, J. R. (1975). *Behavior in organizations*. New York: McGraw-Hill.

Robinson, J. P., Athanasiou, R., & Head, K. B. (1969). *Measures of occupational attitudes and occupational characteristics*. Ann Arbor, MI: Institute for Social Research.

Smith, P. C., Kendall, L. M., & Hulin, C. L. (1969). *The measurement of satisfaction in work and retirement*. Chicago: Rand McNally.

Thibaut, J. W., & Kelley, H. H. (1959). *The social psychology of groups*. New York: Wiley.

In Pursuit of Happiness

Why Study General Job Satisfaction?

PATRICIA CAIN SMITH

General job satisfaction is an important part of a system of interrelated satisfactions, analogous to a river with small tributaries converging into ever-larger branches and eventually into a lake or sea. Satisfactions with specific aspects of a job situation cause satisfaction with facets of the job, with the job in general, and eventually with life. In this analogy, the specific leads to the general.

But the analogy breaks down because specific satisfactions are also consequences of general satisfactions. Moreover, general satisfaction may be a quasi moderator of the relationship between aspects of a situation and a person's reactions to it.

General job satisfaction involves components not caused by the immediate job situation. One is temperamental; I call it happiness. Another is trust in management. Both can act as causes, effects, or quasi moderators, and each is likely to be related to cooperative and adaptive behavior. Since neither can be changed easily by manage-

Throughout this chapter the first-person plural is used to refer to the JDI research team. The initial membership, at Cornell University in 1959, was Patricia Cain Smith, Lorne Kendall, Chuck Hulin, and Ed Locke; it continued unbroken, but with changing membership, first at Cornell and later at Bowling Green (with a branch at South Florida) and involved at least twenty-five graduate and postdoctoral students. Bill Balzer has played a major role in recent years as codirector.

Inquires should be directed to Smith, Sandman, and McCreery, P. O. Box 931, Perrysburg, OH 43551-0931.

ment, both should be measured and the extent of their influences estimated. A data set is described on which some of these interrelationships can be explored.

Organizations measure job satisfaction primarily because of its presumed direct relationship to the short-term goals of cost reduction through increased individual productivity and reduced absences, errors, turnover, and so on. Long-term improvements in employee adjustment and health or contributions to scientific understanding are regarded as mere spinoffs, useful principally in public relations releases. When management discovers that there is no guarantee of a one-to-one correlation between individual satisfaction and individual productivity, interest usually wanes.

In the current period of economic and technological change, however, I propose that management should reconsider the economic value of satisfaction and seek to understand its components. In this era of takeovers, shifts toward a service economy, changing tasks, and downsizing, managers would be wise to think about the kind of organization they want after the transition is completed. Perhaps it makes no sense to some managers to worry about the satisfaction of employees who are about to be retired or discharged, but if the organization is to survive, the nature of the remaining work force becomes crucial.

The employees of the future will need to be adaptable, cooperative, and willing to accept change; they must work together productively. We have evidence that such people are likely to be satisfied with their jobs and with their lives. I have chosen the general term happiness, or *H,* to describe this characteristic. Furthermore, adaptable people are likely also to trust the management of their organization, a characteristic I call trust or *T.* My choice of vague words is deliberate. Both *H* and *T* need further study before the concepts can be clarified, even though recent work has revived interest in affectivity, disposition, citizenship, mood, and other concepts related to temperament, or to *H* (see Bateman & Organ, 1983; Brief, Burke, George, Robinson, & Webster, 1988; George, 1989; Organ, 1988; Organ & Near, 1985; Pulakos & Schmitt, 1983; Schmitt & Pulakos, 1985; Schmitt & Schneider, 1983; Schneider, 1976; Staw, 1984; Staw & Ross, 1985; Tellegen, 1985, for examples). Arvey, Bouchard, Segal, & Abraham (1989) have cited evidence from studies of twins that some aspects of this component are in part genetically determined. I consider both H and T to be important as consequences of a job situation, as causes of subsequent reactions to it, and as influences on the way in which employees react to changes.

General Satisfactions and Behaviors as Results of the Situation

General feelings such as H and T seem to be hard to change. It is much easier to alter various aspects of a job situation and the feelings about them. For example, management may approve changes in job design to improve satisfaction with the task characteristics, or introduce training to improve supervisors' interpersonal skills. We would hope for such immediate outcomes as increased satisfaction with these particular areas, and with the more general aspects or facets of the job, such as the work itself or supervision.

Changes are usually introduced in the hope that improvements in facet satisfaction will in turn affect broader areas of employee satisfaction and eventually improve behavior and reduce costs. For example, job enrichment may lead to reduced turnover and substantial cost savings.

We concentrated our first efforts at measuring satisfaction upon five fairly specific facets, which represent a compromise between the very specific and the very general. We developed and recently revised the JDI, or Job Descriptive Index, which covers five principal facets: work, pay, promotions, supervision, and coworkers (Smith, Kendall, & Hulin, 1969, 1985). This index has proved reliable and valid, and is very widely used.

Such facet scales have helped to target the kinds of changes needed in particular situations and to evaluate the success of interventions designed to improve satisfaction. The scales also permit an ongoing quality control over the effectiveness of procedures involving employees.

Because management usually conceptualizes cause and effect as moving in one direction, we tend to discuss the effects of changes in the situation in the same sequential manner. The picture we present resembles the path of a major river system (See figure 1–1.), in which rain falls on the terrain throughout the river basin and dissolves particles of soil and rock, a process that corresponds to the actual events

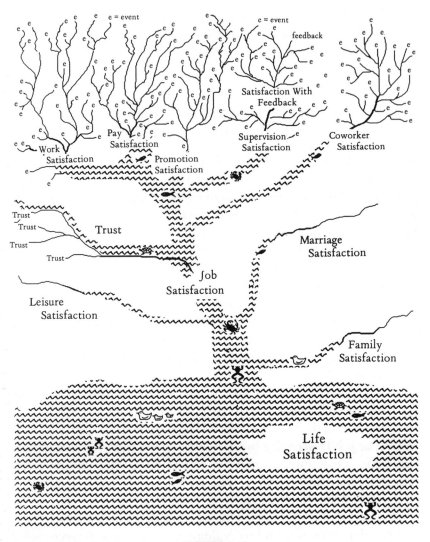

FIGURE 1–1

The River of Satisfaction

The flow from events at work
through facet satisfactions to general
job satisfaction and life satisfaction

(e) the person experiences. Small rivulets collect into creeks—such as satisfaction with feedback—and then the creeks combine to form small rivers—such as supervisory consideration—until we have tributary streams comparable to the facets of job satisfaction: work, pay, promotion, supervision, and coworkers. (We chose to construct the JDI scales at this level of generality.) These tributaries in turn combine to form a major river—general job satisfaction. General job satisfaction is one of the components of life satisfaction. Together with satisfactions with marriage, family, leisure, and other nonwork satisfactions, it makes up the effluent into the gulf of life satisfaction.

This analogy is useful in several ways. Of course, it captures direct effects of policy. Increased pay usually is followed by an increase in pay satisfaction, a clarification of promotion policy by a change in promotion satisfaction, and so on. The river analogy implies that the process takes time; thus the behavioral consequences of improvements may be delayed. The effects of different changes mix together completely as they combine to form more general feelings. The particular behaviors of an individual will thus not necessarily show an obvious logical connection to their antecedents. The unfair act of a supervisor, for example, may decrease satisfactions and eventually be reflected in absence, errors, or even failure to cooperate with another employee. Further investigation is needed on these implications.

General Satisfactions as Causes of Subsequent Satisfactions and Behaviors

The unidirectional picture of the river ignores the well-established observation that a person brings to the job each day general feelings that are related to how he or she will react to what happens. A little of my own personal intellectual history may be in order at this point. I first became interested in general satisfactions when I chose a topic for my doctoral dissertation. The reports of the British Industrial Fatigue and Health Research Boards (Wyatt, Fraser, & Stock, 1929; Wyatt, Langdon, & Stock, 1938) had indicated that there were individual differences in susceptibility to industrial monotony. I thought that these findings needed clarification and amplification.

First I tried to "validate" workers' reports of boredom by correlating the reports with slumps in output. I watched and made complete records of the behavior of each of a number of machine operators throughout every working day for an entire week. Production did indeed change during the day, but the changes were related to the person's self-set goals for the day, not to her subjective feelings. On the other hand, positive attitudes toward the job were reflected in small acts of helpfulness and even in cleaning up the work area. Negative feelings were accompanied by minor acts of sabotage and cheating on the time clock. I learned that, although there is no simple relationship between a particular attitude and a particular behavior, people are likely to express attitudes in some way. This expression has been frequently noted. Only by knowledge of the behavioral alternatives available can we guess what behaviors will appear. I learned further that verbal reports do not have to be validated against behavior—they are valid in their own right (Cain, 1942; Smith, 1953).

I tested my hypotheses concerning individual differences in susceptibility to monotony by a correlational study on a larger sample (Smith, 1955). The principal results have since been replicated and extended. Satisfactions with home life, with personal life, and with other aspects of the job are correlated, and reports of boredom are closely related to all three. The idea that general nonwork satisfactions cause satisfaction and behavior at work has been around for a long time and still remains, although the direction of causation has not been proven. (See, for example, Pulakos & Schmitt, 1983; Schmitt & Pulakos, 1985.)

There is strong evidence for a general factor in satisfaction measures, and different measures of satisfaction are almost always positively correlated. A second-order general factor or common underlying continuum emerges from analyses. Everyday observations, moreover, suggest that a general temperamental or personality characteristic distinguishes the employees who are generally optimistic and cheerful from the chronic grouches, doomsayers, and complainers.

For a long time, we regarded H largely as an unwanted and uncontrolled source of variance in research. Then an article by Weitz (1952) on a "neglected concept of job satisfaction" intrigued us. He had devised a scale for measuring satisfaction with a large number of very specific aspects of everyday nonwork life. People rated their satisfaction with such items as "The high school you attended," "Our foreign policy," "Radio programs," "Restaurant food," and "8½ × 11 paper." He intended to use the scores as a base line to correct for his subjects' overall rating tendency, so that job satisfaction scales would measure only feelings associated with the job and not those arising from individual personality characteristics. The idea was later abandoned when it turned out that using the correction actually reduced the correlation between satisfaction and turnover.

I see now that it was mistaken to give up the attempt. Weitz had measured that portion of job satisfaction I call *H,* and had concluded that it should remain in the measures because it was correlated with turnover. Indeed, it should be included if the goal is to predict turnover. But this factor should be regarded as unwanted variance if the goal is to estimate **how much of individual differences in job satisfaction could be eliminated by management actions.** The overall mean score across individuals might be increased, but relative positions would remain the same to the extent that they are associated with *H*. The inclusion of *H* in a job satisfaction measure might actually displace the wanted variance. Figure 1–2 illustrates the situation. An event may change the job-related part of a measure of job satisfaction (Sj), but not the non-job-related happiness part (Hn). Only the job-related satisfaction would affect turnover (Tj), despite the correlation between non-job happiness (Hn) and non-job-related turnover (Tn).

Thus, if we are contemplating an expensive intervention, we need to know how much change in satisfaction is possible at each level of specificity. If most of the differences among individuals on a measure are attributable to non-job factors, we may still expect to raise the average somewhat, but we cannot expect to raise the scores of the lowest-scoring persons to the level of the higher-scoring ones. We

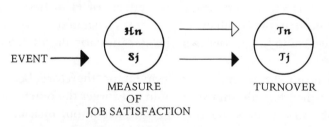

MEASURE
OF
JOB SATISFACTION TURNOVER

Hn = Happiness not related to job events.
Sj = Job satisfaction related to job events.
Tn = Turnover related to happiness, but not to job events.
Tj = Turnover related to job events, but not to happiness.

FIGURE 1–2

Effects of Job Events upon Job-Related and Non-Job-Related Satisfactions and Turnover

cannot use a low mean score to justify the proposed intervention. If, however, the variability is related to situational characteristics, we can hope the intervention will be effective in reducing the percentage of discontented persons.

For a long time we shelved the idea of partialling out H. Nevertheless, we continued to need to measure general satisfactions as consequences—near the mouth of the river—because they were more closely related to intentions to behave than more specific measures, covered areas not covered by the facets, and had theoretical implications. Recently Gail Ironson and I, and our students, constructed a reliable Job in General scale (JIG) (Ironson, Smith, Brannick, Gibson, & Paul, 1989). Since job satisfaction contributes to life satisfaction, we constructed an even more general measure, the Survey of Life Satisfaction (SOLS) (Ironson & Smith, 1978).

We had not forgotten what I had first learned in my dissertation. General satisfactions are not only effects, but also causes of other satisfactions and behaviors. The river analogy breaks down here. The relationships associated with satisfaction are not analogous to the sun distilling the water from the river before releasing it as rain. Instead, a gigantic waterspout sucks the water upward, complete with sewage, toxic spills, fish, algae, and so on. This mixture from the entire river basin is dumped on the land and recycled through the system, thereby eroding the land again. H is a component of all the water in the system. Both individual and situational factors must be included in any conceptualization.

If we were to include the causal effects of H in figure 1–1, we would need arrows from every part of the system to every other. Indeed, we could find evidence in the literature for almost any connection.

Measuring the general satisfaction factor, therefore, becomes important theoretically. But we should not forget the potential usefulness of knowing how much of the variance in our measures can be readily changed by our actions versus how much is either individually determined (H) or is very slow-moving (T). T is relatively easily measured; H may be measured by a modernized Weitz (1952) questionnaire, by some general life satisfaction scale such as SOLS (Ironson & Smith, 1978), or by the Life Orientation Test (LOT) (Scheier & Carver, 1985).

The way these components affect different measures is not at all clear. Moreover, the schematic picture in figure 1–1 omits many factors such as alternatives available for comparison and for job choice, interests, expectations, values, and reactions to stress (see Sandman, chapter 10 in this volume). The picture is not, therefore, a complete model of job satisfaction.

General Satisfactions as Moderators of Satisfactions and Behaviors

The simple river analogy fails even further when we consider that general satisfaction may alter a person's reactions to a situation (a polluted stream will kill the fish). We hypothesize what Stone (1988) terms a quasi moderator. The happy person not only tends to be more satisfied with everything, including his or her experiences and behavior, but also views events differently. According to this admittedly crude concept of personality, the happy person tends to be optimistic and hence to facilitate change. The main effect and this interaction are schematized in figure 1–3 as a comparison of happy with unhappy subgroups. Changes intended to improve the job situation may increase satisfaction for the happy group, while having a small or even negative effect on the unhappy group, who may see the change as reflecting on their competence or as an attempt to manipulate them.

To the network of the already-confused figure 1–1, we would

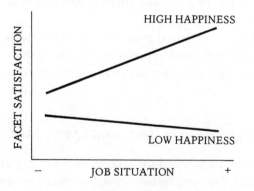

FIGURE 1–3

Hypothesized Influence of General Happiness (H) on the Relations between the Favorableness of the Job Situation and Satisfaction with a Facet of the Job

have to draw arrows intersecting the connections between each situation and the satisfaction with it, between that satisfaction and the next more general stage, and so forth throughout the system. We need to find out where such interactions actually matter, and how much they matter. Fortunately, we already have data to check both the direct and moderating effects of general satisfaction. We have three possible times to administer a set of measures—before an intervention, during it, and later. When we complete the matching of individuals, we can estimate what happens over time and whether general satisfactions affect the extent of improvement. We included in our battery measures of perceived job characteristics (JCI) (Sims, Szilagyi, & Keller, 1976) the five facets of the JDI, the JIG scale (Ironson, Smith, et al., 1989), the SOLS (Ironson & Smith, 1978), and Intent to Leave (modified and extended from Mobley, Horner, & Hollingsworth, 1978).

As usual, all of the satisfaction measures proved to be positively correlated at each time they were studied. Above the top of our picture (figure 1–1), indicating the power of the waterspout, are very strong relationships between the job in general and perceived job characteristics. Off the bottom of the schematic view are even stronger relationships between the job in general and the intent to quit. Since intent to quit is correlated with turnover, as are satisfactions, we can hypothesize a common stream running through all of these measures. In addition to these correlations, we hypothesize interactions, despite the generally small moderator effects reported in the literature.

Our hypotheses are based primarily on repeated observations in field situations. Until these hypotheses have been shown to be untenable we have to include a number of dams and diverting dikes in the system.

Trust as Cause, Effect, and Quasi Moderator

So far we have not discussed the second major but neglected component of general job satisfaction: trust in management, or T. Although highly correlated with H, it is disinguishable from it. T may even run downstream for a time as a distinctive aspect of the stream, just as glacial water does not immediately mix with other components in a larger stream.

Psychologists have considered trust primarily as an effect, or outcome variable, resulting from events in the job situation, but it may also serve as a direct cause, being caught up in the same huge waterspout. Here, however, I want to call attention to its importance in affecting the relationship between actual conditions and employees' reactions to them. When I first began consulting full time, I worked in a single industry. I saw many plants with closely similar jobs and objective conditions. Nevertheless, in some plants the employees quickly adapted to changes and accepted management's statements at face value; in others, they were extremely suspicious of almost anything management suggested or did. In one plant where mistrust was particularly pervasive, I felt obliged to point out to the client that my consulting services would be a waste of money because it would be impractical even to try to change the atmosphere.

Although the term "moderator" was not yet in use, it is now clear that I was considering trust as a powerful moderator in the relationship between policy and either satisfaction or behavior. The trusting person views a change in the job situation as an attempt to improve the situation, while the mistrusting person perceives either managerial incompetence or an attempt to get more work for less money. The interaction effect would look much like that in figure 1–3, except that the lines would represent high and low trust. I would predict, moreover, that the slopes would be even steeper, with high levels of trust facilitating the intended effect of any management intervention and low levels even reversing the direction of the effect substantially. To return to figure 1–1, we need to add another series of dams cutting the flow between each tributary and the larger stream.

Fortunately, we have data that may permit a limited check on the importance of the main effect of T and its possible moderating influence. We already have evidence that trust is substantially related to acceptance of job changes at any one of our three times of administration—that is, a very high correlation exists between a Trust in Management scale (modified from Cook & Wall, 1980) and an Index of Acceptance of Job Changes (Patchen, Pelz, & Allen, 1965). Next we will test whether persons with initially high trust scores show greater increases in satisfaction after our intervention than do those with low initial scores (despite ceiling effects).

I now think that trust can be changed, if only slowly. The first step, of course, is for management to act competently and ethically, and to make this behavior evident. But attempts to improve may be more effective if relatively small changes are spaced judiciously than if they are combined and presented at one time. The areas for action should probably correspond to those facets with the lowest levels of satisfaction. Announcements of policy need to be integrated with appropriate actions in a planned manner. We need to research practical approaches to what may be a truly crucial variable.

Implications for the Future

I shall follow a time-honored tradition by calling for further research on important problems. Some of this research may start with case studies and observations to help form the framework for more controlled studies of specific questions.

It is easy to make a list of areas that need investigation and of applications that should be tried. A few examples may be:

1. Can we measure the cooperative behavior we are seeking? Can we separate it from the bias and prejudice of the rater or observer? Can we translate it into monetary terms, as we have for production, absences, turnover, and so on?
2. Which components of general satisfaction can be most readily modified, and how?
3. Will measuring aspects of general satisfaction such as trust and happiness actually improve our ability to predict the extent of change that will follow an intervention?
4. Will such measurement increase our accuracy in tracking the changes through time?
5. Which, if any, interventions are followed by significant improvements in trust? If trust can be improved, is it changed more rapidly using some schedules of intervention than using others?
6. Does H actually moderate the relationship between measured aspects of the situation and perceptions of it? (figure 1–1) Between perceptions and facet satisfactions? Between facet and general job satisfaction? Between general

job satisfaction and intentions? Between intentions and actions?

7. Does *T* moderate these relationships?
8. More generally, where do *H* and *T* fit into the complex pattern of relationships between the job situation, the person, and his or her adjustment? Could more sophisticated personality dimensions serve better than *H* and *T*? Where do values, interests, expectations, and so on, fit in? How are *H* and *T* related to stress and stressors? To alternatives available or potential?
9. Do any of the satisfaction measures differentially predict which negative behaviors will appear with low satisfaction or which positive behaviors will appear with high satisfaction?

Greater understanding of general satisfaction becomes more important when organizations are facing rapid change. Of course, if management plans to accept a takeover bid or to shut down operations, it can ruthlessly decide that satisfactions make no difference. But most managements feel some responsibility toward their employees. They want them to be as happy as is reasonably possible, whether on or off the job. And, if they hope to maintain their organizations, they want their employees to be cooperative, constructive, and open to innovations. It then makes economic sense—while conforming to humanitarian values—to consider whether trust and happiness can be improved by administrative action and, if so, how.

References

Arvey, R. D., Bouchard, T. J., Jr., Segal, N. L., & Abraham, L. M. (1989). Job satisfaction: Environmental and genetic components. *Journal of Applied Psychology, 74,* 187–192.

Bateman, T. S., & Organ, D. E. (1983). Job satisfaction and the good soldier: The relationship between affect and employee "citizenship." *Academy of Management Journal, 26,* 587–595.

Brayfield, A. H., & Rothe, H. F. (1951). An index of job satisfaction. *Journal of Applied Psychology, 35,* 307–311.

Brief, A. P., Burke, M. J., George, J. M., Robinson, B., & Webster, J. (1988). Should negative affectivity remain an unmeasured variable in the study of job stress? *Journal of Applied Psychology, 73,* 193–198.

Cain, P. A. (1942). *Individual differences in susceptibility to monotony.* Unpublished doctoral dissertation, Cornell University, Ithaca, NY.

Cook, J. M., & Wall, T. D. (1980). New work attitude measures of trust, organizational commitment, and personal need non-fulfillment. *Journal of Occupational Psychology, 53,* 39–52.

George, J. M. (1989). Mood and absence. *Journal of Applied Psychology, 74,* 317–324.

Ironson, G. H., & Smith, P. C. (1978). *The Survey of Life Satisfaction (SOLS).* Bowling Green State University, Department of Psychology, Bowling Green, OH 43403.

Ironson, G. H., Smith, P. C. (1987). *The Stress in General scale (SIG).* Smith, Sandman, & McCreery, P. O. Box 931, Perrysburg, OH 43551.

Ironson, G. H., Smith, P. C., Brannick, M. T., Gibson, W. M., & Paul, K. B. (1989). Construction of a "Job in General" scale: A comparison of global, composite, and specific measures. *Journal of Applied Psychology, 74,* 193–200.

Mobley, W. H., Horner, S. O., Hollingsworth, A. T. (1978). An evaluation of precursors of hospital employee turnover. *Journal of Applied Psychology, 63,* 408–414.

Organ, D. (1988). *Organizational citizenship behavior. The good soldier syndrome.* Indianapolis, IN: Lexington.

Organ, D., & Near, J. P. (1985). Cognition vs. affect in measures of job satisfaction. *International Journal of Psychology, 20,* 241–253.

Patchen, M., Pelz, D., & Allen, C. (1965). *Some questionnaire measures of employee motivation and morale.* Ann Arbor, MI: Institute for Social Research.

Pulakos, E. D., & Schmitt, N. (1983). A longitudinal study of a valence model approach for the prediction of job satisfaction of new employees. *Journal of Applied Psychology, 68,* 307–312.

Scheier, M. F., & Carver, C. S. (1985). Optimism, coping, and health: Assessment and implications of generalized outcome expectancies. *Health Psychology, 4,* 219–247.

Schmitt, N., & Pulakos, E. D. (1985). Predicting job satisfaction from life satisfaction: Is there a general satisfaction factor? *International Journal of Psychology, 29,* 155–167.

Schmitt, N., & Schneider, B. (1983). Current issues in personnel selection. In K. M. Rowland & J. Ferris (Eds.), *Research in personnel and human resources management.* Vol. 1 (pp. 85–125). Greenwich, CT: JAI Press.

Schneider, B. (1976). *Staffing organizations.* Santa Monica, CA: Goodyear.

Sims, H. P., Szilagyi, A. D., & Keller, R. T. (1976). The measurement of job characteristics. *Academy of Management Journal, 19,* 195–212.

Smith, P. C. (1953). The curve of output as a criterion of boredom. *Journal of Applied Psychology, 37,* 69–74.

Smith, P. C. (1955). The prediction of individual differences in susceptibility to industrial monotony. *Journal of Applied Psychology, 39,* 322–329.

Smith, P. C., Kendall, L. M., & Hulin, C. L. (1969). *The measurement of satisfaction in work and retirement.* Chicago: Rand McNally.

Smith, P. C., Kendall, L. M., & Hulin, C. L. (1985). *The Revised Job Descriptive Index*. Bowling Green, OH: Department of Psychology, Bowling Green State University.

Staw, B. M. (1984). Organizational behavior. *Annual Review of Psychology, 35,* 627–666.

Staw, B. M., & Ross, J. V. (1985). Stability in the midst of change: A dispositional approach. *Journal of Applied Psychology, 70,* 469–480.

Stone, E. F. (1988). Moderator variables in research: A review and analysis of conceptual and moderator variables. In K. M. Rowland & G. R. Ferris (Eds.), *Research in personnel and human resources management.* Vol. 6 (pp. 191–229). Greenwich, CT: JAI Press.

Tellegen, A. (1985). Structures of mood and personality and their relevance to assessing anxiety, with an emphasis on self-report. In A. H. Tuma & J. D. Maser (Eds.), *Anxiety and the anxiety disorders* (pp. 681–706). Hillsdale, NJ: Erlbaum.

Weitz, J. (1952). A neglected concept in the study of job satisfaction. *Personnel Psychology, 5,* 201–205.

Wyatt, S., Fraser, J. A., & Stock, F. G. L. (1929). *The effects of monotony in work.* (Report No. 56.) London: Industrial Fatigue Research Board.

Wyatt, S., Langdon, J. N., & Stock, F. G. L. (1938). *Fatigue and boredom in repetitive work.* (Report No. 77.) London: Industrial Health Research Board.

A Critical Analysis of Social Information Processing Models of Job Perceptions and Job Attitudes

EUGENE F. STONE

Empirical studies dealing with relationships between job character-istics, job attitudes, and numerous other types of criterion variables (for example, absenteeism, turnover, worker health) are numerous. In addition, literature relevant to these topics has been reviewed sev-eral times (for example, Locke, 1976). As a result, no attempt is made here to present a comprehensive review of this literature. It de-serves noting, however, that previous reviews of both the narrative and quantitative literature show consistent support in laboratory and field settings for relationships between job characteristics, job attitudes (for example, satisfaction), and several other variables (Stone, 1986). In spite of this fact, research on job design and worker responses has been harshly criticized by Salancik and Pfeffer (1977, 1978) in papers that deal, respectively with (a) need-satisfaction models in industrial and organizational psychology and organiza-tional behavior, and (b) social information processing (SIP) ap-proaches to job design and job-related attitudes. The general nature

This chapter is based in part upon presentations made at the meeting of the Society for Industrial and Organizational Psychology, Boston, Massachusetts, April 1989, and the conference entitled Job Satisfaction: Advances in Theory, Research, and Application, held in Bowling Green, Ohio, October 1987.

of their concerns about need-satisfaction models is captured in their argument that "need satisfaction models, while having almost universal, current acceptance, are founded on questionable assumptions that have been studied in such a way as to almost guarantee the results, as a consequence of the methods used" (Salancik & Pfeffer, 1977, p. 428).

If this and other views presented by Salancik and Pfeffer (1977, 1978) are indeed valid, then we need to find alternative ways of explaining how and why people respond to jobs or other features of their work environments—as extant theory and research suggests that they do. As is shown below, however, in many cases the validity of the arguments presented by Salancik and Pfeffer (1977, 1978) appears suspect. This chapter, therefore, considers theory and research relevant to the assumptions, arguments, interpretations, and conclusions offered in the works of Salancik and Pfeffer and selected other proponents of the SIP approach. Among the issues that are considered are (a) the validity of the contention that research on relationships between job characteristics and job attitudes is plagued by priming and consistency artifacts, (b) the problem of demand characteristics in job characteristics and job satisfaction research that purportedly supports SIP approaches, (c) the erroneous way in which some SIP proponents view workers' needs, and (d) the inaccurate views of some SIP enthusiasts about constructs in scientific research and the means used to operationally define them.

Consistency Artifacts in Research on Job Characteristics, Needs, and Job Satisfaction Research

The Consistency Artifact

The arguments that Salancik and Pfeffer (1977, 1978) presented in denigrating need-satisfaction models of job attitudes were predicated in large part on the belief that all studies of relationships between job characteristics and job attitudes are plagued with the artifact of consistency. According to them, "Consistency effects refers to the phenomenon in which individuals, when interviewed about their attitudes and beliefs, tend to organize information in consistent ways" (p. 447). For example, they would argue that if a person is first asked about the degree of variety in his or her work and is then asked about how satisfied he or she is with the job, answers to the first question would force artifactually consistent responses to the second question. Interestingly, however, they failed to cite a single published study showing this consistency effect in the literature dealing with either job characteristics or job satisfaction. More interestingly, the research they did cite mostly comprised unpublished studies that had serious problems in the validity of their statistical conclusions. (see Cook & Campbell, 1979). For instance, they described studies in which multiple significance tests were used along with a nominal type I error rate of .20. Although the use of such liberal type I error rates may be appropriate when testing for the interactive effects of two or more variables, it is seldom justified in tests of main effects. It is especially inappropriate when evidence from such nonstringent tests is used to bolster support for unorthodox views.

It deserves noting, moreover, that a series of studies by Stone and Gueutal (1984), Stone and Hollenbeck (1982), Spector and Michaels (1983), and Brief and Aldag (1977) show that the consistency artifact is not a problem of consequence in the empirical literature on job characteristics and job satisfaction. Thus, there is good reason to question the SIP-based view that relationships between job characteristics and job attitudes are a function of a response consistency artifact.

However, there is indeed something systematic in the way individuals respond to measures of such constructs as needs, job characteristics, and job satisfaction. This consistency is undoubtedly more a function of the realities that individuals with different personalities encounter on their jobs than it is a consequence of consistency artifacts. That is, when people cannot secure the outcomes they want from a job they become dissatisfied and leave it if acceptable alternatives are available (see, for example, Lofquist & Dawis, 1969; Stone, 1986; Porter & Steers, 1973). That individuals behave in this fashion makes good psychological sense and can be explained and predicted using a variety of extant theories (see Thibaut & Kelley, 1959).

Findings in Studies Where Consistency Doesn't Operate

As reviews of the relevant literature (for example, Locke, 1976; Stone, 1986) show, research findings that are quite consonant with extant theoretical treatments of job design and job satisfaction have been reported in a host of studies in which consistency effects could not be assumed to operate. For instance, research shows that (a) turnover rates are higher among jobs with low job complexity (based on Dictionary of Occupational Titles) than jobs that are higher on complexity, (b) physiological reactions to job characteristics correlate in expected ways with subjective reactions to jobs, and (c) experimental manipulations of job characteristics (both in laboratory and field settings) yield anticipated affective consequences. Taken together, these theory-consistent findings cast serious doubt on the arguments for response consistency artifacts presented by Salancik and Pfeffer and other SIP proponents.

Priming Artifacts in Job Satisfaction Research

The Priming Artifact

The arguments that Salancik and Pfeffer (1977) made in assailing need-satisfaction models of job attitudes were predicated in large part on the belief that all studies of the relationships between job characteristics and job attitudes are plagued with the artifact of priming. In their own words, "Priming means that in questioning a person about his activities or beliefs, the interviewer orients the respondent's attention to particular information" (p. 449). This tendency, they argue, leads respondents to provide different answers than they might have in the absence of such priming. How real are such effects?

Salancik and Pfeffer argued that the "effect of priming on attitude statements is probably immense" (p. 450). However, the evidence they presented (see Salancik & Pfeffer, 1977, 1978) is primarily from unpublished works that (a) deal with issues other than job design or job satisfaction, and (b) have suspect levels of validity in their statistical conclusions. From this research, it's not possible to derive any sound conclusions about the magnitude of priming effects in job design research. Moreover, experimental research by Stone and Gueutal (1984), Stone and Hollenbeck (1982), and others shows no evidence that measures of job satisfaction or other organizationally relevant attitudes are affected meaningfully by the priming that supposedly stems from the measurement of job characteristics. Thus, there is little reason to suspect that priming has any consequential influence on the results of research on job design and job satisfaction.

Attributes of Jobs as the Real Prime

However, this evidence does not refute the fact that priming effects have been demonstrated in a number of laboratory experiments performed by researchers in experimental social psychology. In research in actual organizations, however, there is little theoretical reason to anticipate that the act of measuring job characteristics would consequentially prime cognitions that were not already accessible to most workers. For example, assembly line workers are well aware of the fact that their jobs are simple, routine, repetitive, and so forth. Asking them to complete measures of such constructs as variety, autonomy, and task identity is unlikely to evoke any cognitions that do not already exist or are not well founded in reality.

Moreover, even if it were argued that questioning workers about their jobs does prime certain cognitions, this factor would probably have little or no impact on the overall pattern of research findings in the area of job design, because all workers who responded to a set of questionnaire items or interview questions would be similarly primed. One might expect effects, however, if different sets of primes were used with different sets of workers. However, it is unlikely that any studies in organizational contexts would use such a strategy. Even if they did, there is little reason to hypothesize that the magnitude of the resulting effects would be anything other than trivial.

In sum, there is virtually no credible evidence showing that priming effects are a problem in need-satisfaction research. Moreover, it is unlikely that researchers working on applied problems would use priming manipulations that would result in such effects. Consequently, the actual importance of such effects seems to have been radically overstated by Salancik and Pfeffer (1977).

Some Research-Related Artifacts in SIP Research

Private Beliefs versus Public Pronouncements

Even if SIP researchers were able to provide credible evidence that subjects' reports of job attitudes could be influenced by socially supplied information there is no reason to believe that this factor would have any important implications for theory or research on such topics as job characteristics and job satisfaction. This is because, as social psychologists have known for at least four decades, there is no necessary correspondence between the public pronouncements of individuals and their private values, beliefs, attitudes, and so on. This lack of correspondence has been vividly illustrated in the seminal work on influence and conformity by such notable social psychologists as Asch (1951, 1956, 1965) and Sherif (1935). Their findings have several important implications for the validity of SIP-related research. One very clear implication is that, while it may be possible to show that questionnaire or interview measures of job characteristics, job attitudes, and so forth can be altered by socially supplied information that is blatantly and forcefully presented to research subjects, the same findings say nothing whatsoever about their privately held views on the same issues (see Kelman, 1961). This principle is especially true of studies in which there are strong demand characteristics. In short, as should be clear from Kelman's (1961) seminal work on social influence, there is a clear and nontrivial difference between the attitude change processes of conformity and internalization. More specifically, research subjects in SIP studies dealing with job characteristics and job attitudes may show conformity by responding to questionnaire items or interview questions in ways that are consistent with powerful cues transmitted verbally or in written form by researchers or confederates; that is, the subjects make public statements that are consistent with the attempts to influence them but are inconsistent with their privately held views. However, these publicly made responses should not be construed as implying that the same subjects have internalized (that is, privately hold) the same views about either the job or their affective reactions to it. Simply put, the results of many SIP-related studies on job characteristics and job satisfaction may represent nothing more than the operation of demand characteristics (see Orne, 1962).

Demand Characteristics

As a review of the literature that purportedly supports the SIP approach clearly indicates, demand characteristics represent a strong rival explanation. More specifically, in the experimental studies dealing with the SIP approach one typically encounters a paradigm in which subjects are presented with rather blatant social cues about task characteristics and expected affective responses to measures of task characteristics and task satisfaction (for example, Griffin, 1983; O'Connor & Barrett, 1980; O'Reilly & Caldwell, 1979; Weiss & Nowicki, 1981; Weiss & Shaw, 1979; White & Mitchell, 1979). More specifically, in a typical SIP study, subjects who are naive about the world of work, anxious to please the researcher, and highly subject to influence are (a) told as part of the experiment that a job is so boring and dull that it provides workers with little or no satisfaction, (b) subsequently asked to work on a simulated job or task for a short period of time, and then (c) asked to provide their responses to measures of job characteristics and job satisfaction. Not surprisingly, the responses to the measures are consistent with the inductions used by the researchers. However, these findings are as easily explained by demand characteristics (Orne, 1962) as they are by the true operation of SIP effects. For more on this issue see Blau and Katerberg (1982) and Stone (1987, 1989).

Some Seemingly Circular Logic

In discussing the findings of their SIP studies, researchers often argue that the social cues provided to subjects are responsible for effects on measures of job characteristics, job attitudes, and so on. If the SIP phenomenon is real, however, it could just as easily be argued that subjects respond as they do to the cues because the experimenter expects them to. This is the previously noted notion of demand characteristics. Thus, one might ask: What have we really learned from the various studies that purport to show support for SIP views? Is it that social cues actually influence subjects' job-related attitudes and their beliefs about the characteristics of their jobs? Or, is it that subjects who adopt such research-related roles as the good subject, the apprehensive subject, and the faithful subject (see Fillenbaum, 1966; Fillenbaum & Frey, 1970; Orne, 1962; Riecken, 1962; Rosenberg, 1965, 1969; Stone, 1989; Weber & Cook, 1972) in SIP studies make public pronouncements about their jobs and job-related attitudes that are motivated primarily by the desire to appear normal and cooperative? The available evidence suggests that the latter of these two alternatives has the greatest degree of plausibility.

Individual Differences and Influence Attempts

Even if it could be shown that SIP influences had meaningfully large effects on some workers in real work contexts, there would still be issues about the generality of such effects. More specifically, as research in personality and social psychology has clearly demonstrated, there are substantial differences in the extent to which people are capable of being influenced by messages of various types (see Blau & Katerberg, 1982; Marlowe & Crowne, 1961; Okun & Sasfy, 1977; Sherman, 1967; Thomas & Griffin, 1983). For instance, we know that individuals who are field-dependent as opposed to independent, low as opposed to high in self-esteem, and high as opposed to low in needs for affiliation are most subject to being influenced by others. Moreover, it is even possible that attempts to influence individuals' beliefs, attitudes, values, and so forth will backfire if individuals who are exposed to strong influence attempts develop psychological reactance (see Brehm, 1972).

The Existence, Conceptualization, and Measurement of Needs

The Existence of Needs

A number of theories and models found in the literature of industrial and organizational psychology, organizational behavior, and allied fields employ need-satisfaction-based explanations of job-related attitudes. More specifically, such theories and models posit that (a) individuals have desires or needs for various types of outcomes, (b) work environments provide individuals with differing levels of such outcomes, and (c) individuals' affective states are determined largely by the correspondence between desired and experienced levels of outcomes (for example, Lofquist & Dawis, 1969; Porter & Lawler, 1968). In spite of the popularity of such theories and models and the hundreds of empirical studies that support them, Salancik and Pfeffer (1977) question their validity because they employ the construct of needs. For instance, they write that the view that people have needs is a "cavalier attitude [that] is scarcely warranted. The concept of needs may be potentially misleading and unnecessary for the development of theories of human behavior" (p. 441).

Parenthetically, it's interesting to note that while they critique the concept of needs, Salancik and Pfeffer offer no credible alternative explanation for the motivation of human behavior in either work or nonwork settings. Viewed generously, therefore, we might interpret the SIP model as suggesting that behaviors spring from the cumulative effects of social influence. If this is the case, then we might ask: Why are individuals responsive to such influence? Could it be that they have needs or wants for the outcomes that can be obtained directly or indirectly from manifesting behaviors that are consistent with the wishes of those in their social milieu?

It may also be that the problem Salancik and Pfeffer have with the need concept is more an issue of the narrow way in which they define the concept than it is with the concept itself. More specifically, it appears that their critique of the needs construct is based upon the view that needs are enduring, difficult to change predispositions in people that stem from either heredity or early socialization (see Salancik & Pfeffer, 1977). However, it is important to note that their interpretation of needs is quite inconsistent with a number of extant views. To illustrate this, consider some recent views on needs or wants: Lofquist and Dawis (1969) view needs as being clusters of self-reported preferences for stimulus conditions. And although Locke (1976) considers needs to be "objective requirements for an organism's survival and well-being" (p. 1303), he regards wants or values as being the outcomes that an organism views as being conducive to its welfare. Needs are innate; wants or values are learned. According to Lawler (1973) needs represent classes of outcomes that people regard as desirable.

It should be clear from these conceptions of needs, wants, and values that one need not view desires for enriched work, more pay, better supervision, safer working conditions, a more powerful computer, or most other work-related outcomes as stemming from needs as Salancik and Pfeffer define them. Rather, they can be looked upon as acquired wants or preferences for outcomes. Viewing needs or wants in this way makes clear the inappropriateness of Salancik and Pfeffer's (1977) critique of the needs component in most contemporary need-satisfaction models. Stated differently, a comprehensive, representative, and up-to-date review of the literature on needs, wants, and values, leaves one with far different views on these constructs than those contained in Salancik and Pfeffer's (1977) critique.

The Assertion That Needs Are Immutable

Salancik and Pfeffer (1977) assume that needs are stable, unchangeable attributes of individuals. It is clear, however, that the literature on needs and wants doesn't suggest this. For instance, the works of McClelland (1965), Argyris (1957), Alderfer (1972), Lawler (1973), Maslow (1954), Lofquist and Dawis (1969), Katz and Kahn (1966), and a host of others all point to the fact that individuals' needs, wants, and preferences can and do change. Moreover, many contemporary views on the formation of needs, values, and wants explicitly recognize the importance of individuals' physical and social environments in the development and maintenance of needs, values, wants, and so forth. Thus, Salancik and Pfeffer's (1977) argument that need-satisfaction models posit the existence of immutable needs or wants has no basis whatsoever. In addition, there's no sound basis for their assertion that need-satisfaction models are oblivious to the effects of the environment on personality. Several such models explicitly consider how the experiences of individuals change their needs or wants (for example, Lofquist & Dawis, 1969; Porter & Lawler, 1968; Lawler, 1973). Moreover, contrary to the arguments of Salancik and Pfeffer (1977), the fact that such needs or wants are stable enough over time to allow for their productive use in job satisfaction research does not imply that they are unchangeable.

The Contention That Needs Are Ambiguous

Salancik and Pfeffer (1977) also argue that the concept of needs in need-satisfaction models is so ambiguous that it leaves the meaning of needs unclear and their role in explaining behavior untestable. Unfortunately, this is quite far from being true. In a variety of works (for example, Hackman & Lawler, 1971; Hackman & Oldham, 1976; Smith, Kendall, & Hulin, 1969; Locke, 1969, 1976; Stone, 1975, 1976; Lofquist & Dawis, 1969) needs, wants, values, and related constructs are defined in a fashion that leaves little doubt about either their constitutive (conceptual) or operational definitions.

Salancik and Pfeffer substantiate their views on the ambiguity of needs by referring solely to the need for self-actualization. However, a review of the literature makes it clear that this supposed need has seldom been pivotal to research on job characteristics, job attitudes, or a host of other constructs of interest to researchers concerned with the behavior of individuals in organizational settings.

Salancik and Pfeffer go on to argue that the fact that needs are ambiguous "makes the possibility of [their] empirical refutation remote and the concept in its present stage of development, of limited utility" (p. 443). Unfortunately, this position neglects a tremendous amount of theoretical and empirical work concerned with improving both the conceptualization and measurement of such constructs as needs, wants, and preferences (for example, Jackson, 1967; Cattell, 1949; Cattell, Eber, & Tatsuoka, 1970; Kuder, 1968, 1979; Ghiselli, 1971; Weiss, Dawis, England, & Lofquist, 1964a, 1964b). In short, Salancik and Pfeffer's views on the conceptual and operational ambiguity of needs are quite inconsistent with what is widely known about that construct.

The Need to Invoke Needs to Explain Behavior

Salancik and Pfeffer argue that when there are visible external causes of behavior (for example, a mother working to pay for her child's operation), then there are no good reasons to view needs as the motivators of behavior. On the other hand, they contend that when there are no immediately apparent external causes of behavior, then theorists in industrial and organizational psychology and organizational behavior must inappropriately resort to needs as explanations. It is clear that both of these positions are suspect. The first is questionable because, even if one views the mother's explanation for why she works as a rationalization or self-perception (as Salancik and Pfeffer would have us do), this leaves unexplained the matter of why she went to work in the first place. What motivated the behavior? Clearly, it could not have been the post-hoc rationale that the mother might offer when questioned about her reasons for working. On the other hand, it might very well have been the mother's desire, want, or need to care for her child. An expectancy theorist (for example, Porter & Lawler, 1968; Vroom, 1964) could have predicted this behavior in advance of its occurrence. On the other hand, the SIP theorist could only explain it in a post-hoc manner by asking the mother for her reasons for (that is, self-perceptions about) working (see Bem, 1967).

The second position, that needs are inappropriate post-hoc explanations of behavior that seem to lack external causes, is also suspect. The reason is that just because an external observer can't see or intuit a cause for behavior doesn't imply that one doesn't exist. For instance, while an external observer may not be able to observe that a person is experiencing a severe headache, the person's desire, want, or need for an analgesic would not be any less real.

Needs versus Cultural Expectations

Another criticism advanced by Salancik and Pfeffer (1977) relates to what are generally considered to be higher-order needs (for example, achievement). They note that "it is difficult to distinguish between needs and cultural expectations for behavior" (p. 442). Even if one takes the position that individuals generally behave in accord with cultural expectations, this does not negate the existence of needs, wants, desires, and values or their role in motivating behavior. In fact, these and similar concepts must be used in explaining why people are sensitive to cultural expectations or norms. For instance, people comply with such expectations because they want to maintain group membership, desire the outcomes that stem from behaving in socially approved ways, fear the punishments that might flow from deviant behavior, and so on. In short, contrary to Salancik and Pfeffer's arguments, neither the existence of cultural expectations nor the presence of agents of social control serve any role as explanatory mechanisms for behavior unless and until we posit that individuals have needs, wants, desires, values, and so forth.

The SIP Model's Implicit Reliance on Needs

It should also be noted that unless one posits the existence of needs, wants, desires, drives, reinforcement mechanisms, or other motivation-based constructs, the SIP model of Salancik and Pfeffer breaks down, totally. After all, if people accept social influence, attend to social cues, behave in socially prescribed ways, and so forth, why do they do so? It is doubtful that Salancik and Pfeffer could answer this question without invoking motivational constructs like needs, wants, desires, and so forth. In doing so they would find themselves in the position of being subject to exactly the same criticism that they levied against need-satisfaction models.

Summary of Issues Surrounding Needs

Thus far, it's clear that Salancik and Pfeffer's interpretation of the construct of needs is inconsistent with the interpretation of the same construct that is implicit and explicit in most contemporary models of job design, job satisfaction, work adjustment, and so forth. It is also clear that their work (1977, 1978) grossly misrepresents what is currently known about needs and their measurement. Finally, it is clear that, in the absence of positing the existence of concepts such as needs, drives, wants, preferences, and the like, Salancik and Pfeffer and other SIP proponents can afford no viable explanation for the motivation of human behavior within or outside of organizational settings, including the behavior suggested in the SIP model.

The Conceptualization and Measurement of Job Characteristics

The Concept of Job Characteristics

In addition to being critical of the needs element in various need-satisfaction models, Salancik and Pfeffer (1977) are also highly critical of both the conceptualization and measurement of job characteristics. More specifically, they assert that job characteristics are "taken as realities in the environment to which the individual responds" (p. 430). They go on to state that, "Present job satisfaction models do not seriously consider the possibility that job characteristics are [nothing more than] socially constructed realities, mediated by the individual's social environment, rather than inherent characteristics of the objective situation" (p. 431). Just how legitimate are these and their related arguments?

Clearly, when individuals are faced with ambiguous stimuli, they'll use information provided by others to aid in the interpretation of such stimuli. This fact has been so well established in social psychology that it hardly needed to be reiterated by Salancik and Pfeffer. However, to argue, as do Salancik and Pfeffer, that job characteristics or other features of a worker's environment have no underlying, objectively measurable reality is not only incorrect, but irresponsible.

For one reason, it's clear that a number of characteristics of jobs and work environments have very clear and unambiguous properties that are independent of any social cues that one might choose to consider. These properties include cycle time, number of operations performed, pace of work, ambient temperature, noise level, opportunity for social interaction, and presence or absence of feedback from outside sources; obviously, these exist independent of any social cues to which a job incumbent might be exposed. Moreover, social cues will do little if anything to alter beliefs or perceptions about many of these properties. For instance, telling a steel mill worker that it is very cool near the blast furnace will do little to alter his or her physiological and concomitant psychological reactions to the tremendous heat generated by the furnace. Moreover, were a malevolent co-worker to pour some molten metal on the worker's arm, their insistence (as an influence agent and provider of social information) that no harm was being done would do little to either assuage the worker's pain or prevent damage to the worker's tissue. Thus, it's very clear that jobs have properties that in most work organizations may only be slightly (if at all) altered by social cues. Salancik and Pfeffer's (1977) contention that job characteristics are nothing more than socially construed realities is, therefore, far too extreme to merit acceptance by researchers and theorists in industrial and organizational psychology, organizational behavior, vocational psychology, and related fields.

Confusion about the Roles of Various Constructs in Theories

Salancik and Pfeffer suggest that extant need-satisfaction models regard such features of work as achievement and personal growth to be job characteristics. Taking issue with this, they contend that such features are nothing more than attributions that workers generate about their work behavior. This view is significantly flawed because extant models of job design do not suggest that accomplishment and personal growth are characteristics of jobs. Instead, these models are unambiguous in characterizing such features as possible outcomes of working on jobs (see for example, Hackman & Lawler, 1971; Hackman & Oldham, 1975, 1976; Lawler, 1973).

Correspondence between Predictors and Criteria

Salancik and Pfeffer (1977) argue that a dominant approach in the job design literature has been to focus on the measurement of job characteristics that have the potential to satisfy workers' needs (p. 444). Put somewhat differently, they bemoan the fact that there is often a moderately high level of correspondence between the concepts referenced both by measures of job characteristics and by job satisfaction. For example, a questionnaire battery may contain items that measure a worker's needs for autonomy, the amount of autonomy that is connected with a job, and the worker's satisfaction with that autonomy. Contrary to the views of Salancik and Pfeffer (1977), however, this is not really a problem, because on the basis of work by Ajzen and Fishbein (1977), Fishbein and Ajzen (1975), and other attitude theorists one would expect that measures of predictors considered by researchers would bear considerable correspondence to the criteria they attempt to predict. Thus, in predicting affective responses to job characteristics, it makes sense to use predictors that are *a priori* believed to be responsible for variability in such responses.

Problems with the Construct of Job Characteristics

Another of Salancik and Pfeffer's (1977) criticisms of the job characteristics concept is that "the characterization of jobs is a process which says as much about the researcher as it does about the jobs [themselves]" (p. 445). According to them, the reason is that researchers typically define the constructs to be measured in a study and develop the measures used to index such constructs. There are at least two flaws with their view. First, in some studies (for example, Stone & Gueutal, 1985; Zaccaro & Stone, 1988), job characteristics are based not on *a priori* conceptualizations about the number and nature of job characteristics, but on techniques (for example, multidimensional scaling) that allow research subjects to determine the characteristics along which job perceptions vary.

Second, even if one accepted the validity of the argument that measured job characteristics reflect researchers' conceptions of jobs rather than those of workers, little harm would ensue. The reason is that evidence from a number of empirical studies shows quite convincingly that measures of job characteristics based upon the concepts developed by researchers do a reasonably good job of predicting a number of important behavioral and affective criteria (see Locke, 1976; Stone, 1986).

Moreover, it is instructive to consider how the findings of empirical research on job characteristics and job satisfaction might be affected by researcher-created measures of predictors (that is, job characteristics) that are conceptually more narrow than those that would result from (a) having research subjects provide conceptual definitions of the predictors and (b) developing measures of the predictors based upon such definitions. Most probably the findings of research employing a set of researcher-based, narrowly defined predictors would lead to rather conservative estimates of the true relationships between job characteristics and job satisfaction.

That we might improve on our predictions, however, is indisputable. Indeed, as research by Zaccaro and Stone (1988) shows, satisfaction with work is better predicted by a set of empirically derived measures of job characteristics than it is by the use of measures derived on a largely *a priori* basis by job design researchers.

The General Role of Constructs and Operational Definitions in Science

The Role of Constructs in Science

One logical consequence of the views of Salancik and Pfeffer is that researchers should abandon attempts to define and measure such constructs as job characteristics, job satisfaction, and needs because these social constructions of reality have no existence of their own. This stance, however, would be most imprudent because from a scientific standpoint there is nothing wrong with either the development of constitutive definitions of constructs or the subsequent development of operational definitions of them. Without constructs and measures of them, work by scientists in the behavioral, physical, and natural sciences would quickly grind to a halt. Interestingly, without the ability to invoke a variety of constructs (for example, social influence, cultural norms), Salancik and Pfeffer would not have been able to prepare their rather scathing critique of need-satisfaction models. Moreover, in view of the fact that they consider such constructs as social influence and cultural norms to be appropriate, it is unclear why they regard such constructs as job satisfaction, job characteristics, and needs as any less legitimate.

On the Use of Multiple Operational Definitions of Constructs

Salancik and Pfeffer (1977) also lamented the fact that their review of the literature revealed that different researchers had (a) used measures of job characteristics that assess different characteristics or (b) manipulated different characteristics of jobs in experimental research on job design. As a result they argued that, "If the way individuals characterize jobs can be controlled by experimental procedures, then jobs have no fixed characteristics" (p. 445). Unfortunately, this is hardly a valid point. A number of real-world constraints (time, money, subjects, research sites, and so on) impose severe limits on what can be manipulated or measured in the context of any given laboratory- or field-based study. Therefore, the fact that all job design researchers have not manipulated or measured exactly the same set of job characteristics cannot be construed as evidence that jobs have no fixed characteristics. Interestingly, the fact that researchers in the field of social psychology have not measured exactly the same set of constructs in their research has not led Salancik and Pfeffer to deny the existence of various social psychological constructs.

Also on the topic of job characteristics, Salancik and Pfeffer (1977) stated that, "The problem with the concept of job characteristics is that it must ultimately be arbitrarily defined. Inevitably, jobs can be characterized along multiple dimensions and the choice of the dimensions used may affect what the researcher observes [on the basis of a study]" (p. 446). This is certainly true. However, it is not an indictment that applies solely to research on need-satisfaction models. Indeed, in any study, the researcher must *a priori* choose to focus on some constructs and neglect others. This selection process is just as true of research purporting to support SIP phenomena as it is of research dealing with job design, job satisfaction, needs, and so forth.

Explained Variance in Job Satisfaction Research

Salancik and Pfeffer (1977) argued that, "It is fair to conclude that in spite of consistency and priming effects, studies of need satisfaction seldom explain more than 10 percent of the variance [in behavioral criteria], and the amount of variance in job satisfaction [that is] explained almost never exceeds 40 percent" (p. 453). Furthermore, they contended that these levels of explained variance were rather low. Taken together, these arguments served as a justification for them to conclude that need-satisfaction models are of little or no utility. For several reasons I don't believe their views merit acceptance.

First, explained variance that ranges from 10 to 40 percent implies zero-order correlation coefficients that range from about .316 to .63. These levels are by no means trivial in comparison with the magnitude of correlation coefficients found in most research in the social sciences, including industrial and organizational psychology, organizational behavior, and social psychology. In fact, Cohen (1969) notes that correlation coefficients with ranges of .10 to .29, .30 to .49, and .50 and above, respectively, represent effect sizes that are small, medium, and large. Thus, the proportions of variance that Salancik and Pfeffer dismiss as trivial are levels that experienced and respected statisticians in the social sciences regard as far from trivial.

Second, even if we accepted that correlation coefficients between .316 and .632 are low in some relative sense, we could not justify the inference that the models connected with such coefficients had low utility (see Brogden, 1949; Cronbach & Gleser, 1965). For example, suppose that in testing a model of turnover, a researcher found a −.30 zero-order correlation between the measure of job enrichment and employee turnover in an organization. If turnover led the same organization to experience high recruitment, selection, and training costs, then there would be considerable utility in redesigning jobs to affect the turnover, especially if the turnover were concentrated among the individuals with the highest levels of performance.

Third, relationships between predictors and criteria in need-satisfaction model studies are often much stronger than Salancik and Pfeffer (1977) characterized them to be. For instance, a meta-analytic study by Stone (1986) revealed an average zero-order correlation of .88 between measures of job scope and job satisfaction across 27 different studies involving a total of 17,209 subjects. This implies about 77 percent shared variance, a figure that is considerably larger than the 40 percent value cited by Salancik and Pfeffer (1978).

Of course, the preceding discussion does not imply that organizational scientists should be content with the current capacity to account for variance in studies of relationships between job characteristics, job satisfaction, and other variables. On the contrary, every reasonable effort should be expended to improve the explanatory power of models, the accuracy of predictions, and the theoretical and applied value of research findings. Implicit in the above, however, is that we should not cast our theoretical models upon the funeral pyre solely on the basis of a criterion for the proportion of explained variance. This is especially true when one considers that (a) there is controversy over what constitutes an acceptable level of explained variance for given phenomena, and (b) correlation coefficients alone cannot serve as a basis for inferences about utility (see Brogden, 1949; Cronbach & Gleser, 1965).

Inaccurate Characterization of Need-Satisfaction Models

Salancik and Pfeffer (1977) presented a figure showing what they regarded as a typical need-satisfaction model as found in the literature of industrial and organizational psychology, organizational behavior, and allied fields. In the interest of brevity, that model is not duplicated here. Readers unfamiliar with the model are referred to the Salancik and Pfeffer (1977) article.

However, one important point about the model deserves mention here: Serious questions can be raised about whether it is prototypical. More precisely, the model fails to accurately represent a variety of linkages that have been hypothesized and subsequently subjected to empirical tests in the literature on job characteristics, needs, job satisfaction, and related variables. These linkages are dealt with in publications that have appeared both prior to and following the publication of the Salancik and Pfeffer (1977, 1978) articles. For instance, the supposedly prototypical model fails to report that the relevant literature shows that individuals' beliefs about their jobs and the job environment are affected by such factors as job experiences, experiences in prior situations, communications from others, and a variety of personality variables (for example, Lawler, 1973; Locke, 1976; Lofquist & Dawis, 1969). Moreover, the model fails to suggest that individuals' affective responses to jobs may at least in part, help to determine their perceptions of job characteristics. In short, what Salancik and Pfeffer (1977) regard as a prototypical need-satisfaction model is not prototypical. Rather, it affords a highly deficient view of what we know about needs, jobs, and individuals' affective and behavioral responses to jobs. It is especially unsettling that, on the basis of their analysis of the need-satisfaction model presented in their 1977 article, they would have us abandon all need-satisfaction models in industrial and organizational psychology, organizational behavior, and related fields. In view of the well-demonstrated utility and validity of such models (see Locke, 1976; Lofquist & Dawis, 1969; Stone, 1986) this is very poor advice.

Conclusions

As a result of their analysis of theory and research on need-satisfaction models, Salancik and Pfeffer concluded that, "The evidence and argument is offered that the need satisfaction model must be seriously re-examined and does not warrant the unquestioning acceptance it has attained in the organizational psychology literature" (p. 453). Two points about this conclusion deserve noting. First, it is not at all clear that need-satisfaction models have ever enjoyed unquestioned acceptance by industrial and organizational psychologists and organizational behaviorists (Stone & Gueutal, 1984). If anything, consistent with patterns found in the literatures of various sciences, the literature related to various need-satisfaction models shows a slow but steady stream of critical work that has frequently resulted in the modification of different versions of such models (see

Locke, 1976). Consider, for example, how researchers and theorists in such fields as industrial and organizational psychology and organizational behavior responded to Herzberg, Mausner, and Snyderman's (1959) two-factor model of job satisfaction.

The second very important point is that while there may be some merit in explicitly considering the impact of socially supplied information on individuals' work-related beliefs, values, and attitudes, there is no sound reason to abandon need-satisfaction models in the process. This conviction is especially true when one considers the myriad serious problems inherent in Salancik and Pfeffer's (1977, 1978) critiques of such models.

References

Ajzen, I., & Fishbein, M. (1977). Attitude-behavior relations: A theoretical analysis and review of empirical research. *Psychological Bulletin, 84,* 888–918.

Alderfer, C. P. (1972). *Existence, relatedness, and growth.* New York: Free Press.

Argyris, C. (1957). *Personality and organization.* New York: Harper.

Asch, S. E. (1951). Effects of group pressure upon the modification and distortion of judgments. In H. Guetzkow (Ed.), *Groups, leadership and men* (pp. 177–190). Pittsburgh: Carnegie Press.

Asch, S. (1956). Studies of independence and conformity: A minority of one versus a unanimous majority. *Psychological Monographs, 70,* 177–190.

Asch, S. (1965). Effects of group pressure upon modification and distortion of judgments. In H. Proshansky & B. Seidenberg (Eds.), *Basic studies in social psychology.* (pp. 393–401). New York: Holt, Rinehart & Winston.

Bem, D. J. (1967). Self-perception: An alternative interpretation of cognitive dissonance phenomena. *Psychological Review, 74,* 183–200.

Blau, G. J., & Katerberg, R. (1982). Toward enhancing research with the social information processing approach to job design. *Academy of Management Review, 7,* 543–550.

Brehm, J. (1972). *Responses to loss of freedom: A theory of psychological reactance.* Morristown, NJ: General Learning Press.

Brief, A. P., & Aldag, R. J. (1977). *Order effect and organizational research.* Paper presented at the meeting of the Academy of Management, Orlando, FL.

Brogden, H. E. (1949). When testing pays off. *Personnel Psychology, 2,* 171–183.

Cattell, R. B. (1949). *Manual for forms A and B: Sixteen Personality Factor Questionnaire.* Champaign, IL: Institute for Personality and Ability Testing.

Cattell, R. B., Eber, H. W., & Tatsuoka, M. M. (1970). *Handbook for the Sixteen Personality Factor Questionnaire (16PF).* Champaign, IL; Institute for Personality and Ability Testing.

Cohen, J. (1969). *Statistical power analysis for the behavioral sciences.* New York: Academic Press.

Cook, T. D., & Campbell, D. T. (1979). *Quasi-experimentation: Design & analysis issues for field studies*. Chicago: Rand McNally.

Cronbach, L. J., & Gleser, G. (1965). *Psychological tests and personnel decisions* (2nd ed.). Urbana, IL: University of Illinois Press.

Fillenbaum, S. (1966). Prior deception and subsequent experimental performance: The "faithful" subject. *Journal of Personality and Social Psychology, 4,* 532–537.

Fillenbaum, S., & Frey, R. (1970). More on the faithful behavior of suspicious subjects. *Journal of Personality, 38,* 43–51.

Fishbein, M., & Ajzen, I. (1975). *Belief, attitude, intention and behavior*. Reading, MA: Addison-Wesley.

Ghiselli, E. E. (1971). *Explorations in managerial talent*. Pacific Palisades, CA: Goodyear.

Griffin, R. W. (1983). Objective and social sources of information in task design: A field experiment. *Administrative Science Quarterly, 28,* 184–200.

Hackman, J. R., & Lawler, E. E. (1971). Employee reactions to job characteristics. *Journal of Applied Psychology, 55,* 259–286.

Hackman, J. R., & Oldham, G. R. (1975). Development of the Job Diagnostic Survey. *Journal of Applied Psychology, 60,* 159–170.

Hackman, J. R., & Oldham, G. R. (1976). Motivation through the design of work: Test of a theory. *Organizational Behavior and Human Decision Processes, 16,* 250–279.

Herzberg, F., Mausner, B., & Snyderman, B. (1959). *The motivation to work*. New York: Wiley.

Jackson, D. N. (1967). *Personality Research Form manual*. Goshen, NY: Research Psychologists Press.

Katz, D., & Kahn, R. L. (1966). *The social psychology of organizations*. New York: Wiley.

Kelman, H. C. (1961). Processes of opinion change. *Public Opinion Quarterly, 25,* 185–214.

Kuder, G. F. (1968). *Manual, Kuder Occupational Interest Survey, Form DD*. Chicago: Science Research Associates.

Kuder, G. F. (1979). *Manual, Kuder Occupational Interest Survey, 1979 revision*. Chicago: Science Research Associates.

Lawler, E. E., III. (1973). *Motivation in work organizations*. Monterey, CA: Brooks/Cole.

Locke, E. A. (1969). What is job satisfaction? *Organizational Behavior and Human Performance, 4,* 309–336.

Locke, E. A. (1976). The nature and causes of job satisfaction. In M. D. Dunnette (Ed.), *The handbook of industrial and organizational psychology* (pp. 1297–1349). Chicago: Rand McNally.

Lofquist, L. H., & Dawis, R. V. (1969). *Adjustment to work: A psychological view of man's problems in a work-oriented society*. New York: Appleton-Century-Crofts.

Marlowe, D., & Crowne, D. P. (1961). Social desirability and response to perceived situational demands. *Journal of Consulting Psychology, 25,* 109–115.

Maslow, A. H. (1954). *Motivation and personality.* New York: Harper.

McClelland, D. C. (1965). Toward a theory of motive acquisition. *American Psychologist, 20,* 321–333.

O'Connor, E. J., & Barrett, G. V. (1980). Informational cues and individual differences as determinants of subjective perceptions of task environment. *Academy of Management Journal, 23,* 697–716.

Okun, M. A., & Sasfy, J. H. (1977). Performance cue, approval motivation, and adoption of subject roles. *Journal of Social Psychology, 101,* 317–318.

O'Reilly, C. A., & Caldwell, D. F. (1979). Informational influences as a determinant of task characteristics and job satisfaction. *Journal of Applied Psychology, 64,* 157–165.

Orne, M. T. (1962). On the social psychology of the psychological experiment: With particular reference to demand characteristics and their implications. *American Psychologist, 17,* 776–783.

Porter, L. W., & Lawler, E. E., III. (1968). *Managerial attitudes and performance.* Homewood, IL: Irwin-Dorsey.

Porter, L. W., & Steers, R. M. (1973). Organization, work, and personal factors in employee turnover and absenteeism. *Psychological Bulletin, 80,* 151–176.

Riecken, H. W. (1962). A program for research on experiments in social psychology. In N. F. Washburne (Ed.), *Decisions, values, and groups.* Vol. 2. (pp. 25–41) New York: Macmillan.

Rosenberg, M. J. (1965). When dissonance fails: On eliminating evaluation apprehension from attitude measurement. *Journal of Personality and Social Psychology, 1,* 28–42.

Rosenberg, M. J. (1969). The conditions and consequences of evaluation apprehension. In R. Rosenthal & R. L. Rosnow (Eds.), *Artifact in behavioral research* (pp. 279–349). New York: Academic Press.

Salancik, G. R., & Pfeffer, J. (1977). An examination of need-satisfaction models of job attitudes. *Administrative Science Quarterly, 22,* 427–456.

Salancik, G. R., & Pfeffer, J. (1978). A social information processing approach to job attitudes and task design. *Administrative Science Quarterly, 23,* 224–253.

Sherif, M. (1935). A study of some social factors in perception. *Archives of Psychology, 27* (187), 1–60.

Sherman, S. R. (1967). Demand characteristics in an experiment on attitude change. *Sociometry, 30,* 246–260.

Smith, P. C., Kendall, L. M., & Hulin, C. L. (1969). *The measurement of satisfaction in work and retirement.* Chicago: Rand McNally.

Spector, P. E., & Michaels, C. E. (1983). A note on item order as an artifact in organizational surveys. *Journal of Occupational Psychology, 56,* 35–36.

Stone, E. F. (1975). Job scope, job satisfaction, and the Protestant ethic: A study of enlisted men in the U. S. Navy. *Journal of Vocational Behavior, 7,* 215–224.

Stone, E. F. (1976). The moderating effects of work-related values on the job-scope–job satisfaction relationship. *Organizational Behavior and Human Performance, 15,* 147–167.

Stone E. F. (1986). Job scope–job satisfaction and job scope–job performance relationships. In E. A. Locke (Ed.), *Generalizing from laboratory to field settings:*

Research in industrial/organizational psychology, organizational behavior, and human resources management (pp. 189–206). Lexington, MA: Lexington Books.

Stone, E. F. (1987). *A further consideration of the supposed invalidity of need-satisfaction models of job design and job attitudes.* Paper presented at the conference Job Satisfaction: Advances in Theory, Research, and Application. Bowling Green, OH.

Stone, E. F. (1989). *Problems with the social information processing framework of job attitudes.* Paper presented at the meeting of the Society for Industrial and Organizational Psychology, Boston.

Stone, E. F., & Gueutal, H. G. (1984). On the premature death of need satisfaction models: An investigation of Salancik and Pfeffer's views on priming and consistency artifacts. *Journal of Management, 10,* 237–258.

Stone, E. F., & Gueutal, H. G. (1985). An empirical derivation of the dimensions along which characteristics of jobs are perceived. *Academy of Management Journal, 28,* 376–396.

Stone, E. F., & Hollenbeck, J. R. (1982). An empirical investigation of priming and consistency artifacts in need satisfaction model based research. In N. Weiner & R. Klimoski (Eds.), *Proceedings of the 25th Annual Conference of the Midwest Academy of Management,* (pp. 301–312). Columbus, OH: Midwest Academy of Management.

Thibaut, J. W., & Kelley, H. H. (1959). *The social psychology of groups.* New York: Wiley.

Thomas, J., & Griffin, R. (1983). The social information processing model of task design: A review of the literature. *Academy of Management Review, 8,* 672–682.

Vroom, V. H. (1964). *Work and motivation.* New York: Wiley.

Weber, S. J., & Cook, T. D. (1972). Subject effects in laboratory research: An examination of subject roles, demand characteristics, and valid inference. *Psychological Bulletin, 77,* 273–295.

Weiss, D. J., Dawis, R. V., England, G. W., & Lofquist, L. H. (1964a). Construct validation studies of the Minnesota Importance Questionnaire. *Minnesota Studies in Vocational Rehabilitation, XVIII.*

Weiss, D. J., Dawis, R. V., England, G. W., & Lofquist, L. H. (1964b). The measurement of vocational needs. *Minnesota Studies in Vocational Rehabilitation, XVI.*

Weiss, H. M., & Nowicki, C. (1981). Social influences on task satisfaction: Model competence and observer field dependence. *Organizational Behavior and Human Performance, 27,* 345–366.

Weiss, H. M., & Shaw, J. B. (1979). Social influences on judgments about tasks. *Organizational Behavior and Human Performance, 24,* 126–140.

White, S. E., & Mitchell, T. E. (1979). Job enrichment versus social cues: A comparison and competitive test. *Journal of Applied Psychology, 64,* 1–9.

Zaccaro, S. J., & Stone, E. F. (1988). Incremental validity of an empirically based measure of job characteristics. *Journal of Applied Psychology, 73,* 245–252.

PART TWO

Antecedents of Job Satisfaction

Managers, supervisors, human resource specialists, employees, and citizens in general are concerned with ways of improving job satisfaction. Greater job satisfaction means better quality of life, better health (both mental and physical), more job stability, and probably greater cooperativeness. The first step toward improving job satisfaction is determining its causes and correlates. Practitioners need to know what we can change in the work situation to improve satisfaction and what is immutable. Theorists also want to understand how feelings of satisfaction arise and change.

The three papers in this section concern some of these antecedents and causes, which the authors analyse by employing different methods, different measures, and different antecedents. The consensus among the authors, nonetheless, is considerable. There are numerous points with which few of them would disagree.

1. *As a first step, job satisfaction must be measured reliably.* Schneider, Gunnarson, and Wheeler base their measure on the five-scales Job Descriptive Index (JDI) (Smith, Kendall, & Hulin, 1969, 1975, 1985), but propose to expand these facet measures by adding items concerning opportunities in each facet. Dawis and James and James, use various scales derived from the Minnesota Satisfaction Questionnaire (MSQ) (Weiss, Dawis, England, & Lofquist, 1967). All of these scales are adequately reliable.

2. *Different results may be expected according to the scales used.* The scales discussed in this part vary in length, descriptive and evaluative content, complexity, completeness, format, and so on. Some ask for overall evaluations of the job, others ask about quite specific aspects of it, and some are inbetween.

3. *Satisfaction cannot be judged in absolute terms, but involves comparison or comparisons.* Schneider, Gunnarson, and Wheeler and Dawis explicitly invoke P–E fit, or the comparison of what the person needs with what the environment offers. James and James match the climate general

factor to the satisfaction general factor. The other authors also recognize the importance of comparisons.

4. *The relationship between person and environment (including that between person and job) is interactive.* The person acts to shape (and choose) the environment, which acts in turn upon the person. James and James envision the interaction as an explicit step in which the person compares ("valuates") environmental attributes in terms of work-related values. Dawis also invokes individual motivation (needs) when he uses the MSQ (Weiss, Dawis, England, & Lofquist, 1967), since its scales are based in part upon Murray's (1938) needs. Other authors in this volume also point out the interactive nature of job satisfaction.

5. *Job satisfaction can be broken down into facets or components.* All researchers agree, but choose to focus on varying numbers of scales and contents of facets. For example, Schneider chooses an extension of the five scales of the JDI (Smith, Kendall, Hulin, 1969, 1975, 1985). The Minnesota Satisfaction Questionnaire can be scored for twenty facets; scores from one question for each facet provide a single overall composite score. James and James factor sixteen of these twenty facets into four group factors, the fourth of which, satisfaction with organization, has no corresponding JDI scale. Conversely, the pay and promotions scales of the JDI are not represented in the MSQ either in the twenty scales or in the group scales.

6. *Each of these facets can be tied to one or more aspects of the work environment and of the job.*

7. *Satisfactions with these aspects are intercorrelated, defining a general overall factor.* (The size of these intercorrelations varies with the measures, but they are in all these cases statistically significant.)

8. *Some of this general factor can be attributed to relatively permanent characteristics of the individual* (Arvey, Bouchard, Segal, & Abraham, 1989; Smith, chapter 1 of this volume; Staw & Ross, 1985). The work of Arvey et al. suggests that these traits are at least partly genetic. To the extent that these characteristics account for satisfactions, the employer and the industrial-organizational (I-O) psychologist must realize that changes in policy or conditions cannot be expected to change relative satisfactions. The overall level for all persons, however, can be changed, even if there is a large genetic component.

Some of the intercorrelations among various facet scales can be attributed to a person's generally favorable (or unfavorable) reaction to all aspects of the job—and to life—as a correlate of his or her overall disposition or temperament.

This general factor may well enter into different measures of satisfaction to a greater or lesser extent. It is notable that the intercorrelations among the four factors derived by James and James from the MSQ (.34 to .83 with mean $r = .59$) are significantly larger than those for the five JDI scales (.28

to .42, mean $r = .39$; Smith, Kendall, & Hulin, 1969). If these differences imply more representation of a general factor in the MSQ, and by inference a more heritable component, then one would expect less response to specific situational changes.

We should point out two other possible sources of a general factor in measures of job satisfaction.

9. *Job level is typically correlated with satisfaction with all aspects of the job.* Evidence from studies of job evaluation plans shows that desirable job characteristics (as evaluated by observers) are correlated to the extent that almost all of the variance in numerous "factors" can be accounted for by two or three underlying factors (Lawshe, 1945; Lawshe & Alessi, 1946; Lawshe & Salter, 1944). Jobs that are more complex also have better working conditions, pay, promotion prospects, and supervision (as well as greater autonomy and responsibility).

Later work on the Position Analysis Questionnaire showed that job duties are related to job satisfaction (Pritchard & Peters, 1974).

10. *Community characteristics can account for a large proportion of the intercorrelation of satisfactions when the sample has been drawn from a number of communities.* The alternatives available to the individual serve as a basis for comparison and hence account for a good deal of variance in job satisfaction. The greater the community prosperity and rate of growth, the poorer the individual's own job appears (Kendall, 1963).

Schneider, Gunnarson, and Wheeler, in particular, emphasize the importance of context and alternatives in determining what is satisfying. They point out that employers cannot usually select poor, decaying communities for plant locations, but that they can offer opportunities within the organization.

Each of the propositions 6 through 10 applies to intent to quit as well as to overall job satisfaction.

The papers in this section also highlight different aspects of the antecedents of job satisfaction. The theme of the paper by Schneider, Gunnarson, and Wheeler is that perception of the availability of opportunity for desirable aspects of a job is a principal (and largely unmeasured) aspect of job satisfaction. They define opportunity as "the availability of valued states and/or outcomes in the work situation . . . both . . . those things that people can presently have if they choose to (present opportunities) and . . . those things that people expect to have opportunity to choose some day (future opportunities)."

They consider opportunity in relation to each of the traditionally measured aspects of job satisfaction, and, in the process, furnish us an excellent outline of the personal correlates of job satisfaction and the fit of person to environment (P–E fit). In addition, Schneider, Gunnarson, and Wheeler pose several propositions that deserve investigation:

1. Global job satisfaction would be predicted more accurately if opportunities in each of the facets were measured explicitly as well as implicitly. In other words, the multiple correlation (R) of facet with global satisfaction will be greater if opportunities in all of the facets are added to the predictive side of the equation.
2. Opportunities are important not only in promotions but also in each of the other facets of job satisfaction. The increment in R will be significant if opportunity in any facet is added.
3. The availability of options has a favorable effect on overall satisfaction whether or not the employee elects the option. Specifically, the addition of items concerning availability of options will increase R even if the options are not chosen. (This relationship could also be predicted from other hypothesized effects, such as the increase in trust in management associated with management's providing options.)
4. Age, sex, and race affect job satisfaction in part because of their relation to opportunities.
5. Opportunities will predict some of the variance in overall job satisfaction not predicted from facet satisfactions (Scarpello & Campbell, 1983; Ironson, Smith, Brannick, Gibson, & Paul, 1989).

Schneider, Gunnarson, and Wheeler hypothesize that there is additional variance in global measures of satisfaction due to as-yet unidentified components of job satisfaction. Others have proposed other explanations. For example, Smith (chapter 1 of this volume) proposed differences in weighting of components, differences between short- and long-term satisfactions, and the components happiness and trust in management. Arvey and his associates (Arvey, Bouchard, Segal, & Abraham, 1989) attribute this variance to both genetic and environmental factors (partly following Staw & Ross, 1985). Most of these authors would concede that opportunities are at least part of the missing variance, particularly in work satisfaction.

Opportunity seems, at first blush, to have quite different meaning when applied to work (opportunities for autonomy, growth, achievement) than when applied to pay (potential pay), coworkers (potential support), supervision (help in achieving outcomes and feedback), and promotions (all of these). Schneider and his colleagues will, we hope, stimulate attempts to measure opportunities in all these aspects and to determine how closely they are related to each other, to overall job satisfaction, and to intention to change jobs or to retire.

Dawis provides a thoughtful survey of theories and approaches to job satisfaction. He describes the systematic and programmatic research at the University of Minnesota while exploring a sophisticated concept—Person–Environment Interaction. Although a person and his or her Environment are clearly mutually dependent and interactive, the dynamic relationship is at present too complex to measure. Its surrogate is Person–Environment fit (P–E fit). At any given time, the discrepancy between Person and Environment can be taken as the end product of the interaction. The Minnesota researchers consider this discrepancy to be a cause of job dissatisfaction, as well as of other attitudes and behaviors related to work adjustment.

The Minnesota research group working with Dawis have based their measures on their eight aspects of work and on Murray's (1938) twelve needs. Both the individual's needs and his or her actual job situation are measured. The greater the discrepancy between scores on these values, the poorer the P–E fit. The actual job situation is estimated by averaging the ratings of a group of persons on the job. The best method of evaluating the discrepancy in order to predict job satisfaction is still being investigated.

A promising aspect of the work on P–E fit is the development of Occupational Reinforcer Pattern (ORP), which allows a counselor to estimate whether a client's needs match the ORP of a given occupation. An employer could also use these patterns for placement purposes.

James and James concern themselves with the relationship between what is common to all perceptions of an environment and what permeates the measures of satisfaction. This approach is in sharp contrast to that of Dawis, who considers specific comparisons of what a person wants with what the environment provides. James and James use their Psychological Climate Scales (James & James, 1989), which group into four factors: role stress and lack of harmony; job challenge and autonomy; leadership facilitation and support; and workgroup cooperation, friendliness, and warmth. These four factors are highly intercorrelated (.62 to .69; mean = .67), providing a second-order general factor that is higher in the hierarchy than the group factors, which in turn are more general than the specific climate scales.

The job satisfaction measures form a similar hierarchy. Sixteen satisfaction items group into four intercorrelated factors, which again prove to have in common a general satisfaction factor. Path analyses show that for a heterogeneous sample of 1,046 nonsupervisory personnel, each general factor causes the other. They are significantly both cause and effect. These general factors account for a large portion, but by no means all, of the variance in their respective measures of affect and perception. The nature of these interactive general factors is not yet clear, but James and James recognize a strong emotional component that has yet to be precisely defined. They regard a person's values as the essential basis of evaluation of his or her situation.

These three chapters raise more questions than they answer, and further research should address these major questions. The principal problem is how management can change a situation to effect changes in satisfactions, with concomitant changes in behavior and in individual outcomes. Addressing this problem requires answers to several other issues.

1. What changes in a situation are most likely to be followed by changes in what kinds of satisfactions? For example, will the announcement of a systematic promotional plan be followed by an immediate increase in satisfaction with promotions? We know (from largely unpublished studies) that greater mean promotion satisfaction is found in organizations with alternative promotional ladders. Causation cannot be proved, but only inferred. Similarly, we know that a change in feedback is followed by an increase in satisfaction with supervision (see in Ironson, Smith, Brannick, Gibson, & Paul, 1989), but changes have not been tracked longitudinally for individuals. Correlational evidence abounds for the relationship between situational characteristics and satisfactions, but little experimental or even pseudoexperimental evidence can be cited.

2. What aspects of job satisfaction are related to measurable changes in what kinds of behavior or other outcomes, and with what lag in time? For example, will an increase in satisfaction with promotions be accompanied by an increase in overall job satisfaction, and if so, when? When can one expect changes in intention to quit and in turnover rate? Is it reasonable to expect any changes in short-term behaviors such as absences, lateness, or volunteering for extra tasks? It seems likely that task characteristics will affect these behaviors more directly. For example, lot size has been shown in a field experiment to have an immediate effect on spacing of rest pauses. (Smith & Lem, 1955).

3. As implied above, another question to be answered is whether change occurs more rapidly or readily in facet satisfaction than in global satisfaction. Is it faster in some facets and measures than in others?

4. Since there is general agreement that job satisfactions are correlated and that a general factor can be derived, several questions arise about that factor:

   a. How large is it?
   b. Is it larger in some types of scales (for example, MSQ or JDI format, global or specific questions)?
   c. Is it larger in some facets than in others (for example, in work more than in pay)?
   d. How much of the general factor is attributable to environment, how much to the person, and how much to their interaction?
   e. Of that portion attributable to the person, how much is genetic? And of that, how much is related to temperament or disposition, how much to values, how much to abilities, and how much to job–ability fit?
   f. How much (if any) does the use of discrepancy or difference scores improve the prediction of overall satisfaction (and, potentially, of behavior)? Dawis reports that P–E difference correlates typically between .20 and .30 with satisfaction. These

values are not greater than those usually found when individual needs are correlated with satisfaction without including environment in the computation. Similarly, the original JDI studies (Smith, Kendall, & Hulin, 1969) found that nothing was gained by scoring each item in the direction of individual preference (triadic or diadic scoring).

g. For measures of interactions in which the proportion attributable to the person is relatively great, do changes in the interaction actually have a smaller effect on overall mean satisfaction?

Conclusions

How far have we come in determining the causes and correlates of job satisfaction, and where are we going? We have laid most of the foundation for a comprehensive model. We have developed reliable and valid measures of both facet and global job satisfactions. We have posed several hypotheses about how these measures can be improved even further. We have identified a number of factors in the individual, the organization, the community, and their interactions that may modify or limit the effectiveness of various possible changes introduced into the job or the situation.

It is high time to start collecting the building blocks for the substantive model on this foundation. We need hard data about what changes are followed by what improvements (or decrements) in which measures of job satisfaction, how rapidly, and how much. Further, we need facts about the relation of expressed feelings to sets of behaviors. These field experiments may guide us in deciding which types of measures are most sensitive to which kinds of change and give us direction for further improvements in measurement. The definition and meaning of job satisfactions will thus be further clarified.

Moreover, and crucially, these data will begin to provide decision-makers with a firm basis for selecting treatments in particular situations in order to achieve particular outcomes. Objective decisions based on a factually derived model may finally replace subjective reliance on the latest and most publicized "cutting edge."

References

Arvey, R. D., Bouchard, T. J., Jr., Segal, N. L., & Abraham, L. M. (1989). Job satisfaction: Environmental and genetic components. *Journal of Applied Psychology, 74,* 187–192.

Ironson, G. H., Smith, P.C., Brannick, M. T., Gibson, W. M., & Paul, K. B. (1989). Construction of a "Job in General" scale: A comparison of global, composite, and specific measures. *Journal of Applied Psychology, 74,* 193–200.

James, L. R., & James, L. A. (1989). Causal modeling in organization research. In C. L. Cooper & I. Robertson (Eds.), *International Review of Industrial and Organizational Psychology* (pp. 371–404). Chichester, Eng.: Wiley.

Kendall, L. M. (1963). *Canonical analysis of job satisfaction and behavioral personal background, and situational data.* Unpublished doctoral dissertation, Cornell University.

Lawshe, C. H., Jr. (1945). Studies in job evaluation: 2. The adequacy of abbreviated point ratings for hourly-paid jobs in three industrial plants. *Journal of Applied Psychology, 29,* 177–184.

Lawshe, C. H., Jr., & Alessi, S. L. (1946). Studies in job evaluation: 4. Analysis of another point ratings system for hourly-paid jobs and the adequacy of an abbreviated scale. *Journal of Applied Psychology, 30,* 310–319.

Lawshe, C. H., Jr., & Salter, G. A. (1944). Studies in job evaluation: 1. Factor analyses of point ratings for hourly-paid jobs in three industrial plants. *Journal of Applied Psychology, 28,* 189–198.

Murray, H. A. (1938). *Explorations in personality.* New York: Oxford University Press.

Pritchard, R. D., & Peters, L. H. (1974). Job duties and job interests as predictors of intrinsic and extrinsic satisfaction. *Organizational Behavior and Human Performance, 12,* 315–330.

Scarpello, V., & Campbell, J. P. (1983). Job satisfaction: Are all the parts here? *Personnel Psychology, 36,* 577–600.

Smith, P. C., Kendall, L. M., & Hulin, L. L. (1969, 1975, 1985). *The Job Descriptive Index.* Bowling Green, OH: Psychology Department, Bowling Green State University.

Smith, P. C., & Lem, C. (1955). Positive aspects of motivation in repetitive work: Effects of lot size on spacing of voluntary work stoppages. *Journal of Applied Psychology, 39,* 330–333.

Staw, B. M., & Ross, J. (1985). Stability in the midst of change: A dispositional approach to job attitudes. *Journal of Applied Psychology, 70,* 469–480.

Weiss, D. J., Dawis, R. V., England, G. W., & Lofquist, L. H. (1963). Manual for the Minnesota Satisfaction Questionnaire. *Minnesota Studies in Vocational Rehabilitation,* XXIII.

Weiss, D. J., Dawis, R. V., England, G. W., & Lofquist, L. H. (1967). Manual for the Minnesota Satisfaction Questionnaire. *Minnesota Studies in Vocational Rehabilitation, XXIII.*

3

The Role of Opportunity in the Conceptualization and Measurement of Job Satisfaction

BENJAMIN SCHNEIDER

SARAH K. GUNNARSON

JILL K. WHEELER

An alternate title for this chapter, albeit a long one, is "Job satisfaction is function of not only what people have but also of what people have the *opportunity* to have." We argue that most of the job satisfaction literature considers only how employees appraise their current situation without considering how employees feel about what they *could have* either in their current situation or in the future. Further, we show that in the assessment of job satisfaction, the only questions regarding opportunity have concerned promotion and career advancement. We propose, however, that (a) when people think about their job satisfaction, they think of past and present happenings as well as available opportunities; and (b) opportunities are relevant to all facets of job satisfaction, not just career promotion and advancement.

In the following sections, a definition of opportunity is first presented, and then, three perspectives on job satisfaction are reviewed and the role of opportunity in each is explored. Finally, the implications of including opportunity in the measurement of job satisfaction are discussed and suggestions for future research are made.

What Is Opportunity?

The American Heritage Dictionary defines opportunity as "a favorable or advantageous combination of circumstances." Although we do not disagree with this definition, our definition of opportunity includes another component. This additional component concerns choices or options.

Choice is the most crucial aspect of opportunity. Opportunity here refers to a favorable or advantageous combination of circumstances that presents an individual with the chance to choose among valued alternatives. What is especially fascinating about opportunity is that an individual need not partake of an opportunity (that is, choose an option) for it to be satisfying. In other words, we propose that the mere perception of the availability of an opportunity can be satisfying.

The idea that opportunities are in themselves satisfying has empirical support. For example, Miller and Monge (1986) found that working in a participative climate—defined as having the opportunity to participate—had a more positive effect on worker satisfaction than did actual participation in specific decisions. This research suggests that the availability of an opportunity may be even more satisfying than experiencing the event or circumstance offered by the opportunity.

In summary, we define opportunity as the availability of valued states and/or outcomes in the work situation. That is, opportunity refers both to those things that people can presently have if they choose to (present opportunities) and to those things that people expect to have opportunity to choose someday (future opportunities). An example of a present opportunity is: "In my organization, I can choose to join the union." Present opportunities are those among which employees can currently choose. An example of a future opportunity is: "If I remain with this organization, I will have the opportunity to stay in my current department or join the management track." We propose that when employees are unhappy with aspects of their current situation, including present opportunities, but perceive that the future will offer attractive opportunities, employees will report a higher level of current satisfaction than if they did not perceive the future opportunities.

Despite the proposed importance of the opportunity construct for job satisfaction, opportunity has received little attention in the conceptualization and, thus, the assessment of job satisfaction. In fact, a review of the measures reproduced and discussed in Cook, Hepworth, Wall, and Warr's (1981) compendium of measures revealed that only one measure uses the word opportunity in reference to anything other than career advancement. This measure is Porter's (for example, 1961) Need Satisfaction Questionnaire (NSQ). For example, the NSQ asks about "opportunity for personal growth and development." Porter's reference to opportunity, however, was inadvertent (L. W. Porter, personal communication, April 30, 1989) and was not a point of focus in his work on job satisfaction.

The role of opportunity in job satisfaction may help to explain interesting empirical findings cited by Scarpello and Campbell (1983). Based on the literature regarding relationships between global measures of job satisfaction and summed facet measures, Scarpello and Campbell concluded that "the global measure of job satisfaction and the sum of the facet measures, are by no means equivalent measures" (p. 578). We hypothesize that the reason summed facet measures and global measures do not correlate more highly is that global measures implicitly tap everything relevant to employees, including present and future opportunities, as well as other unidentified components of job satisfaction. This leads us to Proposition One: *The addition of present and future opportunities to the measurement of job facet satisfaction will improve the relationships between the sum of facet satisfaction and an index of overall job satisfaction.*

As will be shown later, the concept of opportunity is an underlying component of job situations that has been only partially captured by existing job satisfaction measures. To demonstrate the role opportunity has played in theory and research, three contemporary conceptual approaches to job satisfaction will be reviewed here. First, the situational approach to job satisfaction, upon which most satisfaction measures are based, will be presented. Then, the literature concerning the role of person variables in job satisfaction will be explored for evidence of opportunity as an underlying construct. Finally, the person–environment (P–E) fit perspective on job satisfaction will be examined to show how opportunity is relevant to the understanding of job satisfaction.

Situational Correlates of Job Satisfaction

The situationist perspective on job satisfaction maintains that satisfaction is determined by characteristics of both the job and the larger environment in which the job exists. This view has dominated the literature since the first studies by Hauser (1927). Taylor's (1911) attempts to increase job satisfaction through job design and pay incentives were also situationally focused, as were the various projects at the Western Electric plants in Hawthorne (see Roethlisberger & Dickson, 1939). Up to the present, the majority of research studies make the assumption that when a particular set of job conditions exists, a particular level of job satisfaction will follow.

One of the most popular and extensively researched measures of job satisfaction is the Job Descriptive Index (JDI) (Smith, Kendall, & Hulin, 1969). This measure identifies five facets of job satisfaction. For convenience, the discussion of the role opportunity plays in situational approaches to job satisfaction will be organized around the five facets of the JDI.

The work itself. Research has found that the facet that correlates most highly with overall job satisfaction is the work itself. Satisfaction with the work itself is usually measured in terms of the core job characteristics proposed by Hackman and his colleagues (Hackman & Lawler, 1971; Hackman & Oldham, 1975). It can be shown that measures of the presence of autonomy, skill variety, feedback, task identity, and task significance in the work itself implicitly address present opportunity.

For example, a meta-analysis conducted by Fried and Ferris (1986) on the job characteristics model found that task feedback (when compared with other characteristics of the work itself) was the strongest correlate of job satisfaction. One interpretation of this finding is that feedback is the mediator through which people perceive opportunities in their work; in the absence of feedback, one does not know how one is doing, so it is impossible to perceive opportunity. The lack of feedback creates uncertainty; uncertainty does not permit plans; and the absence of plans is the absence of opportunity (Miller, Galanter, & Pribram, 1960).

Trist and Bamforth's (1951) report of the change to the longwall method of coal mining was perhaps the first to highlight the importance of opportunities for autonomy in the workplace. Prior to implementation of the longwall method, colliers had made contracts with management to work their own small face of the mine. This contract, in effect, established numerous miniorganizations. Colliers chose their own work mates, and work groups were autonomous. Groups were free to set their own goals and had flexibility in determining their work pace. All of this ended when the longwall method was instituted. Groups were disbanded; choice in how to do the work was lost. These changes caused by the longwall method can be conceptualized as changes that decreased opportunities for workers.

Supervision. The concepts of opportunity and supervision have been closely linked in the theoretical literature on job satisfaction. For example, in Locke's (1976) theoretical discussion of satisfaction with supervision, he suggested that the relationship between supervisors and subordinates is based partially on what he called functional attraction. Functional attraction refers to the extent to which subordinates perceive that their supervisor is helping them obtain valued job outcomes. Evans (1970) and House (1971) present similar conceptualizations of leadership. Thus, supervisors can control opportunities on the job through the assignments they make and the feedback they give to subordinates. For example, Landau and Hammer (1986) found that young clerical employees who received high levels of feedback about their job performance from their supervisors perceived greater opportunities for within-organizational mobility than did employees who received lower levels of feedback.

In summary, opportunities at work are mediated through supervision in many ways: supervisors provide feedback, assess employees' performance with ratings that may affect employees' future opportunities, and assign work that can influence the opportunities with which employees are presented. Conceptually, then, when employees think about their satisfaction with supervision, a portion of the functional attraction toward supervisors should be a function of how supervisors mediate present and future opportunities for their employees. When viewed from a functional attraction or opportunity perspective, contemporary measures of satisfaction with supervision appear to fail to capture the opportunity construct. Little or no attention is paid to the various kinds of opportunities supervisors may make available to workers or the ways supervisors can facilitate or constrain the attainment of future opportunities.

Coworkers. People seek friendly, warm, and cooperative relationships with others not only for what they produce in some immediate sense, but also for what those relationships provide in times of need—that is, social support (LaRocco, House, & French, 1980). We argue that people are aware of their ties to others at least partially because of the possible, not only the actual, benefits attached to those relationships. This is what opportunity refers to: something available even if not used. Perhaps the best example of opportunities concerning coworkers is networking. One establishes networks at work not necessarily for what they immediately provide, but rather for what they have the potential to produce. Networks provide opportunity.

Pay. Pay is an important source of satisfaction at work. In addition to salary providing a potential source of self-esteem (Brockner, 1988), pay provides the generic opportunity for anything money can buy (Lawler, 1971). Most, if not all, research on satisfaction with pay focuses on current income. However, current pay, even though it provides current opportunities, it not the only conceptually important determinant of satisfaction with pay. People's satisfaction with pay would also be influenced by what they will be able to obtain (that is, how their standard of living will improve) as their salary increases.

To better understand the influences of future salary on present satisfaction with pay, consider the two professions of nursing and accounting. Although nurses earn a starting salary of about $21,000, the maximum for an experienced nurse averages only about $29,000. In contrast, accountants can expect to almost triple their income from the same starting base in the same period of time to more than $61,000 (Trafford, 1988). No research on this contrast in opportunity seems to exist, but it can be hypothesized that a nurse and an accountant making the same salary at the onset of their careers might be differentially satisfied with their pay because of their differential future earning opportunities.

Promotion. Promotion is the one facet of the JDI that explicitly assesses how perceptions about the future can affect job satisfaction. Studies have shown that employees who perceive few opportunities for advancement have negative attitudes toward their work and their organizations (Kanter, 1977; Kipnis, 1964; Larson, 1982). For example, Kanter (1977) found that career opportunity at all hierarchical levels can account for the ways people involve themselves in their work. Further, it is likely that an individual's satisfaction with promotion opportunities is influenced by more than just the next promotion in the line of progression. Opportunities for promotion throughout an individual's tenure with an organization are probably reflected in an individual's satisfaction with promotion.

The typical way that promotion opportunities are assessed, however, is very general. For example, consider "opportunity somewhat limited" (Job Descriptive Index; Smith, Kendall, & Hulin, 1969), and "chance for advancement on this job" (Minnesota Satisfaction Questionnaire; Weiss, Dawis, England, & Lofquist, 1967). Because of the lack of an explicit reference for what promotion may yield (for example, in the way of increased job challenge, better supervision, more cooperative coworkers, more pay), these items also are likely to be assessing an individual's perceptions of the opportunities promotions may present in the other four facets of job satisfaction. Perhaps the concept of promotion opportunity is more encompassing than the other facets and implicitly captures opportunities associated with the other satisfaction components of a job.

In summary, we propose that measures of job satisfaction from the situationist perspective, in the future, contain items that explicitly assess perceptions of opportunity in all facets of work, not just promotion opportunities.

If the situationist perspective formed the key to understanding job satisfaction completely, the following dilemma would not remain: Why, in what appears to be the same situation, are some people more generally satisfied than others? The literature on individual differences in job satisfaction provides some answers to this interesting question.

Personal Correlates of Job Satisfaction

Understanding individual differences and the relationship between individual differences and the availability of opportunities can help resolve the dilemma stated above. Personal correlates of job satisfaction have become a recent focus of at least some researchers' interest.

Investigators have examined such individual correlates of job satisfaction as physical, mental, and dispositional differences.

Although physical characteristics such as sex, age, and race and their relationships to job satisfaction have been investigated extensively, results have not been consistent or conclusive (see Dalton & Marcis, 1987; Forgionne & Peeters, 1982; Mottaz, 1986; Murray & Atkinson, 1981; Quinn, Staines, & McCullough, 1974; Smith, Kendall, & Hulin, 1969). It is possible, however, that sex, age, or race are not the key variables. The better predictor of satisfaction may be the availability of opportunities—the availability of opportunities mediated differently in different situations because of an individual's sex, age, or race. That is, individuals of different sexes, age groups, or races may be offered varying opportunities because of prejudiced notions about what a particular "type" of person is capable of.

Ability is another individual variable that has been shown to be correlated with job satisfaction. For example, Schneider, Reichers, and Mitchell (1982) found that the relationship between ability requirements for a job and job satisfaction is as strong as the relationship between job rewards (for example, identity, autonomy, feedback) and satisfaction. It seems logical to propose, then, that ability provides opportunity because the more one is capable of doing, the more one has the opportunity to do.

We also believe that there are individual differences in how important opportunity is to people. One theory that deals with this individual difference in the form of a personality variable is the Myers-Briggs Type Indicator (MBTI) (Myers & McCaully, 1985). One of the four preferences exhibited by people is called the "sensing- intuitive" dimension. A person who is an intuitive type is particularly intrigued with possibilities and what is "just around the corner" rather than with the facts or reality of the current situation. For example, the preference for intuition appears to be conducive to the pursuit of higher education (Myers, 1980). Logically, a person who deeply values opportunity would also value education because of the options education provides.

Recently, another personal attribute, dispositional characteristics, has become a focus in the study of job satisfaction and related topics. A seemingly close link between personality traits and job satisfaction has been demonstrated by Pulakos and Schmitt (1983) and Staw and his colleagues (Staw, Bell, & Clausen, 1986; Staw & Ross, 1985).

Pulakos and Schmitt (1983) showed that instrumentality perceptions (that is, the perceived likelihood of obtaining valent outcomes from being employed) predicted job satisfaction. The instrumentality perceptions were obtained from high school juniors and seniors and correlated with job satisfaction measures twenty months later. Staw and his colleagues found similar stability in attitudes. A generally positive disposition correlated .40 with job satisfaction data collected forty to fifty years later. Given that job satisfaction data have, at best, stability of about .70 over eighteen months (Schneider & Dachler, 1978), the findings of Staw and his colleagues and Pulakos and Schmitt are quite impressive.

At least two explanations exist for why these findings are so strong. One possibility is that there is a true disposition such that, regardless of the setting, more positively disposed people will be more satisfied. Genetic theorists support this view. Research by Arvey, Bouchard, Segal, and Abraham (1989) has shown that genetic factors explained 32 percent of the shared variance in job satisfaction of monozygotic (identical) twins reared apart. An alternate interpretation of these data is that identical twins look alike and are therefore likely to be treated similarly. For example, twins with "intelligent" faces may be treated as if they are very capable (that is, receive similar opportunities), and therefore may feel more satisfied with their jobs as a result of this special treatment.

Another alternative to Arvey, et al.'s (1989) view is that people who are more positive, whether identical twins or not, choose to work in environments in which they are more likely to be satisfied. This argument proposes that people seek environments in which their positive affect is reinforced and rewarded and, if they are in an environment that fails to provide such reinforcement, they seek it elsewhere. This leads to Proposition Two: *People are predisposed to seek opportunity in their work and work worlds.* This proposition is especially true for people who are dispositionally more positive, intuitive (in the MBTI sense of the concept), and who have greater ability.

Finally, we turn to the literature that attempts to integrate the situational and the individual perspectives on job satisfaction—the person–environment fit perspective (P–E fit).

P–E Fit and the Prediction of Job Satisfaction

The vocational choice P–E fit literature shows that people will be satisfied with their vocational choices when those choices offer them the opportunity to implement or actualize their interests, personality, self-image, abilities, or needs (Super, 1953). The most influential theory of vocational choice, Holland's (1985), posits, for example, that careers and career environments are logically and conceptually groupable into six categories: realistic, investigative, artistic, social, enterprising, and conventional. The challenges for a person making a vocational choice are to acquire self-knowledge and to correctly choose the appropriate career environment. In a similar vein, Super's early framework argues that people choose to enter occupations that will allow them self-expression.

In the I-O and human resources literatures, there has also been evidence showing the validity of the P–E fit perspective. For example, investigators (Hackman & Lawler, 1971) have examined the relationships between growth need strength (GNS) and job satisfaction. They have found that the strength of the relationship between the work itself and overall job satisfaction is moderated by GNS. That is, people with high GNS are more likely to react favorably to job characteristics with high motivating potential, such as skill variety and task identity, than people with low GNS. In addition, Loher and Noe (1985) found that situational rather than job characteristics appear to be more important in determining satisfaction for employees low in GNS than for employees high in GNS.

The P–E fit perspective acknowledges that both the situation and the individual determine various outcomes, such as job satisfaction. To take this perspective even further, Kohn and Schooler's (1982) work has demonstrated that the relationship between the two variables, the situation and the individual, is dynamically reciprocal. Kohn and Schooler found that individuals' tendency to choose a complex versus a simple job is influenced by their cognitive complexity. Their cognitive complexity, however, is partially a reflection of the complexity of their present and previous jobs (for example, diversity of stimuli, number of decisions required). The findings of Kohn and Schooler regarding reciprocal relationships in cognitive complexity and job attributes can be applied to the relationships between future opportunities and job satisfaction. An individual who is exposed to many opportunities early in life may become more positively disposed to anticipate opportunities in future situations and, therefore, will more actively seek them out. It follows that people who actively seek opportunities will find more opportunities.

The research on personal correlates of job satisfaction and P–E fit correlates of satisfaction reveal a number of shared themes. Both emphasize the importance of individuals actively influencing and selecting their environments. By seeking positive situations, expectations can be met, abilities can be used, growth can come to fruition, desires can be attained, feelings can be actualized, personality can be implemented, and the self can be enacted. All of these, we argue, are variations on the theme of opportunity. These themes share a focus on possibilities, not just actualities, and on opportunities for what can be, rather than only what exists now or has already happened.

When the situationist perspective is added to these more personalogical ideas regarding the role of opportunity in satisfaction, it becomes clear how absent the construct has been in our conceptualization and measurements of satisfaction. Proposition One suggests that inclusion of opportunity in our measures would improve relationships between facet and global measures of satisfaction. In what follows, other contributions of the opportunity construct are explored.

Suggestions for Future Research

One area of research to which the concept of opportunity might provide additional insight is that of turnover. Numerous studies have shown that the relationship between job satisfaction and turnover is moderated by the alternatives people perceive in the work world. For example, Carsten and Spector (1987) found that a low correlation between job satisfaction and turnover exists during periods of high unemployment, while a much stronger relationship exists between job satisfaction and turnover during periods of expanded economic opportunity. They interpret these data as supporting the hypothesis of Hulin and his associates (Hulin, Roznowski, & Hachiya, 1985) that job opportunities influence turnover directly. In an article titled "The "Greener Grass" Phenomenon," J. Schneider (1976) showed that predictions of turnover were strongest when thoughts about perceived opportunities in an alternate job were included in the prediction.

> As Vroom (1964, p. 178) stated more than 20 years ago: It seems reasonable to assume that simultaneous measurements of the valence of one's present position (i.e., job satisfaction), the valence of the other positions, and the expectancy that these other positions can be attained would yield a better prediction of the outcomes of an individual's decision to stay or resign from his job than would measurements of job satisfaction alone.

Indeed Vroom anticipated the Carsten and Spector (1987) findings by proposing that: "If the probability of resignation is affected not only by job satisfaction but also by the availability of other positions, one should find higher turnover in times of full employment than in times of considerable unemployment" (p. 178).

These ideas can be incorporated with earlier logic to suggest that turnover may be more accurately predicted from job satisfaction data when the latter data include assessment of current and future opportunities. These ideas and findings lead to Proposition Three: *Measures of job satisfaction would be better predictors of turnover if items concerning the presence of present and future opportunities within the employing organization and outside that organization were included.* A second area of important research regarding opportunity concerns operationalization of the construct itself. Assessment of satisfaction with present and future opportunities would require the development of a new measure that would explicitly distinguish among the current situation, present opportunities, and future opportunities for each relevant facet of the job. For example, the following items might be used to assess satisfaction with pay.

> *Current Situation:* My present pay is adequate for my expenses.
> *Present opportunity:* I presently have opportunities available to me at which I could earn more money.
> *Future opportunity:* In the future, I will have the opportunity available to me to increase my pay on this job.

An obvious goal of these attempts to operationalize opportunity would be to test whether those measures designed to assess opportunities increase the prediction of turnover and correlate more highly with global indices of job satisfaction than do exiting facet measures.

Future research could also address questions such as: What opportunities are considered important by employees? Is there a point at which a future opportunity is irrelevant to one's current level of satisfaction? Are there individual differences governing the importance people place on opportunities available or expected to be available at different points in time?

Conclusion

The preceding issues are important for obtaining a better understanding of the opportunity construct and, ultimately, of job satisfaction. It is time for industrial-organizational psychologists to move beyond examining only existing job situations and individual differences in their efforts to understand job satisfaction and to begin measuring opportunity as well. Muchinsky (1987) expressed the importance of opportunity when he wrote:

> As a nation we value individual freedom, personal growth and "opportunity." Such values stem from formal documents like the Bill of Rights, a doctrine that has guided the political and social evolution of this country for over 200 years. They also stem from the belief that America is the "land of opportunity." . . . We believe implicitly that everyone has the right to a rewarding, satisfying job. Opportunity, we believe, is the great satisfier; it is in our culture and in our dispositions. Why isn't it more fully developed and represented in our theories and measures?

References

Arvey, R. D., Bouchard, T. J., Segal, N. L., & Abraham, L. M. (1989). Job satisfaction: Environmental and genetic components. *Journal of Applied Psychology, 74,* 187–192.

Brockner, J. (1988). *Self esteem at work: Research, theory and practice.* Lexington, MA: Lexington Books.

Carsten, J. M., & Spector, P. E. (1987). Unemployment, job satisfaction, and employee turnover: A meta-analytic test of the Muchinsky model. *Journal of Applied Psychology, 73,* 374–381.

Cook, J. D., Hepworth, S. J., Wall, T. D., & Warr, P. B. (1981). *The experience of work.* New York: Academic Press.

Dalton, A. H., & Marcis, J. G. (1987). Gender differences in job satisfaction among young adults. *Journal of Behavioral Economics, 16,* 21–32.

Evans, M. G. (1970). The effects of supervisory behavior on the path-goal relationship. *Organizational Behavior and Human Performance, 5,* 277–298.

Forgionne, G. A., & Peeters, V. E. (1982). The influence of sex on managers in the service sector. *California Management Review, 25,* 72–83.

Fried, Y., & Ferris, G. (1986). The validity of the job characteristics model: A review and meta-analysis. *Personnel Psychology, 40,* 287–322.

Hackman, J. R., & Lawler, E. E. (1971). Employee reactions to job characteristics. *Journal of Applied Psychology, 55,* 259–286.

Hackman, J. R., & Oldham, G. R. (1975). Development of the Job Diagnostic Survey. *Journal of Applied Psychology, 60,* 159–170.

Hauser, J. D. (1927). *What the employer thinks.* Cambridge, MA: Harvard University Press.

Hill, J. M., & Trist, E. L. (1953). A consideration of industrial accidents as a means of withdrawal from the work situation. *Human Relations, 6,* 357–380.

Holland, J. (1985). *Making vocational choices: A theory of careers.* Englewood Cliffs, NJ: Prentice-Hall.

Houser, R. J. (1971). A path-goal theory of leadership effectiveness. *Administrative Science Quarterly, 16,* 321–338.

Hulin, C. L., Roznowski, M., & Hachiya, D. (1985). Alternative opportunities and withdrawal decisions: Empirical and theoretical discrepancies and an integration. *Psychological Bulletin, 97,* 233–250.

Kanter, R. M. (1977). *Men and women of the corporation.* New York: Basic Books.

Kipnis, D. (1964). Mobility expectations and attitudes toward industrial structure. *Human Relations, 17,* 57–71.

Kohn, M. L., & Schooler, C. (1982). Job conditions and personality: A longitudinal assessment of their reciprocal effects. *American Journal of Sociology, 87*(6), 1257–1286.

Kulik, C. T., Oldham, G.W., & Langer, P.H. (1988). Measurement of job characteristics: Comparison of the original and the revised Job Diagnostic Survey. *Journal of Applied Psychology, 73,* 422–466.

Kunin, T. (1955). The construction of a new type of attitude measure. *Personnel Psychology, 8,* 65–78.

Landau, J., & Hammer, T. H. (1986). Clerical employees' perceptions of intraorganizational career opportunities. *Academy of Management Journal, 29,* 385–404.

LaRocco, J. M., House, J. S., & French, J.R.P., Jr. (1980). Social support, occupational stress, and health. *Journal of Health and Social Behavior, 2,* 202–218.

Larson, E. (1982). *Employee commitment to an organization and the effects of perceived ease of movement.* Unpublished doctoral dissertation, State University of New York at Buffalo.

Lawler, E. E., III. (1971). *Pay and organizational effectiveness.* New York: McGraw-Hill.

Locke, E. A. (1976). The nature and causes of job satisfaction. In M. D. Dunnette

(Ed.), *Handbook of industrial and organizational psychology* (pp. 1297–1349). Chicago: Rand McNally.

Loher, B., & Noe, R. (1985). A meta-analysis of the relation of job characteristics to job satisfaction. *Journal of Applied Psychology, 70,* 280–289.

Miller, G. A., Galanter, E., & Pribram, K. H. (1960). *Plans and the structure of behavior.* New York: Holt.

Miller, K. I., & Monge, P. R. (1986). Participation, satisfaction, and productivity: A meta-analytic review. *Academy of Management Journal, 29,* 727–753.

Mottaz, C. (1986). Gender differences in work satisfaction, work-related rewards and values, and the determinants of work satisfaction. *Human Relations, 39,* 359–378.

Muchinsky, P. (1987). *Psychology applied to work: An introduction to industrial and organizational psychology.* Chicago: Dorsey Press.

Murray, M. A., & Atkinson, T. (1981). Gender differences in correlates of job satisfaction. *Canadian Journal of Behavior Sciences, 13,* 44–52.

Myers, I. B. (1980). *Gifts differing.* Palo Alto, CA: Consulting Psychologists Press.

Myers, I. B., & McCaulley, M. (1985). *Manual: A guide to the development and use of the Myers-Briggs Type Indicator.* Palo Alto, CA: Consulting Psychologists Press.

Porter, L. W. (1961). A study of perceived need satisfaction in bottom and middle management jobs. *Journal of Applied Psychology, 45,* 1–10.

Pulakos, E. D., & Schmitt, N. (1983). A longitudinal study of a valence model approach for the prediction of job satisfaction of new employees. *Journal of Applied Psychology, 68,* 307–312.

Quinn, R. P., Staines, G. L., & McCullough, M. R. (1974). *Job satisfaction: Is there a trend?* Washington, DC: U.S. Department of Labor.

Roethlisberger, F. J., & Dickson, W. J. (1939). *Management and the worker.* Chicago: Harvard University Press.

Scarpello, V., & Campbell, J. P. (1983). Job satisfaction: Are all the parts there? *Personnel Psychology, 36,* 577–600.

Schneider, B., & Dachler, H. P. (1978). A note on the stability of the Job Descriptive Index. *Journal of Applied Psychology, 63,* 650–653.

Schneider, B., Reichers, A. E., & Mitchell, T. M. (1982). A note on some relationships between the aptitude requirements and reward attributes of tasks. *Academy of Management Journal, 25,* 567–574.

Schneider, J. (1976). The "greener grass" phenomenon: Differential effects of a work context alternative on organizational participation and withdrawal intentions. *Organizational Behavior and Human Performance, 116,* 303–333.

Smith, P. C., Kendall, L. M., & Hulin, C. L. (1969). *The measurement of satisfaction in work and retirement.* Chicago: Rand McNally.

Staw, B. M., Bell, N. E., & Clausen, J. A. (1986). The dispositional approach to job attitudes: A lifetime longitudinal test. *Administrative Science Quarterly, 31,* 56–77.

Staw, B. M., & Ross, J. (1985). Stability in the midst of change: A dispositional approach to job attitudes. *Journal of Applied Psychology, 70,* 469–480.

Super, D. E. (1953). A theory of vocational development. *American Psychologist, 8,* 185–190.

Taylor, F. W. (1911). *The principles of scientific management.* New York: Harper.

Trafford, A. (1988). What do nurses want? For starters, try doubling their salary. *The Washington Post,* July 19, p. H11.

Trist, E. L., & Bamforth, K. W. (1951). Some social and psychological conse-quences of the longwall method of coal-getting. *Human Relations, 4,* 3–38.

Vroom, V. H. (1964). *Work and motivation.* New York: Wiley.

Weiss, D. J., Dawis, R. V., England, G. W., & Lofquist, L. H. (1967). *Manual for the Minnesota Satisfaction Questionnaire.* Minneapolis: Industrial Relations Center, University of Minnesota.

4

Person–Environment Fit and Job Satisfaction

RENE V. DAWIS

This chapter is about research on person–environment fit (P–E fit) and job satisfaction, part of an ongoing research program on work adjustment that is being conducted at the University of Minnesota. The resulting theoretical ideas that have been shaped by this research, which in turn now guide our research efforts, are also described. "Our" refers to the Work Adjustment Project, initially led by G. W. England and L. H. Lofquist (1957–1964), then by Lofquist and R. V. Dawis (1964–1988), and now by Dawis and D. J. Weiss.

Only a generation ago, job satisfaction was studied not so much as a variable in its own right but as a predictor variable or as a moderator variable. In those days, job satisfaction was (and still is) seen as important for its consequences and for its contribution to the prediction of productivity and job performance. Nowadays, we are also interested in predicting job satisfaction as a criterion variable.

This paper is about P–E fit as a predictor of job satisfaction. P–E fit is, of course, only one of several possible predictors of job satisfaction. Conversely, job satisfaction is only one of several possible consequences of P–E fit.

P–E fit by itself is not particularly interesting from a theoretical standpoint, and has been derided as the "square-peg-in-square-hole" idea. The concept derives whatever theoretical attractiveness it possesses from being a proxy variable for person-environment interaction. P–E interaction is the mechanism that underlies, and is manifested in, P–E fit.

P–E interaction theory has attracted attention recently as the dialectic resolution of the trait-versus-situation controversy (Mischel, 1968; Bowers, 1973). This controversy, in turn, is only the most recent instance of the "paradigm clash" between two antithetical schools of thought in psychological theory (Ekehammer, 1974): the personologist school, which espouses the formula, $B = f(P)$, and the environmentalist school, whose basic formula is $B = f(E)$, where B stands for behavior, P for person, and E for environment. These two formulas are also frequently expressed as $B = f(O)$ and $B = f(S)$, respectively, where O stands for organism and S for stimulus. One notes, in passing, that the two schools correspond in a crude way to Cronbach's (1957) two "disciplines," the correlational and the experimental. The synthesis is, of course, $B = f(P,E)$ or $B = f(O,S)$, which is where P–E interaction comes in.

Far from being of recent origin, P–E interaction theory is one of the more venerable lines of psychological theorizing, as Ekehammar (1974) has pointed out. An early example is Kantor (1924, 1926) who wrote about the "mutual interaction" of the organism and the environment. Lewin's (1936) field theory is, perhaps, one of the best articulated of the early P–E interaction theories, in which the reciprocal dependence of P and E on each other is one of the basic features. Lewin's theory (influenced by Gestalt thinking) contrasts with Kantor's (which was behavioristic) in at least one major respect: whereas Kantor defined the environment in physical terms, Lewin insisted on the primacy of the phenomenological or "psychological" environment. The contrast between physical and psychological environments constitutes one of the major issues for P–E interaction theorists. For example, Tolman's early behavior theory focused on the physical "environmental variables" (Tolman, 1932); his later, more cognitively oriented writing stressed the psychological "behavior space" (Tolman, 1951). Murray (1938) resolved the problem in his need-press schema by including both: as alpha press (physical) and beta press (psychological). Furthermore, Murray introduced the idea of commensurate description—that is, describing both person and environment on parallel dimensions.

P–E interaction theory is arguably more interesting and more intellectually satisfying than P–E fit formulations, but it is also the more difficult to get data about, to instrument, to observe, to test, and to disconfirm or verify. With our current methodological capabilities, usually only P–E fit data can be obtained, and P–E interaction has to be inferred or assumed. At the least, P–E fit data can be used in prediction, which in any event is the acid test for theories.

Accurate prediction is also the first step toward control and intervention. It should come as no surprise, therefore, that the idea of P–E fit has been entertained and used in applied psychology from the earliest times. In vocational psychology, the "matching model" was first proposed by one of the field's founders, F. Parsons (1909). A few years later, Strong (1927) developed the "empirical scale" in his well-known measure of vocational interests. The "empirical scale" in effect described the work environment (occupation) in person terms (in terms of the interests of people engaged in the occupation). A high score on the scale meant that one "matched" the occupation.

With the development of more psychological tests, other test data began to be used in the matching. Viteles (1932), one of the pioneers in industrial psychology, proposed the use of the "job psychograph" (a forerunner of the test profile) to describe work environments in psychological-test terms. By 1935, the "differential occupational ability pattern" had been developed by Paterson (Paterson & Darley, 1936) and his student, Dvorak (1935) to describe occupations in terms of ability requirements. From that point on, the idea of matching people and jobs via patterns of ability requirements became accepted practice in both personnel selection and vocational guidance.

Relating P–E fit to job satisfaction did not occur until almost twenty years later, in the mid-1950s. In an early influential study of needs and satisfaction, Schaffer (1953) used the construct "need satisfaction" to refer to the extent to which each of twelve "Murray" needs was being satisfied on the job, in effect a measure of P–E fit. He also obtained data on "need strength," the strength of each of the twelve needs for a given individual. Schaffer found that (a) need strength and need satisfaction were correlated at different levels for different individuals, (b) average need satisfaction correlated modestly ($r = .44$) with overall job satisfaction (a separate measurement, not a score derived from need satisfaction), and (c) need satisfaction for the most important (highest strength) needs correlated strongest with overall job satisfaction.

Porter (1961) also saw job satisfaction as resulting from "perceived need-fulfillment"—that is, from need satisfaction. The notion of P–E fit was explicit in Porter's operationalization of need satisfaction, which was calculated from responses to two questions: "How much is there now?" (environment) and "How much should there be?" (person).

French and his Michigan colleagues (French & Kahn, 1962; French, Rodgers, & Cobb, 1974; Harrison, 1978) defined adjustment as the "goodness of fit" between person and environment. The Michigan group differentiated "objective" person and environment from "subjective" person and environment, thereby leading logically to two kinds of P–E fit, objective and subjective. In both cases, P–E fit is assessed by comparing "demands" and "supplies" on commensurate dimensions. There are two kinds of demands and two kinds of supplies to meet these demands: (a) the person's motives (for example, needs) are person demands to be met by environmental supplies; and (b) the environment's role requirements (as well as requests from other people) are environment demands to be met by the person's supplies (abilities). Objective P–E fit is assessed from objectively measured demands and supplies, and subjective P–E fit is assessed from subjective reports (the person's perception) of demands and supplies. A third measure of P–E fit can also be obtained by asking the person to report on perception of fit ("perceived fit").

The Michigan group has used the construct of P–E fit in the study of job stress and strain. Job stress (or, more correctly, the stressfulness of the job) is inferred from lack of P–E fit (the extent to which the job does not provide supplies to meet the person's motives, and/or the extent to which the person's abilities fall below the job's demands). Job stress, in turn, results in "strain," which is deviation from normal response or behavior. There are physiological strains, such as high blood pressure and elevated serum cholesterol; there also are psychological strains, of which job dissatisfaction is an example (others include anxiety, depression, and boredom).

The Michigan group has reported finding relationships between P–E fit and overall job satisfaction. For instance, Caplan (in French, Rodgers, & Cobb, 1974) reported significant F-values for analyses of variance with job satisfaction as the dependent variables and ten P–E fit scores as independent variables. Harrison (1978) reported that P–E fit (more correctly, "misfit") correlated 0.47 with job dissatisfaction and contributed more than half of the explained variance in the multiple correlation of job dissatisfaction with person, environment, and P–E fit. An interesting finding by the Michigan researchers was the observation of "curvilinearity" in the relationship of P–E fit with job dissatisfaction. For example, Harrison (in the study just cited) found significant etas between P–E fit on workload and job dissatisfaction for three different occupational groups (assembly line workers, administrators, and police officers). Though not symmetrical in effect, underload as well as overload can produce job dissatisfaction.

The Job Descriptive Index (JDI) group, under the leadership of P. C. Smith (Smith, Kendall, & Hulin, 1969), conceptualized job satisfaction as being associated with the perception of a difference between what is expected (or aspired to) and what is experienced—in other words, subjective P–E fit. Furthermore, the perceived characteristics of the job are evaluated in relation to the person's frame of reference, which, in turn, is shaped by the available alternatives, by expectations, by experience, and by the person's general adaptation level. The interrelationships of person variables (individual capacities, experience, values) and environment variables (objective factors of the job, available alternatives) are seen as the major predictors of satisfaction and performance as well.

Katzell (1964) stressed the important role that values (personal values) play in determining job satisfaction. Values, in turn (for Katzell), derive from the person's frame of reference and adaptation level. Thus, one might infer that Katzell favored subjective P–E fit as the predictor of job satisfaction. However, Katzell favored the separate assessment of job characteristics and personal values over the linked assessment that Porter (1961) and Schaffer (1953) used. Only by the former approach, Katzell believed, could we determine how given job features provide or deny the fulfillment of basic personal values.

Holland's (1966, 1985) popular theory of vocational choice is a P–E fit concept in which environments are "defined" by the characteristics of persons who customarily inhabit them. Vocational satisfaction, according to Holland, depends on the "congruence between one's personality and the environment in which one works" (1985, p. 10). Evidence supporting this proposition has been compiled in reviews by Spokane (1985) and by Assouline and Meir (1987). Most studies report finding statistically significant correlations between P–E fit and job satisfaction, averaging (in Assouline and Meir's meta-analysis) about .21, but with a wide range, from essentially zero (−.10) to .50. According to Assouline and Meir, the wide range of correlations was due to (or moderated by) how broadly or narrowly environment was defined, and how congruence (that is, P–E fit) was measured.

Pervin (1968), in an early and influential review of the literature on satisfaction as a function of P–E fit, raised three questions as the most important issues for P–E fit researchers to address: (a) Should one consider the perceived or the "actual" environment? (b) What units should be employed and should they be the same units of analysis for individuals and environments? (c) What is the nature of the processes involved in individual–environment relationships?

At the University of Minnesota, we began our study of work adjustment by, among other things, identifying "satisfaction" as one of the generic indicators of adjustment to work. "Satisfaction," we recognized, could be specified further as, for example, job satisfaction, occupational satisfaction, or career satisfaction. Satisfaction, we thought, logically called for its complement, need. Thus, we developed a measure of job satisfaction (which measured satisfaction with eight aspects of work; Carlson, Dawis, England, & Lofquist, 1962) and a measure of needs (which measured the importance of Murray's twelve needs, following Schaffer's lead; Weiss, Dawis, England, & Lofquist, 1964).

Shortly after doing this, we realized the pivotal significance of P–E fit in the prediction of work adjustment and, hence, of satisfaction. We also realized that the most practical way to operationalize P–E fit (which we called "individual-environment correspondence") was via commensurate measurement. We therefore combined the eight satisfaction aspects with the twelve needs to produce twenty "dimensions" on which to measure both satisfaction and needs (Weiss, Dawis, England, & Lofquist, 1967; Gay, Weiss, Dawis, & Lofquist, 1971). However, we still needed a measure of environment.

At this point, we decided that, if being satisfied meant staying on the job—that is, if job satisfaction maintained work behavior—then the "satisfiers" must be reinforcers. Therefore, it followed that the twenty dimensions referred to twenty different reinforcers, that "satisfaction" meant satisfaction with reinforcers, that "needs" referred to requirements for reinforcers (albeit measured as preferences for reinforcers), and that therefore the measure of environment—if commensurate with the measure of the individual's needs—should reflect the presence or absence, and degree, of each of the twenty reinforcers in the environment. Thus, we could use the same twenty statements, modified to suit grammatical requirements, in questionnaires that differed only in question stem, as follows:

For satisfaction: How satisfied are you with (x reinforcer)?
For need (person): How important to you in your ideal job is (x reinforcer)?
For reinforcer (environment): How well is this job described by (x reinforcer)?

Table 4–1 shows the twenty reinforcer statements and their scale titles.

Thus, with regard to Pervin's second question about units, we chose reinforcers: reinforcer requirements (or needs) on the person side, and reinforcer patterns on the environment side. Factor analysis studies of the three measures (of satisfaction, needs, and reinforcer systems), conducted on several large data sets and with the data obtained on separate samples for each measure, found that the factor structures mapped onto each other rather well. This finding is shown in table 4–2. (Details can be obtained from Weiss, Dawis, England, & Lofquist, 1967; Gay, Weiss, Dawis, & Lofquist, 1971; Dawis & Lofquist, 1984; and Shubsachs, Rounds, Dawis, & Lofquist, 1978.)

Table 4–2 shows that satisfaction tends to be organized around two factors, usually identified as intrinsic and extrinsic satisfaction (Campbell & Pritchard, 1976). However, we prefer to call them satisfaction with internal reinforcers (Factor I) versus satisfaction with external reinforcers (Factor II) to reflect origin of reinforcer as the primary differentiating characteristic between the factors.

Needs, or reinforcer requirements, are shown in table 4–2 to be organized around six factors. We subsequently labeled these factors as "values" (Lofquist & Dawis, 1978) to reflect our belief that values (that is, importance) underlie particular choices (preferences or requirements) of reinforcers. The need factor structure might be interpreted as follows (after Lofquist & Dawis, 1978):

Factor I: Safety value—the importance of structure, stability, and predictability in the work environment.

TABLE 4-1

Twenty Reinforcer Statements Used in Measures
of Satisfaction, Needs (Reinforcer Requirements),
and Reinforcer Systems, with Corresponding Scale Titles

Scale Title	Statement
1. Ability utilization	I could do something that makes use of my abilities.
2. Achievement	The job would give me a feeling of accomplishment.
3. Activity	I could be busy all the time.
4. Advancement	The job would provide an opportunity for advancement.
5. Authority	I could tell people what to do.
6. Company policies and practices	The company would administer its policies fairly.
7. Compensation	My pay would compare well with that of other workers.
8. Coworkers	My coworkers would be easy to make friends with.
9. Creativity	I could try out my own ideas.
10. Independence	I could work alone on the job.
11. Moral values	I could do the work without feeling it is morally wrong.
12. Recognition	I could get recognition for the work I do.
13. Responsibility	I could make decisions on my own.
14. Security	The job would provide for steady employment.
15. Social service	I could do things for other people.
16. Social status	I could be "somebody" in the community.
17. Supervision—human relations	My boss would back up the workers (with top management).
18. Supervision—technical	My boss would train the workers well.
19. Variety	I could do something different every day.
20. Working conditions	The job would have good working conditions.

TABLE 4–2

Scales Defining Factors for Measures of Satisfaction, Needs (Reinforcer Requirements), and Reinforcer Systems

	Factors										
	Satisfaction		Needs (Reinforcer Requirements)						Reinforcer Systems		
Scale Title	I	II	I	II	III	IV	V	VI	I	II	III
1. Ability utilization	1						1		1		
2. Achievement	2						2		2		
3. Activity	3				3						
4. Advancement		4						4	4	4	
5. Authority	5							5	5		
6. Company policies and practices		6	6							6	
7. Compensation		7			7					7	
8. Coworkers		8				8					8
9. Creativity	9			9					9		
10. Independence	10			10							
11. Moral values	11					11					11
12. Recognition		12						12	12	12	
13. Responsibility	13			13					13		
14. Security		14			14						
15. Social service	15					15					15
16. Social status	16							16	16		
17. Supervision—human relations		17	17							17	
18. Supervision—technical		18	18							18	
19. Variety	19				19				19		
20. Working conditions		20			20					20	

Factor II: Autonomy value—the importance of control exercised by self, of self-initiative.

Factor III: Comfort value—the importance of a comfortable and nonstressful work environment.

Factor IV: Altruism value—the importance of harmony with others and opportunity to be of service to others.

Factor V: Achievement value—the importance of accomplishment via use of one's abilities.

Factor VI: Status value—the importance of social recognition and prestige.

The data on reinforcer patterns (called Occupational Reinforcer Patterns, or ORPs) are organized around three factors (Shubsachs, Rounds, Dawis, & Lofquist, 1978), as shown in table 4–2. Factor I is defined predominantly by self or internal reinforcers. Factor II reflects reinforcers from the organizational environment. Factor III is the reinforcer equivalent of the Altruism value.

By 1964, we felt confident enough to describe the relationship between P–E fit and satisfaction as a formal proposition in our Theory of Work Adjustment. "Proposition III. Satisfaction is a function of the correspondence between the reinforcer system of the work environment and the individual's needs" (Dawis, England, & Lofquist, 1964).

With regard to Pervin's first question about perceived versus "actual" environments, we chose the "actual" or, more accurately, the "consensually validated" (as Pervin described it). That is, we chose to use the aggregated data of a group of raters, rather than the person's own ratings of the environment, in the calculation of P–E fit. We were aware that the aggregated data of a group of raters are, in a real sense, perceptions as well. However, because they are consensually validated, they can be called "objective," as contrasted with the person's own "subjective" data. Objective data have advantages over the subjective: (a) Group data tend to be more reliable and more accurate than individual data; (b) Linked measurement—that is, obtaining *P* and *E* scores from the same source—has its psychometric problems, as Cronbach and Furby (1970) point out; and (c) Inexperienced or uninformed individuals, such as adolescents or young adults, may have little knowledge of work environments or, worse, have distorted stereotypes about them. On the other hand, subjective data have the advantage of being temporally as well as spatially closer to job satisfaction in the causal chain. It is therefore not surprising to find that when objective and subjective P–E fits are compared in the same study, for the same set of subjects, subjective P–E fit is found to be the better predictor of job satisfaction (see, for example, Pazy & Zin, 1987; Holt, 1984). Nonetheless, our theoretical preference was for the objective.

Furthermore, because our research problem at that time was the prediction of future, rather than current, work adjustment (hence, future job satisfaction), the choice of objective rather than subjective P–E fit made more sense, inasmuch as our vocational client population would not yet have experienced the work environment and therefore could not provide the data on the perceived or subjective environment as required for P–E fit measurement. This choice, in turn, required us to collect objective reinforcer data in the form of Occupational Reinforcer Patterns (ORPs) on a large number and a broad range of occupations. Figure 4–1 shows an example of an Occupational Reinforcer Pattern. (For technical details about the construction of ORPs and their psychometric properties, see Borgen, Weiss, Tinsley, Dawis, & Lofquist, 1968).

ORPs have been developed for 185 occupations, based on data obtained primarily from supervisors (Stewart et al., 1986). These 185 ORPs have been grouped, using cluster analysis, into six groupings called Occupational Reinforcer Clusters (ORCs). ORCs are, in effect, broader definitions of environment than are ORPs. (For research purposes, we developed a rating procedure that enabled "expert" raters to classify occupations according to ORC reliably.)

An even broader definition of environment (or, in other terms, less specific definition) is obtained from using the Minnesota Occupational Classification System III (or MOCS III, our third effort at occupational classification; see Dawis, Dohm, Lofquist, Chartrand, & Due, 1987). MOCS III classifies occupations (almost 2,000) according to two facets or axes: ability requirements and reinforcer patterns. The classification system is based on three categories of ability (perceptual, cognitive, motor) and three categories of reinforcer (internal, social, environmental), using three levels (high, average, not significant) for each category. One classification combination is called a taxon, an example of which is shown in figure 4–2.

Over the years, we have collected sizeable amounts of data show-

ELECTRICAL ENGINEER

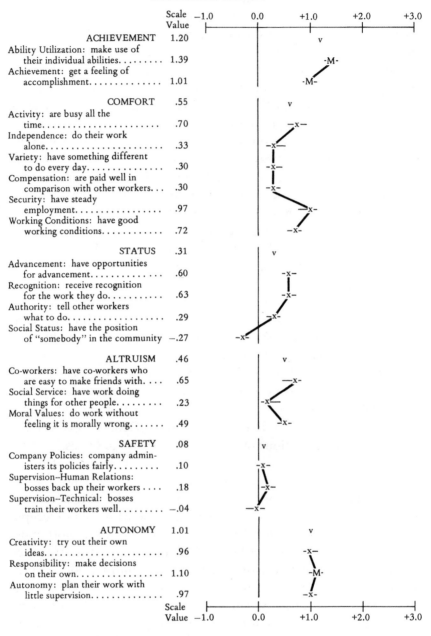

	Scale Value
ACHIEVEMENT	1.20
Ability Utilization: make use of their individual abilities.	1.39
Achievement: get a feeling of accomplishment.	1.01
COMFORT	.55
Activity: are busy all the time.	.70
Independence: do their work alone.	.33
Variety: have something different to do every day.	.30
Compensation: are paid well in comparison with other workers. . .	.30
Security: have steady employment.	.97
Working Conditions: have good working conditions.	.72
STATUS	.31
Advancement: have opportunities for advancement.	.60
Recognition: receive recognition for the work they do.	.63
Authority: tell other workers what to do.	.29
Social Status: have the position of "somebody" in the community	−.27
ALTRUISM	.46
Co-workers: have co-workers who are easy to make friends with. . . .	.65
Social Service: have work doing things for other people.	.23
Moral Values: do work without feeling it is morally wrong.	.49
SAFETY	.08
Company Policies: company administers its policies fairly.	.10
Supervision–Human Relations: bosses back up their workers	.18
Supervision–Technical: bosses train their workers well.	−.04
AUTONOMY	1.01
Creativity: try out their own ideas.	.96
Responsibility: make decisions on their own.	1.10
Autonomy: plan their work with little supervision.	.97

FIGURE 4–1

Occupational Reinforcer Pattern for Electrical Engineer

PCM/IS   TAXON: 095
Primary Taxon: 02   Level code: 111.120

OCCUPATIONAL REQUIREMENTS

Left margin vertical labels: OCCUPATIONAL REINFORCERS — Internal: ACH AUT STA AVERAGE — Social: ALT HIGH — Environment: SAF COM NOT SIGNIF

	Perceptual Abilities S, P, Q AVERAGE		Cognitive Abilities G, V, N AVERAGE		Motor Abilities K, F, M AVERAGE											
DOT Title	DOT Code			DOT Profile			Job Des		Additional Data							
	GRP	DPT	EC	INT	TMP	PHY	DOT	OOH	FX	PR	OAP	SCH	ORP	ORC	INV
MEDICAL TECHNOLOGIST, TEACHING SUPERVISOR	078	121	010	476	547	L45 6	061	183	HI	HI	00	VR	NO		S
NURSE, GENERAL DUTY nurse, staff nurse, professional	075	374	010	47	5Y	LM4 6	058	174	MOD	HI	50	V	YES	F	SK
NURSE, LICENSED PRACTICAL	079	374	014	47	5Y	LM4 6	065	196	MOD	HI	50	V	YES	F	SK
NURSE, SUPERVISOR	075	127	022	476	547	L45 6	057	174	HI	HI	50	VR	NO		
RADIOLOGIC TECHNOLOGIST x-ray technologist	078	362	026	47	5Y	LM4 6	062	200	MOD	HI	50	VI	YES	F	S
SECRETARY secretarial stenographer secretary (general office)	201	362	030	26	159	S45 6	153	281	MOD	MH	35	VI	YES	F	SK

GRP–DOT (1977) Occupational Group (3-digit code)
DPT–DOT (1977) Worker-Function Code for data, people, things
  EC–DOT (1977) extended code (last three digits)
INT–Interests (DOT, Vol. II. Occupational Classification--third edition 1965)
TMP–Temperaments (DOT, Vol. II., Occupational Classification--third edition 1965)
PHY–Physical Demands (DOT, Vol. II., Occupational Classification--third edition 1965)
DOT–Page number for Occupational Description in the DOT (1977)
OOH–Page number in the Occupational Outlook Handbook (1986-1987)
  FX–Estimated Flexibility of the Work Environment
  PR–Occupational Prestige Level
OAP–Occupational Aptitude Pattern (where available)
SCH–Schedule of Reinforcement
ORP–Availability of Occupational Reinforcer Pattern
ORC–Occupational Reinforcer Cluster (where available)
INV–Interest Inventory Containing Occupational Scale (where available)

FIGURE 4–2

A Taxon from the Minnesota Occupational Classification System III

ing that both concurrent and subsequent job satisfaction can be predicted from P–E fit (for example, Betz, 1968; Holt, 1984; Lichter, 1980; Rounds, 1981; Salazar, 1981; Vessey, 1973). Correlations are typically between .20 and .30, with occasional .30s and .40s or higher. This level of prediction is not much different from that reported for the Holland studies cited earlier (Spokane, 1985; Assouline & Meir, 1987). Like Assouline and Meir, we also observed that level of prediction (predictive efficiency) appeared to be related to level of specificity in defining environment and type of P–E fit measure used. Table 4–3 illustrates this finding. The data come from Rounds' (1981) study of vocational counseling clients. ORP ratings represent the most narrow definition of environment, whereas taxon grouping refers to its broadest definition. With respect to P–E fit measure, the well-known Euclidian-distance measure of profile similarity, d^2, incorporates all three profile components of level, shape, and scatter, whereas Pearson r reflects only the shape component (that is, rank order).

Table 4–3 shows that the more narrowly environment is defined, the better the prediction; also, that Pearson r does a better job as a predictor than does d^2. Table 4–3 also shows that in Rounds' (1981) study, the prediction of job satisfaction before vocational counseling was possible only for the female clients, that level of prediction was higher after counseling, and that gender interacted with type of P–E fit measure in the prediction of job satisfaction after, as well as before, counseling. (Restriction of range was not observed for job satisfaction and therefore was not a factor in these results. As expected, job satisfaction improved after counseling.)

In the early 1960s, when we first began to use P–E fit as a predictor, the P–E fit measure we chose was d^2, the favored measure of profile similarity (Cronbach & Gleser, 1953). We soon became aware (as Rounds' data illustrate) that d^2 had shortcomings as a predictor. We therefore experimented with several P–E fit measures, culminating in an extensive study in 1975 that involved six occupational groups and nineteen different P–E fit measures.

Our development of P–E fit measures were governed by several considerations. Given commensurate measurement, a P–E fit measure is some function of the difference scores between corresponding (parallel) person and environment measures—in our case, measures of needs and reinforcers. The P–E fit measure may take account of

TABLE 4–3

Correlation of P-E Fit and Job Satisfaction Before and After Vocational Counseling, by Client Gender, Environment Measure, and P-E Fit Measure

Environment Measure	P-E Fit Measure			
	Before Counseling		After Counseling	
	d^2	r	d^2	r
ORP Ratings				
Female Sample	−05	21[b]	−15	52[b]
Male Sample	09	−13	−32[a]	55[b]
ORC Ratings				
Female Sample	−07	21[b]	−18	46[b]
Male Sample	06	−04	−27[a]	33[b]
Taxon Grouping				
Female Sample	−06	12[a]	−14	36[b]
Male Sample	03	−09	−21[a]	16[a]

Notes: Samples were clients of a fee-for-service university-run vocational assessment clinic. Female sample numbers ranged from 57 to 170; for male samples, from 41 to 190. Decimal points omitted. Data taken from Rounds, 1981, tables 31 and 32.

[a]$p < .05.$
[b]$p < .01.$

the direction of the difference in the difference scores, or it may not. The difference scores may be weighted according to some factor like importance, or they may not. Inasmuch as our scales had zero points (they were constructed according to Thurstone's method of comparative judgment), the zero point may be taken into account (only scores above the zero point are used), or it may not. Inasmuch as two profiles (for needs and for reinforcers) were being compared, correlational methods (including indexes of agreement) could be used as measures of P–E fit.

The results of this study were finally published recently (Rounds, Dawis, & Lofquist, 1987). Table 4–4 summarizes these findings.

As table 4–4 shows, level of prediction differed for different types

TABLE 4-4

*Average Correlation of P-E Fit Measures and Job Satisfaction,
by Type of P-E Fit Measure and Occupation*

Type of P-E Fit Measure	Occupation					
	A	B	C	D	E	F
Nondirectional						
1. Agreement $(n = 3)$	02	11	02	−07	02	−06
2. Rank order $(n = 4)$	25[b]	12	18[b]	12	26[b]	19[a]
3. d^2	−10	−25[a]	−05	−03	−03	−13
4. Level	00	−20	05	02	19	30[a]
Directional						
1. $R > N$ $(n = 5)$	−13	05	−08	−18	−25[b]	−26[a]
2. $N > R$ $(n = 5)$	05	−24[a]	06	06	13	24[a]

Notes: Agreement P–E fit measures included high point index and two Holley's G indexes of agreement. Rank-order measures included Pearson r, Spearman *rho*, Kendall *tau*, and d^2 prime. Directional P–E fit measures included eight configurations of weighted versus unweighted, without zero point, and $R > N$ versus $N > R$, where N = needs and R = reinforcers. Two final directional measures used zero points for both needs and reinforcers, for $R > N$ and $N > R$.

Occupations were: A = cashier $(n = 91)$, B = checker-marker $(n = 64)$, C = counselor $(n = 196)$, D = salesperson $(n = 117)$, E = service representative $(n = 89)$, and F = telephone operator $(n = 78)$. Decimal points omitted.

[a]$p < .05$.
[b]$p < .01$

of P–E fit measures. The type with the best prediction record across all six occupations was the group of four rank-order measures (Pearson *r*, Spearman *rho*, Kendall *tau*, and d^2 prime). Directional measures were not better than the nondirectional. Level of prediction also appeared to differ by occupation. (Sampling could be a factor.) The highest level of prediction was obtained with different P–E fit measures for different occupations, a finding that bears further investigation.

One can conclude from table 4–4 that more study has to be devoted to the question of operationalizing P–E fit. Proposition III of the theory of work adjustment (mentioned previously), taken literally, implies that degree of difference (between P and E scores), rather than direction, is what matters. This, in turn, implies curvilinearity in the relationship between P–E fit and job satisfaction. Furthermore, if, as posited by the Theory of Work Adjustment, reinforcers are involved in job satisfaction, there may be a difference in the relationships observed for positive versus negative reinforcers, if these can be identified. Also, Rounds, Dawis, and Lofquist (1987) found that weighting by the importance of the need did not materially improve prediction. This finding, together with the finding that the best P–E fit measures were the rank-order measures, indicates that our P and E scales remain very much at the ordinal level of measurement. We have a long way to go in the measurement of P–E fit.

With regard to Pervin's third question, a conjecture can at least be offered. If reinforcement is involved in job satisfaction, Premack's (1965) interpretation of reinforcement as response rather than as stimulus makes for some interesting speculation. It would imply that job satisfaction itself, and not the environmental conditions of work, is the reinforcer. As reinforcer, job satisfaction maintains work behavior, whereas job dissatisfaction triggers other behavior (adjustment behavior, according to the Theory of Work Adjustment). The differential satisfaction/dissatisfaction response must, in turn, be brought about by some cause, and the best candidate so far is perception of P–E fit. Construction of "objective" or "consensually validated" measures of E (still important to obtain for reasons outlined above) should therefore start with job satisfaction. There is an analogy here to the way ability requirements for jobs are determined at present, which is by starting with performance. That is, when we determine the required abilities for a job, we do better to infer them from performance than by having "expert" raters estimate them; in the same way, determining "reinforcing conditions" (conditions that produce job satisfaction, the reinforcer) might be better done by comparing more versus less satisfied groups, rather than having raters estimate them, as is currently done in the case of the ORPs. Ironically, this was a method considered and tried out early in the Work Adjustment Project, with some success (Weiss, Dawis, England, & Lofquist, 1965). Things change and yet remain the same.

More to the point of Pervin's third question: If satisfaction or dissatisfaction is a trigger to behavior, it is implicated in the motivation of behavior. Satisfaction can play a role in all three aspects in motivation—energizing, sustaining, and directing behavior. Thus, satisfaction plays a pivotal part in the processes involved in P–E interaction. P–E fit also plays a role in motivation in its capacity as an antecedent of job satisfaction. As such, it contributes probably to directing behavior, possibly to sustaining behavior, and it can be the occasion for energizing behavior, although other factors (genetic inheritance, experience, learning, memory) may play more decisive roles. Thus, the relationship between P–E fit and satisfaction gets turned around, and satisfaction can be used to infer contemporaneous P–E fit. But P–E fit remains useful as a predictor of future satisfaction in environments with which the person has not yet interacted.

References

Assouline, M., & Meir, E. I. (1987). Meta-analysis of the relationship between congruence and well-being measures. *Journal of Vocational Behavior, 31,* 319–332.

Betz, E. L. (1968). *Occupational reinforcer patterns and need-reinforcer correspondence in the prediction of job satisfaction.* Unpublished doctoral dissertation, University of Minnesota, Minneapolis.

Borgen, F. H., Weiss, D. J., Tinsley, H. E. A., Dawis, R. V., & Lofquist, L. H. (1968). The measurement of occupational reinforcer patterns. *Minnesota Studies in Vocational Rehabilitation, XXV.*

Bowers, K. S. (1973). Situationism in psychology: An analysis and a critique. *Psychological Review, 80,* 307–336.

Campbell, J. P., & Pritchard, R. D. (1976). Motivation theory in industrial and organizational psychology. In M. D. Dunnette (Ed.), *Handbook of industrial and organizational psychology* (pp. 63–130). Chicago: Rand McNally.

Carlson, R. E., Dawis, R. V., England, G. W., & Lofquist, L. H. (1962). The measurement of employment satisfaction. *Minnesota Studies in Vocational Rehabilitation, XIII.*

Cronbach, L. J. (1957). The two disciplines of scientific psychology. *American Psychologist, 12,* 671–684.

Cronbach, L. J., & Furby, L. (1970). How should we measure "change"—or should we? *Psychological Bulletin, 74,* 68–80.

Cronbach, L. J., & Gleser, G. C. (1953). Assessing similarity between profiles. *Psychological Bulletin, 50,* 456–473.

Dawis, R. V., Dohm, T. E., Lofquist, L. H., Chartrand, J. M., & Due, A. M. (1987). *Minnesota Occupational Classification System III.* Minneapolis: Department of Psychology, University of Minnesota.

Dawis, R. V., England, G. W., & Lofquist, L. H. (1964). A theory of work adjustment. *Minnesota Studies in Vocational Rehabilitation, XV.*

Dawis, R. V., & Lofquist, L. H. (1984). *A psychological theory of work adjustment.* Minneapolis: University of Minnesota Press.

Dvorak, B. J. (1935). *Differential occupational ability patterns.* Bulletins of the Employment Stabilization Research Institute, *3*(8), Minneapolis: University of Minnesota.

Ekehammer, B. (1974). Interactionism in personality from a historical perspective. *Psychological Bulletin, 81,* 1026–1048.

French, J. R. P., Jr., & Kahn, R. L. (1962). A programmatic approach to studying the industrial environment and mental health. *Journal of Social Issues, 18,* 1–48.

French, J. R. P., Jr., Rodgers, W., & Cobb, S. (1974). Adjustment as person–environment fit. In G. V. Coelho, D. A. Hamburg, & J. E. Adams (Eds.), *Coping and adaptation* (pp. 316–333). New York: Basic Books.

Gay, E. G., Weiss, D. J., Dawis, R. V., & Lofquist, L. H. (1971). Manual for the Minnesota Importance Questionnaire. *Minnesota Studies in Vocational Rehabilitation, XXVIII.*

Harrison, R. V. (1978). Person–environment fit and job stress. In C. L. Cooper & R. Payne (Eds.), *Stress at work* (pp. 175–205). New York: Wiley.

Holland, J. L. (1966). *The psychology of vocational choice.* Waltham, MA: Blaisdell.

Holland, J. L. (1985). *Making vocational choices* (2nd ed.). Englewood Cliffs, NJ: Prentice-Hall.

Holt, N. C. L. (1984). *The relation between individual vocational needs and work environment reinforcers in a sample of food service workers.* Unpublished doctoral dissertation, University of Minnesota, Minneapolis.

Kantor, J. R. (1924). *Principles of psychology.* Vol. 1. Bloomington, IN: Principia Press.

Kantor, J. R. (1926). *Principles of psychology.* Vol. 2. Bloomington, IN: Principia Press.

Katzell, R. A. (1964). Personal values, job satisfaction, and job behavior. In H. Borow (Ed.), *Man in a world at work* (pp. 341–363). Boston: Houghton Mifflin.

Lewin, K. (1936). *Principles of topological psychology.* New York: McGraw-Hill.

Lichter, D. J. (1980). *The prediction of job satisfaction as an outcome of career counseling.* Unpublished doctoral dissertation, University of Minnesota, Minneapolis.

Lofquist, L. H., & Dawis, R. V. (1978). Values as second-order needs in the Theory of Work Adjustment. *Journal of Vocational Behavior, 12,* 12–19.

Mischel, W. (1968). *Personality and assessment.* New York: Wiley.

Murray, H. A. (1938). *Explorations in personality.* New York: Oxford University Press.

Parsons, F. (1909). *Choosing a vocation.* Boston: Houghton.

Paterson, D. G., & Darley, J. G. (1936). *Men, women, and jobs.* Minneapolis: University of Minnesota Press.

Pazy, A., & Zin, R. (1987). A contingency approach to consistency: A challenge to prevalent views. *Journal of Vocational Behavior, 30,* 84–101.

Pervin, L. A. (1968). Performance and satisfaction as a function of individual–environment fit. *Psychological Bulletin, 69,* 56–68.

Porter, L. W. (1961). A study of perceived need satisfaction in bottom and middle management jobs. *Journal of Applied Psychology, 45,* 1–10.

Premack, D. (1965). Reinforcement theory. In D. Levine (Ed.), *Nebraska Symposium on Motivation* (pp. 123–180). Lincoln: University of Nebraska Press.

Rounds, J. B., Jr. (1981). *The comparative and combined utility of need and interest data in the prediction of job satisfaction.* Unpublished doctoral dissertation, University of Minnesota, Minneapolis.

Rounds, J. B., Dawis, R. V., & Lofquist, L. H. (1987). Measurement of person–environment fit and prediction of satisfaction in the Theory of Work Adjustment. *Journal of Vocational Behavior, 31,* 297–318.

Salazar, R. M. C. (1981). *The prediction of satisfaction and satisfactoriness for counselor training graduates.* Unpublished doctoral dissertation, University of Minnesota, Minneapolis.

Schaffer, R. H. (1953). Job satisfaction as related to need satisfaction in work. *Psychological Monographs: General and Applied, 67*(364).

Shubsachs, A. P. W., Rounds, J. B., Jr., Dawis, R. V., & Lofquist, L. H. (1978). Perception of work reinforcer systems: Factor structure. *Journal of Vocational Behavior, 13,* 54–62.

Smith, P. C., Kendall, L. M., & Hulin, C. L. (1969). *The measurement of satisfaction in work and retirement.* Chicago: Rand McNally.

Spokane, A. R. (1985). A review of research on person–environment congruence in Holland's theory of careers. *Journal of Vocational Behavior, 26,* 306–343.

Stewart, E. S., Greenstein, S. M., Holt, N. C., Henly, G. A., Engdahl, B. E., Dawis, R. V., Lofquist, L. H., & Weiss, D. J. (1986). *Occupational reinforcer patterns.* Minneapolis: Department of Psychology, University of Minnesota.

Strong, E. K., Jr. (1927). *Vocational interest blank,* Palo Alto, CA: Stanford University Press.

Tolman, E. C. (1932). *Purposive behavior in animals and men.* New York: Appleton-Century.

Tolman, E. C. (1951). A psychological model. In T. Parsons & E. A. Shils (Eds.), *Toward a general theory of action* (pp. 279–361). Cambridge, MA: Harvard University Press.

Vessey, T. M. (1973). *A longitudinal study of the prediction of job satisfaction as a function of the correspondence between needs and the perceptions of job reinforcers in an occupation.* Unpublished doctoral dissertation, University of Minnesota, Minneapolis.

Viteles, M. S. (1932). *Industrial psychology.* New York: Norton.

Weiss, D. J., Dawis, R. V., England, G. W., & Lofquist, L. H. (1964). The measurement of vocational needs. *Minnesota Studies in Vocational Rehabilitation,* XVI.

Weiss, D. J., Dawis, R. V., England, G. W., & Lofquist, L. H. (1965). An inferential approach to occupational reinforcement. *Minnesota Studies in Vocational Rehabilitation,* XIX.

Weiss, D. J., Dawis, R. V., England, G. W., & Lofquist, L. H. (1967). Manual for the Minnesota Satisfaction Questionnaire. *Minnesota Studies in Vocational Rehabilitation,* XXIII.

Psychological Climate and Affect

Test of a Hierarchical Dynamic Model

LAWRENCE R. JAMES

LOIS A. JAMES

Cognitive approaches to the study of environments are based on the hypothesis that individuals respond affectively and behaviorally to situational events as a function of how they perceive these events (see Ekehammar, 1974; Endler & Magnusson, 1976; James & Jones, 1974; Lewin, 1938). Specifically, it is believed that individuals interpret environmental events in ways that are psychologically meaningful to them, such as interpreting a pay raise in terms of its equity (James, 1982; James, Hater, Gent, & Bruni, 1978; Stotland & Canon, 1972; Mandler, 1982). It is the "meaning" (for example, equity) that an individual imputes to an environment that links "objective" environmental events (for example, a pay raise) to individual attitudes and/or behaviors (for example, job satisfaction, initiating a search for another job). Our objective in this chapter is to continue our recent efforts into the study of meaning as it pertains to work environments (see L. R. James & James, 1989; James, James, & Ashe, 1990). We will begin with an overview of our perspective of meaning. This overview will be followed by the presentation of a hierarchical model of meaning, wherein recent tests for a general factor of meaning of work environment perceptions are described. Discussion proceeds to an empirical test of a proposed reciprocal relationship between the general factor of meaning and overall job satisfaction. This test reflects a continuing belief that affect is both a cause and an effect of perceptions of special salience to individuals (James & Jones, 1980; James & Tetrick, 1986).

Measures of Meaning in Work Environments

Individual perceptions of environmental attributes can range from purely descriptive reports of the work situation to highly complex appraisals of what environmental events mean psychologically to the individual. Perceptions are said to be descriptive, denotative, and cold when the objective of perception is to report the presence or absence of attributes of environmental events (see Lazarus & Folkman, 1984; Mandler, 1982; Osgood, Suci, & Tannenbaum, 1957; Stotland & Canon, 1972; Zajonc, 1980). In contrast, hot cognitions, evaluative meanings, connotative perceptions, cognitive appraisals, and emotionally relevant cognitions require more cognitive information processing than descriptive perceptions and are more personalistically oriented (see preceding references). Of particular interest is the concept of "valuation" (Mandler, 1982), which suggests that individuals cognitively appraise environmental attributes in terms of schemas that are derived from work-related values such as recognition or challenge (L. R. James & James, 1989). Valuation is thus viewed as a product of the integration of perceptions of what is out there (descriptive perceptions) with schemas engendered by work-relevant values. The product of this integration—the valuation—is what is generally thought of as the "meaning" of the environment event(s) for the individual.

To illustrate the processes discussed above, consider job complexity as one objective indicator of job characteristics. Job complexity could be operationalized in terms of the number of complex task problems that must be solved, the degree to which tasks are non-repetitious, the extent to which task goals are difficult to define, the number of opportunities that exist for personal decision making, and the degree to which problem-solving procedures are non-standardized (see James & Jones, 1980). For the sake of this discussion, let us presume that individuals perceive these indicators of job complexity in a reasonably veridical fashion. Such perceptions thus describe actual environmental events. What constitutes a "challenging" job to a particular individual, however, requires valuations of the indicators of job complexity (more technically, valuations of the perceptions of these indicators). The valuative judgments are dependent on an individual's "structural requirements" (Mandler, 1982) for challenging jobs, which is to say the standards that this individual employs to judge whether a job is challenging (Locke, 1976). This, then, is a subjective, value-based process because the structural requirements are personal standards one uses to appraise environmental attributes cognitively in terms of their significance to what one values, wants, or desires (James, Hater, Gent, & Bruni, 1978).

It follows logically that environmental attributes may be identical for two individuals, and perceived that way descriptively, whereas the valuations associated with these attributes may differ reliably. For example, a highly intelligent individual may perceive a task of modest complexity as "nonchallenging," whereas a less-gifted individual may perceive the same task as "challenging." Clearly, the individuals' structural requirements (that is, standards or values) for "challenge" differ reliably. Moreover, this difference underscores the psychological nature of valuation in the sense that values may be defined as those things that one seeks, desires, or needs because they are conducive to one's welfare (Locke, 1976). The psychological nature of welfare is clearly indicated by its being defined in terms of happiness and well-being (L. R. James & James, 1989). We suggest, therefore, that meanings derived from valuation processes are psychological variables that are employed to appraise work environments in terms of their facility to promote personal well-being (welfare). Because we are concerned solely with welfare in the work environment, well-being will hereafter be limited to what we have referred to as Organizational Well-Being (OWB) (L. R. James & James, 1989).

Valuations are believed to be key determinants of affective outcomes (for example, satisfaction) because, in combination with physiological arousal, valuations give rise to a subjective experience of affect (see Reisenzein, 1983; Schachter & Singer, 1962). Of special concern here is the concept of an emotionally relevant cognition (Reisenzein, 1983; Schachter & Singer, 1962), which connotes that meanings reflecting valuations provide relevant input for emotions. Indeed, valuations are emotionally relevant by definition. In valuation, environmental events are appraised in terms of psychological standards that reflect the benefit or detriment of the event(s) for one's (organizational) well-being. The ensuing feeling of happiness or well-being (or lack of such) is the affective, emotional experience (see Lazarus, 1982, 1984; Lazarus & Folkman, 1984). Thus, emotional responses to work environments are regarded as functions of valuations—that is, cognitive appraisals of the significance that environmental events have for one's well-being.

For example, we might say that individuals desire various indicators of the latent psychological value "job challenge" (that is, individuals seek opportunities to make important decisions or to solve novel problems) because individuals have learned that job challenge is emotionally relevant—that is, efficacious—for a feeling of well-being (that is, finding a novel solution to a problem feels good). More specifically, the novel solution is the environmental event of interest. A schema for job challenge comprises a set of standards for judging how challenging the finding of the novel solution is (or was) to the individual. The appraisal of how much challenge was represented in the finding of the novel solution is the valuation. Note that because this valuation is based on standards engendered by values, the perceived challenge intrinsically reflects the benefit or detriment of the environmental event (finding the novel solution) to the individual—that is, the cognition of challenge is emotionally relevant. The relevance is manifested in the affect (for example, feeling good) that follows the valuation of challenge.

The process described previously is believed to be one aspect of an overall reciprocal causation model in which affect is both influenced by emotional cognition (as previously) as well as a cause of emotional cognition. This latter point is addressed later in this chapter. For now, we proceed with the brief review of valuations in work environments.

Perceptual variables popularly employed to assess valuations of work environments are presented in table 5–1. These variables are measures of Psychological Climate (PC), which "furnishes perhaps the most readily identifiable set of variables in Industrial/Organization (I/O) psychology for appraising work environments in terms of schemata based on . . . latent values" (L. R. James & James, 1989, p. 740). A long history of research and development has demonstrated that these PC variables (1) are frequently used by individuals

TABLE 5–1

Psychological Climate (PC) Item Composites Clustered
by Four First-Order Factors

Role Stress and Lack of Harmony	Leadership Facilitation and Support
Role ambiguity	Leader trust and support
Role conflict	Leader goal facilitation
Role overload	Leader interaction facilitation
Subunit conflict	Psychological influence
Lack of organization identification	Hierarchical influence
Lack of management concern and	
awareness	Work Group Cooperation,
	Friendliness, and Warmth
Job Challenge and Autonomy	Work group cooperation
Challenge and variety	Work group friendliness and warmth
Autonomy	Reputation for effectiveness
Job importance	Esprit de corps

to valuate their work environments and (2) cluster within the four factors shown in table 5–1 (invariantly) over diverse work environments (James & Sells, 1981; Jones & James, 1979). The designations given to these four factors are (1) Role stress and lack of harmony, (2) Job challenge and autonomy, (3) Leadership facilitation and support, and (4) Work group cooperation, friendliness, and warmth. It is noteworthy that these designations reflect a compatibility between the four PC factors and four of the more salient work-related, personal values. These values are (desires for) (a) clarity, harmony, and justice; (b) challenge, independence, and responsibility; (c) work facilitation, support, and recognition; and (d) warm and friendly social relations (Locke, 1976, p. 1329). Such compatibility is purposeful in the sense that PC is based on a model in which latent values engender the schemas used by individuals to valuate (that is, to interpret, to impute meaning to) work environments (L. R. James & James, 1989).

It is also interesting that the four PC factors in table 5–1 refer, respectively, to the distinct domain of roles, jobs, leaders, and/or work groups. Historically, the tendency has been to view the role, job, leader, and work group referents as distinct cognitive organizing principles for perceptual variables. Indeed, the use of orthogonal factor rotations (Jones & James, 1979; James & Sells, 1981) has in part reflected at least an implicit belief held by PC researchers and others in I-O psychology that jobs, roles, leaders, and work groups represent different although related domains of organizational behavior (as well as different domains of research in I-O psychology). Alternatively, the theoretical concept of meaning discussed above suggests that the four first-order factors share a common theme. Specifically, each factor, and thus each PC variable, furnishes information pertaining to how efficious the work environment is perceived to be in regard to promoting or detracting from personal welfare. For example, perceptions that a job is challenging, a leader is supportive, role expectations are clear, and work group members are cooperative share the common denominator (underlying appraisal) that this work environment is personally beneficial to the perceiver's welfare. This suggests that, rather than viewing the perceptual PC domains as orthogonal dimensions, the four first-order factors could be viewed as sharing common variance due to a common judgment of how beneficial (detrimental) the work environment is to one's sense of (organizational) well-being.

Until recently (see L. R. James & James, 1989), there had been no attempt to integrate the perceptual variables and factors shown in table 5–1. We tested the hypotheses that (a) the four first-order factors are correlated and (b) the correlations among the four first-order factors could be explained by a single, higher-order (general) factor of meaning. Stated concisely, we proposed and tested the hierarchical model of meaning presented in figure 5–1. The theoretical rationale and the results of the empirical test of the general factor model are presented subsequently, and are then followed by a discussion of the causal relations between the general factor of meaning and affect.

Hierarchical Model of Meaning

To summarize briefly, it has been suggested that PC perceptions are emotionally relevant cognitions that share a common component, namely an appraisal of the degree to which the work environment is personally beneficial versus personally detrimental (damaging, painful) to the self and therefore to one's organizational well-being. This

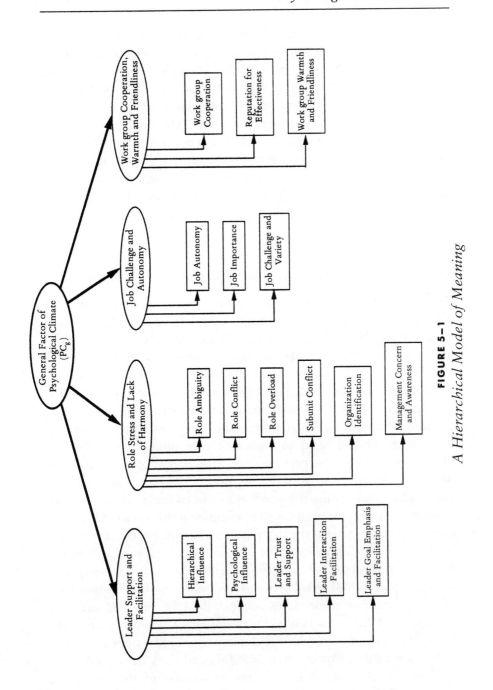

FIGURE 5–1

A Hierarchical Model of Meaning

common variance is especially important at the latent level of analysis because it is believed to be the sole basis for correlations among the first-order PC factors. Such a belief presupposes a hierarchical, integrative model of meaning wherein personal benefit versus personal detriment to organizational well-being serve as a single, higher-order general factor (see figure 5–1). The single, general factor of meaning is designated PC_g (that is, a general factor of psychological climate). The causal arrows extending from PC_g to each of the factors denote that PC_g is a latent, psychological common denominator for the factors. An overview of the empirical test of the model follows.

Empirical Test of the Hierarchical Model of Meaning

Confirmatory factor analysis was used to test the goodness-of-fit of the hierarchical model of meaning. Tests of the model were conducted using both the Unweighted Least Squares (ULS) and the Maximum Likelihood (ML) solutions contained in LISREL VI (Joreskog & Sorbom, 1986). A ULS solution was conducted because it is the recommended procedure when there is possible multicollinearity in relations among the manifest indicators (Joreskog & Sorbom, 1986). Near zero determinants of the variance-covariance matrices in several samples indicated that multicollinearity was likely an issue with the present data. However, because ULS does not have a known statistical distribution, a chi-square statistic was not available for testing the goodness-of-fit of the models. The ML solution was therefore employed to estimate a chi-square. Comparisons were made among the key parameter estimates (that is, factor loadings, correlations among the first-order factors) provided by the ULS solution and the ML solution, and attention was given to possible biasing of the ML results due to multicollinearity. Comparisons of the key parameter estimates between the ULS and ML solutions revealed that the two sets of values were almost identical. Only the ULS solution is reported in this chapter (see L. R. James & James, 1989, for a full set of results). Standardized data were used in all analyses (with the exception of the estimation of the chi-square value) in order to deal with the scale dependency contained in ULS estimation (Long, 1983).

Sample and Instruments. The model was tested on data from four different samples of nonsupervisory personnel. The samples were navy personnel ($n = 422$), systems analysts ($n = 128$), front line firefighters ($n = 288$), and production line personnel ($n = 208$). The perceived work environment variables were measured with the latest version of the PC inventory developed by James, Jones, and colleagues (see James & Sells, 1981). There were seventeen PC item composites or scales common to all samples; each PC scale consisted of three to eleven items. Coefficient alphas were generally acceptable for research purposes (see L. R. James & James, 1989).

Test for PC_g. The standardized ULS solution provided by a first-order Confirmatory Factor Analysis (CFA) on the navy data is presented in table 5–2. These results are representative of those obtained for the other three samples. The four first-order factors reflect the points discussed earlier in regard to table 5–1, namely, the ten-

TABLE 5–2

Standardized Estimates of Relations of Manifest Psychological Climate (PC) Variables on Four First-Order Factors Using an Unweighted Least Squares for Navy Personnel

Role Stress and Lack of Harmony		Leadership Facilitation and Support	
Role ambiguity	.86[a]	Leader trust and support	.93[a]
Role conflict	.76	Leader goal facilitation	.88
Role overload	.48	Leader interaction	
Subunit conflict	.48	facilitation	.84
Lack of organization		Psychological influence	.83
identification	.69	Hierarchical influence	.87
Lack of management			
concern and awareness	.68	Work Group Cooperation,	
		Friendliness, and Warmth	
Job Challenge and Autonomy		Work group cooperation	.71[a]
Challenge and variety	.74	Work group friendliness	
Autonomy	.79[a]	and warmth	.69
Job importance	.72	Reputation for effectiveness	.67
		Esprit de corps	.85

[a]Fixed parameter (not equal to 1.0 because results are presented in terms of a standardized solution such that the Psi has 1.0's on the diagonal).

$n = 422$.

dency for PC data to factor by referent (that is, role, job, leadership, and work group). What was of special interest in this study were the moderate to high correlations among the first-order factors presented in table 5–3. These results were consistent with the hypothesized general (second-order) factor for PC, and underscore the belief that the first-order PC dimensions are not independent.

Assessment of the validity of the general factor model presented in figure 5–1 was based on a second-order CFA, and involved a number of statistical indices. These included (a) coefficients of determination, measures of how well the manifest variables jointly serve as indicators for latent variables; (b) Goodness-of-Fit Indexes (GFI), measures of the relative amount of variance and covariance jointly accounted for by the model; and (c) Root Mean Square Residuals (RMSR), measures of the average residual variances and covariances (Joreskog & Sorbom, 1986). In the case of the ML solution, chi-square indexes were also available to test the fit of the model for each of the four samples. These results are reported fully in L. R. James and James (1989) and are too extensive to be reproduced here. What is important to report is that all of the indexes of overall fit of the hierarchical model satisfied or exceeded standard criteria for confirmation of a model. Thus, the principal hypothesis of a single, higher-order factor for PC (that is, PC_g) was supported. Support here implies that the PC_g model serves as a useful basis for explaining correlations among the four first-order PC factors. It does not suggest that the PC_g model presented in figure 5–1 has been proven to be correct or that this model furnishes a unique explanation for the correlations among the PC factors (James, Mulaik, & Brett, 1982).

TABLE 5–3

Correlations among Four First-Order Factors for Navy Personnel Using an Unweighted Least-Squares Solution

	I	II	III	IV
I. Role stress and lack of harmony	1.00			
II. Job challenge and autonomy	−.62	1.00		
III. Leadership facilitation and support	−.64	.62	1.00	
IV. Work group cooperation and friendliness	−.69	.67	.69	1.00

Estimated loadings of the four first-order PC factors on PC_g are presented (for each of the four samples) in table 5–4. These estimates were generally of high magnitude and suggested that PC_g explained substantial proportions of variance in each of the first-order PC factors. Stated alternatively, each of the four first-order PC factors appeared to reflect a substantial portion of variance attributable to a common underlying factor. As discussed, we have proposed that this factor, PC_g, reflects the degree to which the environment is perceived to be personally beneficial versus personally detrimental to one's sense of organizational well-being.

Indirect Effects of PC_g. The importance of PC_g as an indirect cause of the PC item composites was assessed via the use of path analytic principles (see Alwin & Hauser, 1975; Duncan, 1975). The extent to which PC_g explained variance in the original PC item composites was an indicator of the ability of the general factor to explain variance in manifest indicators. All too often, proposed general factors account for only small portions of variance in the original measurements, a result that calls into question the practical salience of the general factor. This was not the case here, inasmuch as the general factor explained considerable variance in the manifest indicators of PC. The indirect effects of PC_g on the PC item composites are presented in table 5–5. These effects have the form of correlation coefficients and may be interpreted accordingly. With few exceptions,

TABLE 5–4

Standardized Estimates of Relations of the Four First-Order Factors on a Single, Higher-Order Factor for Navy Personnel, System Analysts, Production Line Personnel, and Firefighters Using Unweighted Least Squares

	NA	SA	PL	FF
Role stress and lack of harmony	−.77	−.81	−.95	−.80
Job challenge and autonomy	.80	.71	.67	.92
Leadership facilitation and support	.80	.90	.87	.93
Work group cooperation and friendliness	.87	.78	.75	.72

Note: NA = navy personnel, SA = system analysts, PL = production line personnel, FF = firefighters.

TABLE 5–5

Indirect Effects of PC$_g$ on Manifest Indicators Using an Unweighted Least-Squares Solution

	PC$_g$			
	NA	SA	PL	FF
Role Stress and Lack of Harmony				
Role ambiguity	−.66	−.70	−.72	−.64
Role conflict	−.59	−.52	−.62	−.54
Role overload	−.37	−.31	−.50	−.31
Subunit conflict	−.37	−.50	−.64	−.50
Lack of organization identification	−.53	−.73	−.78	−.54
Lack of management concern and awareness	−.52	−.65	−.83	−.66
Job Challenge and Autonomy				
Challenge and variety	.69	.54	.41	.63
Autonomy	.63	.56	.52	.61
Job importance	.58	.48	.36	.36
Leadership Facilitation and Support				
Leader trust and support	.74	.75	.76	.84
Leader goal facilitation	.70	.77	.65	.79
Leader interaction facilitation	.67	.68	.55	.77
Psychological influence	.66	.65	.72	.73
Hierarchical influence	.69	.68	.68	.73
Work Group Cooperation, Friendliness, and Warmth				
Work group cooperation	.62	.59	.57	.66
Work group friendliness and warmth	.60	.60	.53	.61
Reputation for effectiveness	.58	.70	.57	.55
Esprit de corps	.74			
	Summary Statistics			
Range	.37–.74	.31–.77	.36–.83	.31–.84
Mean[a]	.60	.61	.61	.62

Note: NA = navy personnel, SA = system analysts, PL = production line personnel, FF = firefighters.

[a]Mean was computed on absolute values.

the indirect effects were greater than .50 (the range was from .31 to .84). Moreover, the mean (computed on absolute values) indirect effect of PC_g on the PC item composites was essentially identical over samples. These means suggest that an average of 37 percent of the variance in the PC composites was explained by PC_g.

Measurement Issues. A key measurement issue in this study was whether PC_g lacked the substantive content we have attributed to it and instead is a reflection of a common, systematic bias (for example, social desirability) engendered by the use of a common method. In other words, one might argue that the primary basis for correlation among the PC composites and PC first-order factors was a common method factor. This is a construct validity issue, and was addressed here by investigating relations between PC_g and nonenvironmental variables that were (a) expected to be differentially related to PC_g although (b) assessed by the same method as PC and therefore subject to the same common method bias. The variables employed in this analysis were overall job satisfaction, achievement motivation, rigidity, and self-esteem.

The overall job satisfaction (OJS) measure was based on the Minnesota Satisfaction Questionnaire (Weiss, Dawis, England, & Lofquist, 1977). Some of the wording was changed in the questionnaires used here to ensure that the items were applicable in each sample and that all the areas of PC were represented in the item domains (that is, satisfaction with aspects of jobs, roles, work groups, and leaders). The OJS measure was a composite score based on twenty items, for which alpha coefficients were greater than .89 across all samples.

Item composites were also employed as measures of the following personality variables: achievement motivation, rigidity, and self-esteem. The number of items for these variables ranged from eleven to thirteen and the alpha coefficients ranged from .68 to .74 (see L. R. James & James, 1989). The achievement motivation composite was designed to assess orientation toward success, the rigidity composite was based on a need for certainty and structure (see James, Gent, Hater, & Coray, 1979), and the self-esteem composite focused on assessing confidence in the work place (see James & Jones, 1980).

Prior research had demonstrated differential statistical relationships between the OJS/personality variables and various PC variables. For example, satisfaction with job events and valuations of job attributes (that is, challenge, autonomy, importance) have been shown to be reciprocal causes of one another (James & Jones, 1980; James & Tetrick, 1986). These results suggested that OJS and PC_g would be highly correlated. Conversely, it was expected that the correlations between PC_g and the three personality variables would be small and/or close to zero because the personality variables have been shown to be effective moderators of relations between leadership PC variables and affective/behavioral outcomes (James, Gent, Hater, & Coray, 1979). It follows that if correlations between PC_g and achievement motivation, rigidity, and self-esteem were moderate to high, then method variance could serve as an (alternative) explanation for the covariation among the PC composites and first-order factors.

The squared correlations provided by ULS between the general factor and OJS, and between the general factor and each of the personality variables, are presented in table 5–6. PC_g correlated highly with overall satisfaction, whereas the correlations between PC_g and the three personality variables were close to zero. The large differences between the correlations of PC_g with OJS compared to PC_g with the personality variables suggested that the data did not involve a general method factor.

Summary. Research indicated that a higher-order, general latent variable, designated PC_g, provided a useful basis for explaining co-

TABLE 5–6

Squared Correlations of PC_g with Overall Job Satisfaction and Personality Variables Provided by Unweighted Least Squares

Variables	PC_g			
	NA	SA	PL	FF
Overall job satisfaction	.79	.88	.75	.73
Achievement motivation	.04	.06	.11	.05
Rigidity	.00	.10	.04	.00
Self-esteem	.06	.01	.06	.03

Note: NA = navy personnel, SA = system analysts, PL = production line personnel, FF = firefighters.

variation among four first-order PC factors. This general factor suggested that, in regard to work environments at least, individuals employ a simpler, more integrated cognitive structure to appraise the world than has been indicated by prior research, which suggested multiple, independent, environmental perception domains. Moreover, not only does PC_g connote a simpler, more integrated cognitive structure, but also it suggests what the essential elements of perceptions of environments might be. These elements derive from viewing PC variables as emotionally relevant cognitions and thus as indicators of the efficacy of the environment to enhance (or detract from) well-being. "Stated simply, people respond to work environments in terms of how they perceive these environments, and the key substantive concern in perception is the degree to which individuals perceive themselves as being personally benefitted as opposed to being personally harmed (hindered) by their presence in the environment" (L. R. James & James, 1989, p. 748).

Reciprocal Causation between Perception and Affect

The preceding discussion suggests that psychological climate should be strongly related to affective variables. Indeed, characterizing PC variables as emotionally relevant cognitions denotes that PC perceptions furnish highly salient information for the determination of emotional responses. Causal models relating PC to the affective variable of job satisfaction have supported these predictions; the relationship between PC and job satisfaction is not only strong, but also postcognitive—that is, emotions follow emotionally relevant cognitions (see James & Jones, 1980; James & Tetrick, 1986). A causal order wherein affect follows cognition does not suggest, however, that the model is recursive (that is, emotionally relevant cognitions influence affect but affect has no influence on emotionally relevant cognitions). James and colleagues have proposed multiple means by which affect might influence PC (James & Jones, 1980; James & Tetrick, 1986; James, James, & Ashe, 1990). These include conditions in which desired and/or existing levels of affect cause the individual (a) to attend only to selected situational cues in the interest of increasing (or decreasing), maintaining, or confirming emotions; (b) to impute desirable (undesirable) attributes or events to a work environment; (c) to restructure (cognitively) and redefine situational cues to enhance the probability that they will be interpreted as beneficial (detrimental) to well-being; and (d) to restructure (cognitively) cognitions to make them consistent with implicit theories regarding whether an environment should or should not be beneficial to well-being.

Prior research has supported the general hypothesis that PC and affect are reciprocally related (see prior references). This research was based on one domain of PC, namely perceptions of job autonomy, challenge, and importance, and satisfaction was limited to affect toward events related specifically to performing one's job. The research reported here seeks to extend these prior, focused investigations to more general valuation and affective domains. Specifically, our objective here was to test a hypothesis that PC_g and organizational well-being are reciprocal causes of one another. The development of a measure of organizational well-being is presented subsequently, and is followed by an overview of the results of a test of the reciprocal causation hypothesis.

Development of a Measure of Organizational Well-Being

An overall job satisfaction measure was used to assess organizational well-being. As noted briefly in prior discussion, the measurement of overall job satisfaction was based on sixteen items from the Minnesota Satisfaction Questionnaire, with minor revisions to ensure that satisfaction with *a priori* factors of PC were represented in the items. The satisfaction items, clustered by *a priori* domain, are presented in table 5–7.

The concept of organizational well-being is, as discussed previously, visualized as a general affective factor. This implies that a single, higher-order factor underlies the satisfaction items in table 5–7. A confirmatory factor analysis was conducted on the correlations among the satisfaction items to ascertain if a single, higher-order factor was consistent with the data. The data used to test for a single, higher-order satisfaction factor (or well-being) were based on the sample employed by James and Jones (1980) and James and Tetrick (1986) to test for reciprocal causation between job perceptions and job satisfaction. This sample was based on the samples of systems analysts, firefighters, and production line personnel de-

TABLE 5–7

*Measure of Satisfaction Clustered by the Original
First-Order Factors*

Satisfaction with Job
  Opportunity to do challenging work
  Time given to complete my work
  Prestige of my job in this organization
  Clarity of information I receive on how to do my job
  Work quality requirements for my job
  The amount of authority I have to carry out my responsibilities
  Opportunity for independent thought and action

Satisfaction with Work Group
  Cooperation from the people in my work group
  Friendliness among coworkers

Satisfaction with Organization
  Prestige of my organization
  Training I received for my job
  Opportunity for growth and development
  Opportunity for promotion

Satisfaction with Leader
  Support received from supervisors
  Respect and fair treatment from supervisors
  Opportunity to influence those above me

scribed in the previous section, plus (a) incumbents of less technical jobs (for example, computer operators) from the same private health care program that provided the systems analysts ($n = 40$), and (b) nonproduction personnel (for example, sales persons) from the same four plants that provided the production line personnel ($n = 65$). All samples were combined for the present analysis to ensure wide variation in all data. The total n, based on complete sets of data for all subjects, was 642.

Confirmatory Factor Analysis

Logic and a model similar to that used to test the hierarchical model of meaning were employed to test for a general, higher-order latent variable for satisfaction. The test of the hierarchical model of satisfaction involved a two-step process. A first-order factor model was

tested initially to assess the goodness-of-fit between the sixteen satisfaction items and the four, first-order satisfaction factors indicated
in table 5–7. Each satisfaction item was allowed to load on only one
first-order satisfaction factor. Relations between each item and the
remaining three satisfaction factors were fixed to zero. Once an acceptable level of fit of the first-order model to the data was achieved,
the first-order model was extended to include a single, higher-order
satisfaction factor. Each of the first-order factors served as an indicator of this overall satisfaction factor, which in turn was considered
as one form of assessment of organizational well-being.

As with the PC variables, a near-zero determinant for the item
variance/covariance matrix indicated multicollinearity among the
satisfaction items. Nevertheless, all analyses reported for the satisfaction data are based on a Maximum Likelihood (ML) solution
(rather than an Unweighted Least Squares solution). The ML solution was used to test the model for several reasons. First, and most
important, comparisons among ULS and ML parameter estimates
and all of the shared goodness-of-fit indices were almost identical.
Second, ML provided a chi-square for additional tests of the goodness-of-fit of the model, although these tests should be consistent
with those that do not rely on chi-square values. Third, ML, unlike
ULS, provides modification indexes that, in combination with theoretical rationale, are helpful in the conduct of specification searches
(MacCallum, 1986).

The observed covariance matrix was used to test the higher-order
satisfaction model. A chi-square was determined for the first-order
model (χ_1^2) and the second-order or general factor model (χ_2^2). The χ
was used as a stand-alone index (see Marsh, Balla, & McDonald,
1988) to assess the fit of the first-order model. The test of the hierarchical model was based on (1) a difference chi-square test $\chi_1^2 - \chi_2^2$
with $df_1 - df_2$ degrees of freedom), a measure of the adequacy of
general satisfaction to explain covariation among the first-order factors; and (2) the Tucker-Lewis (1973) index

$$(\chi_n^2/df_n - \chi_2^2/df_n)/(\chi_n^2/df_n - 1.0)$$

where n represents the null model—a measure of covariance accounted for by the hierarchical model relative to the total covariance
among the satisfaction items. Other indexes provided by LISREL VI

were used to assess the overall fit of the model to the observed data. To review briefly, these indexes were (3) the Goodness-of-Fit Index, a measure of the amount of variance and covariance jointly accounted for by the model; (4) the Root Mean Square Residual, the average residual variance and covariance; and (5) R^2, a measure of how well the indicators jointly accounted for the latent variables.

Results. The goodness-of-fit tests of the proposed first-order model presented in table 5–7 furnished the following: χ_1^2 (93, $n =$ 637) = 514.04, GFI = .90, and RMSR = .07. These results generally indicated that the model did not have a good fit to the observed data. Moreover, a large number of normalized residuals had absolute values greater than two, a result that further suggested a less-than-acceptable fit for the first-order model (see Hayduk, 1987; Joreskog & Sorbom, 1986). It was decided, therefore, to conduct a specification analysis on first-order factor model. Guidelines recommended by MacCallum (1986) were followed, with special emphasis placed on attempting to integrate theoretical rationale with the modification indexes furnished by LISREL.

Of note was that covariation among all the satisfaction items could not be accounted for fully by covariation among the first-order satisfaction factors. In other words, the underlying factor pattern appeared to be more complex than the simple structure proposed in table 5–7. Thus, although there may be facets of satisfaction associated with specific domains in the work place (Weiss, Dawis, England, & Lofquist, 1977; Smith, Kendall, & Hulin, 1969), additional theory is needed to explain covariation among some of the satisfaction items. Statistically speaking, several large modification indexes for the factor pattern matrix suggested where complexity of relations between the satisfaction items and the first-order factors might occur. The reasons for possible complexity were generally rather obvious. For example, affect involving such things as opportunities to influence supervisors had both job and leadership referents (see table 5–8). A satisfaction item was thus allowed to load on more than one factor if the modification index indicated that the freed parameter would result in a substantial gain in the fit of the model. We also allowed the unique variances for two satisfaction items (that is, the off diagonal elements of the Theta Epsilon matrix) within the same factor to covary, the rationale being that a subfactor existed for theoretically related items within the more encompassing first-order factor. Finally, recategorization of some satisfaction items was indicated when parameters were freed.

The results of a CFA on the fully respecified model are summarized in table 5–8. Major changes to the model indicated in table 5–8 were as follows:

1. Two satisfaction items were moved from Satisfaction with Organization to Satisfaction with Job and one satisfaction item was moved from Satisfaction with Job to Satisfaction with Leader.
2. Four of the satisfaction items now load on more than one factor.
3. The unique variances between "Prestige of my job in this organization" and "Prestige of my organization" were freed to covary.

The goodness-of-fit indexes for the respecified first-order model reported in table 5–8 were $\chi_1^2 (95, n = 637) = 238.95$, GFI = .95, RMSR = .03, and R^2 = 99. These values were substantially better than those for the original model and indicated an acceptable fit of the model to the data. The correlations among the four first-order factors are presented in table 5–9; these correlations supported the possibility of a single, second-order factor.

The results of the tests for a general factor of satisfaction are presented in tables 5–10 through 5–12. The goodness-of-fit indexes reported in table 5–11 demonstrate that the single, higher-order satisfaction factor adequately explained the covariation among the four first-order factors. Specifically, the difference chi-square was nonsignificant, the Tucker-Lewis index was greater than .90, and the RMSR was low. Additional support for the second-order factor was provided by the generally high factor loadings of the first-order factors on the general factor, reported in table 5–10. The mean factor loading was .76; thus, an average of 58 percent of the variance in the four first-order factors could be explained by the general satisfaction factor.

The final test of the second-order model analyzed the extent to which variance in the original satisfaction items was retained in the second-order factor. This was assessed by computing the total effects of the general factor on the satisfaction items, an effect that is equivalent to the correlation between the general factor and each of

TABLE 5–8

Confirmatory Factor Analysis of Satisfaction Items Following Specification Analysis

	1	2	3	4
Satisfaction with Job				
Opportunity to do challenging work	.30		.31	
Time given to complete my work	.58[c]			
Prestige of my job in this organization	.48		.23	
Clarity of information I receive on how to do my job	.67			
Work quality requirements for my job	.57			
The amount of authority I have to carry out my responsibilities	.66			
Prestige of my organization[a]	.55			
Training I receive for my job[b]	.59			
Satisfaction with Work Group				
Cooperation from the people in my work group		.97*		
Friendliness among coworkers		.63		
Satisfaction with Organization				
Opportunity for growth and development			.89[c]	
Opportunity for promotion			.86	
Satisfaction with Leader				
Support received from supervisors				.82[c]
Respect and fair treatment from supervisors				.76
Opportunity to influence those above me		.32		.43
Opportunity for independent thought and action[b]			.23	.53

$n = 637$

[a]Moved from Satisfaction with Organization to Satisfaction with Job.

[b]Moved from Satisfaction with Job to Satisfaction with Leader.

[c]Fixed parameter (not equal to 1.0 because results are presented in terms of a standardized solution such that the Ψ matrix has 1.0s on the diagonal).

the original satisfaction items. The results of this analysis are presented in table 5–12. With the exception of two work group satisfaction items, all total effects were greater than .50. The actual range was .31 to .67, and the mean (computed on absolute values) was .59. These results demonstrated that reasonable amounts of variance in the satisfaction items were accounted for by the general factor.

In sum, the confirmatory factor analyses supported the hypothesized general affect factor, thus suggesting that a general factor for organizational well-being is a viable possibility. Even though re-

TABLE 5–9

Correlations among Four First-Order Satisfaction Latent Variables

	I	II	III	IV
I. Satisfaction with job	1.00			
II. Satisfaction with work group	.45	1.00		
III. Satisfaction with organization	.70	.34	1.00	
IV. Satisfaction with leader	.83	.41	.63	1.00

TABLE 5–10

Standardized Estimates of Relations of the Four First-Order Latent Variables on a Single, Higher-Order Satisfaction Latent Variable

First-Order Factor	
Satisfaction with job	.96
Satisfaction with work group	.47
Satisfaction with organization	.73
Satisfaction with leader	.86

TABLE 5–11

Goodness-of-Fit Indexes for Second-Order Confirmatory Factor Analysis for the Satisfaction Data

Chi-square for higher-order factor model	239.77 (95 *df*)
Difference chi-square[a]	.82
Tucker-Lewis index	.95
GFI	.95
RMSR	.03
R^2 First-order factors	.99
R^2 Second-order factors	.95

Note: GFI = Goodness-of-Fit Index, RMSR = Root Mean Square Residual.

[a]Chi-square difference between first-order model and higher-order model with 2 *df*.

TABLE 5–12

*Indirect Effects of a Second-Order Satisfaction Latent Variable
on the Satisfaction Manifest Variable*

Satisfaction with Job	
Opportunity to do challenging work	.52
Time given to complete my work	.56
Prestige of my job in this organization	.63
Clarity of information I receive on how to do my job	.64
Work quality requirements for my job	.55
The amount of authority I have to carry out my responsibilities	.63
Prestige of my organization	.54
Training I receive for my job	.59
Satisfaction with Work Group	
Cooperation from the people in my work group	.47
Friendliness among coworkers	.31
Satisfaction with Organization	
Opportunity for growth and development	.67
Opportunity for promotion	.63
Satisfaction with Leader	
Support received from supervisors	.70
Respect and fair treatment for supervisors	.65
Opportunity to influence those above me	.68
Opportunity for independent thought and action	.63

Mean = .59
Range = .32 to .67

specification of the first-order model involved moving manifest indicators from one factor to another and introducing factorial complexity, it was reasonably clear that a higher-order, general factor of satisfaction was consistent with the data. Thus, we proceeded to test the hypothesis that PC_g is reciprocally related to (overall) organizational well-being.

Test of Reciprocal Causation between Perception and Affect

What is presented here represents an initial test of the reciprocal causation hypothesis. It is an imperfect assessment if for no other reason than that archival data were used in the analysis. Specifically, the variables and data used here were generally the same as those employed by James and Jones (1980) and James and Tetrick (1986) to test for reciprocal causation between job perceptions and job satisfaction. It is likely that PC_g has causes above and beyond those identified earlier, and here, for job perceptions (in addition to general affect, of course). The same may be said for causes of organizational well-being, which likely has causes above and beyond PC_g and the causes of job satisfaction used in the earlier studies. In short, the present model was likely subject to problems of unmeasured variables (James, 1980). A mitigating circumstance is that the causal variables identified in the earlier studies cover a wide range of possible causal influences for both overall valuations and overall affect (for example, leadership, structure, personality, age). This point, in combination with the facts that (a) the first-order job perception factor correlated highly with PC_g and (b) the job satisfaction factor correlated highly with the general satisfaction factor, connote that the unmeasured variable problems were not likely to seriously bias parameter estimates in the analyses reported below.

The analyses were based on the same sample of 642 individuals used in the CFA on the satisfaction data. Unfortunately, the present analyses failed to converge (after many iterations) when we attempted to test the reciprocal causation model using full-information, latent variable estimation techniques. Potential reasons for nonconvergence are many (see Anderson & Gerbing, 1988; Bentler & Chou, 1987; L. A. James & James, 1989), but a likely candidate is the inability of a full-information method to distinguish between a high correlation (between perception and affect) due to reciprocal causation and a high correlation engendered by an underlying common factor. To counteract this problem, we used a simultaneous-equation, limited information estimator (Two-Stage Least-Squares, see James & Singh, 1978) in the context of a manifest variable design. The product of this approach is that the model, variables, data, and analytic procedures are generally the same as those employed by James and Jones (1980) and James and Tetrick (1986) in the prior reciprocal causation studies. The one key difference is that the affective measure for organizational well-being is based on the item composite for OJS, while the cognitive measure for PC_g is based on a linear composite of the seventeen PC item composites. No attempt was made to estimate factor scores for either OJS or PC_g, the objective being to avoid the problem of factorial indeterminacy. The correlations between various items, composites, and factors reported in the various CFAs were of sufficient magnitude to suggest that composites of observed data were reasonable surrogates of general factors.

The results of the Two-Stage Least-Squares (2SLS) analysis are summarized in figure 5–2. Estimates of path coefficients (standardized structural parameters) are reported for each hypothesized direct effect. (Results were basically the same for the standardized and unstandardized solutions; the standardized solution includes the Hout corrections [Hout, 1977]). Pearson correlations associated with hypothesized direct effects are shown in parentheses. The key finding was that PC_g and OJS were reciprocally related. The $PC_g \rightarrow$ OJS path coefficient was .35 ($p < .05$). These results support the prediction that a general measure of the degree to which a work environment is perceived to be personally beneficial versus detrimental to one's organizational well-being will be both a cause and an effect of the general level of organizational well-being.

Additional information provided by the 2SLS analysis was that reasonable amounts of variance in the endogenous variables were accounted for in the first- and second-stage analyses (Rs for the first-stage were .60 and .61 for OJS and PC_g, respectively; Rs for the second-stage were .58 and .60 for these same variables). These Rs could be enhanced by the development of a more catholic model to explain the general factors and perhaps by trimming of the exogenous variables with trivial path coefficients in figure 5–2. Goodness-of-fit tests designed to assess overidentifying restrictions (Condition 10 tests, see James, Mulaik, & Brett, 1982) were based on the disturbance-term regression procedure proposed and described by James and Jones (1980). These tests demonstrated that the reciprocal causation model had a good fit to the data. Here again, however, one must be careful about overinterpreting results. The key conclusion provided by this particular analysis is that general factors of meaning and affect may be reciprocally related. It follows that both overall valuations of a work environment as well as more specific emotional cognitions associated with jobs, leaders, work groups, and roles are not only efficacious in regard to affect, but also themselves involve a substantial affective component.

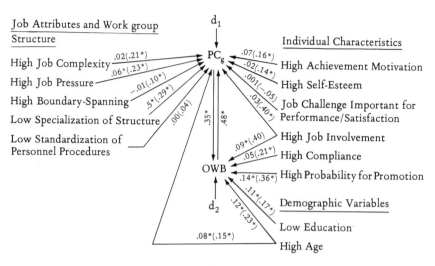

FIGURE 5–2

*Path Coefficients Pertaining to Reciprocal Causation
between PCg and Organizational Well-Being*

Zero-order correlations are in parentheses;
the correlation between PCg and OWB was .81
$^*p < .05.$

Conclusions

The analyses reported here suggest the presence of general factors for both psychological climate and satisfaction. Both such general factors are traceable to values; PC_g reflects the degree to which environmental events are perceived to meet standards engendered by work-relevant values, whereas the general factor of satisfaction reflects a sense of well-being engendered by environmental events having met or exceeded the standards attributable to values. These general factors account for a substantial portion of the variance in manifest measures of perception and affect, although salient portions of unique variance remain in the first-order factors. Nevertheless, the general factors imply that there is much to be learned (gained) by future attempts to view the cognitive system as at least partially integrated and hierarchical. The same may be said for future models that attempt to integrate values more fully into the affective and cognitive systems.

Future development might also consider the mounting evidence that emotionally relevant cognitions, such as are reflected in the PC variables, not only are relevant for the experience of emotions, but also involve a strong emotional component. This is "hot cognition" (see Zajonc, 1980), an area that is only beginning to receive attention but portends possible theoretical revision in areas such as decision making, leadership, and stress (James, James, & Ashe, 1990). More immediate attention should, perhaps, be directed toward attempts to replicate the reciprocal causation studies, for we in the research community need to know whether the reciprocal cognitive-affect relation is generalizable. Assuming this is so, research may extend in numerous directions, including those mentioned above as well as other perceptual and emotional domains.

Finally, the research reported here was based on a number of relatively new analytic techniques. The power and abuses of confirmatory techniques are only beginning to be realized. More importantly, psychologists are no longer bound to latent variable systems that emphasize orthogonality between first-order factors simply because oblique rotational systems are ostensibly more subjective than orthogonal ones. Rotation is not the same kind of issue in confirmatory procedures as it was in exploratory factor analyses, and now perhaps we are in a better position to gain substantive understanding of psychological phenomena with less preordaining of results for purely methodological reasons. Finally, the inclusion of nonrecursive modeling techniques in our methodological repertoire opens the door for testing what has long been believed to be the primary model for behavior in organizations, namely, a reciprocally interacting, dynamic, open system.

References

Alwin, D. F., & Hauser, R. M. (1975). The decomposition of effects in path analysis. *American Sociological Review, 40,* 37–47.

Anderson, J. C., & Gerbing, D. W. (1988). Structural equation modeling in practice: A review and recommended two-step approach. *Psychological Bulletin, 103,* 411–423.

Bentler, P. M., & Chou, C. P. (1987). Practical issues in structural modeling. *Sociological Methods and Research, 16,* 78–117.

Duncan, O. D. (1975). *Introduction to structural equation models.* New York: Academic Press.

Ekehammer, B. (1974). Interactionism in personality from a historical perspective. *Psychological Bulletin, 81,* 1026–1048.

Endler, N. S., & Magnusson, D. (1976). Toward an interactional psychology of personality. *Psychological Bulletin, 83*, 956–974.

Hayduk, L. A. (1987). *Structural equation modeling with LISREL*. Baltimore, MD: Johns Hopkins University Press.

Hout, M. (1977). A cautionary note on the use of two-stage least squares. *Sociological Methods and Research, 5*, 335–346.

James, L. A., & James, L. R. (1989). Integrating work environment of perceptions: Explorations into the measurement of meaning. *Journal of Applied Psychology, 74*, 739–751.

James, L. R. (1980). The unmeasured variable problem in path analysis. *Journal of Applied Psychology, 65*, 415–421.

James, L. R. (1982). Aggregation bias in estimates of perceptual agreement. *Journal of Applied Psychology, 67*, 219–229.

James, L. R., Gent, M. J., Hater, J. J., & Coray, K. E. (1979). Correlates of psychological influence: An illustration of the psychological climate approach to work environment perceptions. *Personnel Psychology, 32*, 563–588.

James, L. R., Hater, J. J., Gent, M. J., & Bruni, J. R. (1978). Psychological climate: Implications from cognitive social learning theory and interactional psychology. *Personnel Psychology, 31*, 781–813.

James, L. R., & James, L. A. (1989). Causal modelling in organizational research. In C. L. Cooper & I. Robertson (Eds.), *International review of industrial and organizational psychology* (pp. 371–404). Chichester, Eng.: Wiley.

James, L. R., James, L. A., & Ashe, D. K. (1990). The meaning of organizations: An essay. In B. Schneider (Ed.), *Climate and culture* (pp. 40–84). San Francisco: Jossey-Bass.

James, L. R., & Jones, A. P. (1974). Organizational climate: Review of theory and research. *Psychological Bulletin, 81*, 1096–1112.

James, L. R., & Jones, A. P. (1980). Perceived job characteristics and job satisfaction: An examination of reciprocal causation. *Personnel Psychology, 33*, 97–135.

James, L. R., Mulaik, S. A., & Brett, J. M. (1982). *Causal analysis: assumptions, models, and data*. Beverly Hills, CA: Sage.

James, L. R., & Sells, S. B. (1981). Psychological climate: Theoretical perspectives and empirical research. In D. Magnusson (Ed.), *Toward a psychology of situations: An interactional perspective* (pp. 275–295). Hillsdale, NJ: Erlbaum.

James, L. R., & Singh, K. (1978). An introduction to the logic, assumptions, and basic analytic procedures of two-stage least squares. *Psychological Bulletin, 85*, 1104–1122.

James, L. R., & Tetrick, L. E. (1986). Confirmatory analytic test of three causal models relating job perceptions to job satisfaction. *Journal of Applied Psychology, 71*, 77–82.

Jones, A. P., & James, L. R. (1979). Psychological climate: Dimensions and relationships of individual and aggregated work environment perceptions. *Organizational Behavior and Human Performance, 23*, 201–250.

Joreskog, K. G., & Sorbom, D. (1986). *LISREL VI analyses of linear structural relationships by maximum likelihood, instrumental variables, and least squares methods*. Mooresville, IN: Scientific Software.

Lazarus, R. S. (1982). Thoughts on the relations between emotion and cognition. *American Psychologist, 37,* 1019–1024.

Lazarus, R. S. (1984). On the primacy of cooperation. *American Psychologist, 39,* 124–129.

Lazarus, R. S., & Folkman, S. (1984). *Stress, appraisal, and coping.* New York: Springer.

Lewin, K. (1938). *The conceptual representation of the measurement of psychological forces.* Durham, NC: Duke University Press.

Locke, E. A. (1976). The nature and causes of job satisfaction. In M. D. Dunnette (Ed.), *Handbook of industrial and organizational psychology* (pp. 1297–1350). Chicago: Rand McNally.

Long, J. S. (1983). *Confirmatory factor analysis: A preface to LISREL.* Beverly Hills, CA: Sage.

MacCallum, R. (1986). Specification searches in covariance structure modeling. *Psychological Bulletin, 100,* 107–120.

Mandler, G. (1982). The structure of value: Accounting for taste. In M. S. Clark & S. T. Fiske (Eds.), *Affect and cognition: The seventeenth annual Carnegie symposium on cognition* (pp. 3–36). Hillsdale, NJ: Erlbaum.

Marsh, H. W., Balla, J. R., & McDonald, R. P. (1988). Goodness-of-fit indexes in confirmatory factor analysis: The effect of sample size. *Psychological Bulletin, 103,* 391–410.

Osgood, C. E., Suci, G. J., & Tannenbaum, P. H. (1957). *The measurement of meaning.* Urbana: University of Illinois Press.

Reisenzein, R. (1983). The Schachter theory of emotion. Two decades later. *Psychological Bulletin, 94,* 239–264.

Schachter, S., & Singer, J. E. (1962). Cognitive, social, and physiological determinants of emotional state. *Psychological Review, 69,* 379–399.

Smith, P. C., Kendall, L. W., & Hulin, C. L. (1969). *The measurement of satisfaction in work and retirement: A strategy for the study of attitudes.* Chicago: Rand McNally.

Stotland, E., & Canon, L. K. (1972). *Social psychology: A cognitive approach.* Philadelphia: Sanders.

Tucker, L. R., & Lewis, C. (1973). Reliability coefficient for maximum likelihood factor–analysis. *Psychometrica, 38,* 1–10.

Weiss, D. J., Dawis, R. V., England, G. W., & Lofquist, L. H. (1977). *Manual for the Minnesota Satisfaction Questionnaire.* Minneapolis: University of Minnesota Industrial Relations Center.

Zajonc, R. B. (1980). Feeling and thinking: Preferences need no inferences. *American Psychologist, 35,* 151–175.

PART THREE

Consequences of Job Satisfaction

The role of the job satisfaction construct in both the theory and the practice of industrial-organizational psychology has often been the subject of debate. Some of this debate has centered on whether the construct should be treated as an independent or a dependent variable in research. That is, is job satisfaction an outcome that is important for its own sake, or is it important because it leads to important organizationally relevant outcomes? This section deals with the latter view by concentrating on the consequences of job satisfaction or dissatisfaction. The five chapters deal with three classes of consequences of job satisfaction: nonwork or "citizenship behaviors" such as attendance, turnover, sabotage, and so on, which are important to the health of the organization; work performance as indicated by the quality and quantity of work; and the mental and physical health of the workers.

The first two chapters discuss the search for relationships between job satisfaction and a number of nonwork behaviors that are important to organizations. Indeed, Roznowski and Hulin take the position that valid measures of job satisfaction for current employees are the most important information an organizational psychologist or manager can have. The chapters by Roznowski and Hulin and by Fisher and Locke both note that correlations between job satisfaction and specific behavioral criteria such as turnover or absenteeism are weak. Both argue persuasively that current attitude theory (for example, Ajzen & Fishbein, 1977) suggests that this result is due to a misguided attempt to predict specific behaviors from a general attitude toward the job or some aspect of the job. They recommend that the level of aggregation of the behavioral measures match that of the attitude (job satisfaction) measures. Thus, Fisher and Locke stress the need for a typology of nontask behaviors and underlying constructs.

Each of the chapters presents a model of response to job satisfaction. The models are similar in that they are cognitive in nature and are affect- rather than need-based; both stress the motivating effect of dissatisfaction and both view the consequent behaviors as attempts at individual adaptation. Fisher and Locke suggest that an integration of affect-based and valence models is possible and argue the superiority of such models over those based on "abstract needs."

Roznowski and Hulin propose four hypothetical behavioral families of functionally similar responses to dissatisfaction. They stress that these are intended to be a first approximation of logical clusters of behaviors in this area. Their description of attempts to develop behavioral scales effectively highlights the problems in such research and offers suggestions for alternative approaches.

Fisher and Locke describe a series of exploratory studies representing efforts to categorize behavioral responses to job dissatisfaction. They follow with an excellent discussion of research problems and suggested directions for further research in this area.

The Katzell, Thompson, and Guzzo chapter deals with the second class of consequences, work performance. They note that the conventional wisdom, exemplified by comments in contemporary textbooks, holds that there is little or no relationship between job satisfaction and work performance. They challenge this view with a model of the conditions moderating the relationship between job satisfaction and job performance, which is presented as a testable path model embedded in a larger model of work motivation. They describe a test of the model and results showing that job satisfaction and job performance have little direct impact on each other, but are each determined by a number of factors, some of which are common to both and furnish indirect links between them. They suggest that treatments that affect those common elements may cause both job satisfaction and job performance to vary. Discussion of intervention studies supports this view and leads the authors to argue that appropriate management practices can result in both high satisfaction and high performance.

Still another class of correlates of dissatisfaction is considered in the chapters by Ironson and by Sandman. Both are concerned with the concept of job stress and its implications for the organization and the individual. While job stress and job satisfaction have not always been clearly distinguished in the literature, it seems clear that the two constructs often involve the same or related antecedents and consequences. As these two chapters show, there is an urgent need to identify the nature of the implications of job stress and job satisfaction for the physical and mental health of workers, and to distinguish clearly the central meaning of each construct. Ironson, with expertise in both psychology and in medicine, deals with the relationship between job stress and health. She discusses problems with the definition and the dimensionality of stress and reviews a variety of suggested determinants of job stress. Her discussion focuses on job stress and coronary disease and on job stress and high blood pressure. She cites the need for an overall paradigm of the process by which job stress is linked to disease outcomes and the lack of sufficient data to effectively target intervention strategies.

Sandman reports on the development of a job stress measure, the Job Stress Index. She notes the considerable confusion between the constructs of job satisfaction and job stress that results from a number of overlapping dimensions or aspects in both theoretical and operational definitions. The work she reports is, in part, an attempt to distinguish between the two constructs. Her results indicate that job satisfaction and job stress can be measured as two separate but related constructs with clear conceptual distinctions. Like Ironson, she cites the need for further research, especially longitudinal research, in this important area.

Taken together, the chapters in this section strongly support the central role that Roznowski and Hulin claim for job satisfaction and the usefulness of valid measures of the construct.

Reference

Ajzen, I., & Fishbein, M. (1977). Attitude-behavior relations: A theoretical analysis and review of empirical literature. *Psychological Bulletin, 84,* 888–918.

The Scientific Merit of Valid Measures of General Constructs with Special Reference to Job Satisfaction and Job Withdrawal

MARY ROZNOWSKI

CHARLES HULIN

The General Usefulness of Intelligence as a Predictor of Behavior

Prior to organizational entry, a job applicant's score on a test of general intelligence (g) is the most useful datum an organizational psychologist can have about that person in terms of predicting organizationally relevant criteria. This statement is equally true for other psychologists—counseling, vocational, clinical, personnel, cognitive, or engineering—and across behavior settings—schools, formal work organizations, informal work groups, human performance laboratories, military units, or space stations—although the apparent usefulness of the datum may be obscured by restrictions of range, questions asked, approaches to data analysis, or experimentally enhanced variance on other competing predictors of behavior.

The authors are grateful to Lloyd Humphreys and James Austin for their input at various stages of this project. Correspondence should be sent to Mary Rosnowski, Department of Psychology, Ohio State University, 1885 Neil Avenue, Columbus, OH 43210-1222.

The general usefulness of valid, well-constructed measures of intelligence can be attributed to a long series of theoretically based, empirical investigations. Theoreticians and empirically oriented researchers carefully developed and refined measures of intelligence. Evidence demonstrating the general validity of these measures is easily obtainable. Applied researchers from nearly all branches of psychology systematically analyzed different measures of intelligence and found they accounted for gratifying amounts of variance in many criteria. Deficiencies in definitions and operations were discovered and researchers iterated through the entire cycle many times over. No one study was crucial in this history, but the cumulative impact has been remarkable.

On a more restricted basis, an argument can be made that the best job satisfaction scales occupy a place in organizational behavior research similar to that held by measures of g in general psychological research. The mechanisms by which g and job satisfaction influence behavior are not necessarily similar. The measure of g may operate to place limits on what an individual is able to do in a given situation during a specified period of time. Affect, on the other hand, may influence what employees choose to do on the job and how persistent they are in doing things that are instrumental in helping them adapt to their work situations.

Job satisfaction shares several characteristics with intelligence; it has been around in scientific psychology for so long and has been researched so extensively that it gets treated by some researchers as a comfortable "old shoe," one that is unfashionable and unworthy of continued research. Many organizational researchers seem to assume that we know all there is to know about job satisfaction; we lose sight of its usefulness because of its familiarity and past popularity. Compared to other variables, such as organizational commitment, organizational climate, social information processing, overjustification effects, or general dispositional constructs, job satisfaction simply does not arrest and maintain the attention of researchers and practitioners. However, like intelligence, well-developed measures of job satisfaction account for variance in organizationally relevant responses far beyond the demonstrated usefulness of the newer and trendier constructs, notions, and variables.

The history of scientific research on job satisfaction has been much shorter than that on intelligence. The consensus on definitions and conceptualizations is less striking, the well-done theoretical research is less extensive, and there is less convergence among investigators' choices of measures. As an example, researchers in the area of human abilities rarely combine ten or twelve home-grown items and call the resulting scale a measure of intelligence. But as Zedeck (1987) has reported, we continue to see such troublesome practices with unfortunate frequency in job attitude research.

The parallels between these two areas of scientific inquiry are many and noteworthy. Even controversies and disagreements about the constructs show remarkable similarities. Can we measure satisfaction (Landy, 1978)? What is its dimensionality (Baehr, 1954; Baehr & Renck, 1958)? Is satisfaction determined by individual differences or environments (Staw, Bell, & Clausen, 1986; Weitz, 1952; Judge, 1990; Hackman & Oldham, 1976)? Can we change satisfaction by interventions? Should satisfaction, as a surrogate for quality of work life, become a target of public policy (Lawler, 1982)? There are also those who have attempted to estimate the extent to which job satisfaction is genetically determined (Arvey, Bouchard, Segal, & Abraham, 1989).

We argue here that the usefulness of measures of g prior to organizational entry is paralleled by the usefulness of measures of job satisfaction after organizational entry. Once an individual joins the organization, a vector of scores on a well-constructed, validated set of job satisfaction scales becomes the most informative data an organizational psychologist or manager can have. The evidence for this bold statement is impressive. Job affect has been demonstrated to influence employee attendance at work (Smith, 1977; Scott & Taylor, 1985), decisions to leave an organization (Mobley, Horner, & Hollingsworth, 1978; Hom & Hulin, 1981; Carsten & Spector, 1987), decisions to retire (Hanisch & Hulin, 1990; Schmitt & McCune, 1981) general behavioral syndromes reflecting pro-organizational orientations (Bateman & Organ, 1983; Farrell, 1983; Smith, Organ, & Near, 1983; Roznowski, Miller, & Rosse, 1990) attempts to change work situations by voting for union representation (Getman, Goldberg & Herman, 1976; Schriesheim, 1978), psychological withdrawal behaviors (Roznowski, Miller, & Rosse, 1990; Fisher & Locke, Chapter 7), and even receptivity to prevote, unionization activity (Hamner & Smith, 1978).

One last introductory remark is in order. This chapter concerns the general usefulness of scores on scales assessing job satisfaction. We are not concerned in this chapter with the most valid predictor of any specific behavior. It is clear that behavioral intentions to engage in a given act at a specified time will probably generate higher validities for that specific behavior occurring within a specified time period than any other predictor (Ajzen & Fishbein, 1977; Fishbein & Ajzen, 1974; Fishbein, 1980). Both the validities of these behavioral intention measures and their limitations are well described by the term *idiot savants* of organizational psychology. We have described behavioral intentions this way, noting that they do one thing and that they do it very well; but that is about all they do (Hulin, in press; Roznowski, 1988). The small but reliable decrements in validities of job satisfaction predicting specific behaviors are more than made up for by the breadth of behaviors that general satisfaction scales are capable of predicting with modest to substantial validity.

The General Usefulness of Satisfaction as a Predictor of Behavior

At this point, we offer figure 6–1, borrowed from Hulin, Roznowski, and Hachiya (1985) and slightly modified, as a framework for this chapter. We will not focus here on the portion of the model specifying the antecedents of job satisfaction. We choose instead to discuss the response portion of the model. Although the entire, fully specified model has not been tested in a study that would permit causal inferences, support has been found for a number of the model's linkages (Roznowski, Miller, Rosse, 1990; Hulin, 1991; Hanisch & Hulin, 1990; Hulin, Roznowski, & Hachiya, 1985). Such support is important; the hypothesized causes of work role satisfaction may suggest which behavioral constructs are likely to prove useful as responses to dissatisfaction.

A general hypothesis of this heuristic model is that work role dissatisfaction motivates individuals to do something to alleviate it; dissatisfaction is unpleasant and stressful. Similar ideas have been advanced elsewhere (March & Simon, 1958; Rosse & Miller, 1984). Rosse and Miller's (1984) adaptation cycle, for example, proposes a specific adaptation process model applied to the satisfaction-absenteeism link.

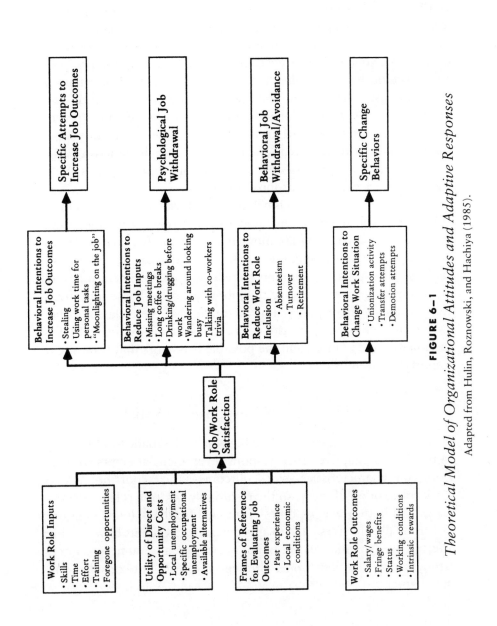

FIGURE 6–1

Theoretical Model of Organizational Attitudes and Adaptive Responses

Adapted from Hulin, Roznowski, and Hachiya (1985).

The model shown in figure 6–1 hypothesizes that dissatisfied workers will do something to alleviate or somehow lessen negative feelings about their job and work role. Viewed in this way, satisfaction has a much different motivational function than other social attitudes. Negative feelings toward an institution are unlikely to provoke specific behaviors directed toward that institution. This is because most behaviors are unlikely to change the institution and have a very limited impact on the attitudes, well-being, or distress of the individual. In the case of formal work roles, dissatisfaction especially should motivate intentions to engage in behavior to change work inputs, outcomes, or related work role characteristics. Substantial evidence for these propositions exists.

The general areas in which behavioral efforts of dissatisfied individuals are likely to be concentrated in order to change their jobs and increase their satisfaction are indicated in the model. Possible areas include (1) attempts to increase work role outcomes, (2) attempts to decrease job inputs, (3) attempts to reduce work role inclusion, and (4) formal attempts to change the job/work role. These four areas constitute hypotheses; no claims are made that these classes of behaviors are definitive, exhaustive, or even mutually exclusive. A discussion of these families and the possible behaviors that they might comprise is given below.

Behavioral Families as Responses to Satisfaction

We describe responses to dissatisfying work roles made by individual employees as adaptive. Such responses represent attempts to alter work role characteristics, work outcomes, their contributions to work roles, or all of these, so the resulting work role is less dissatisfying. In addition, we hypothesize implied feedback loops in figure 6–1 from all behaviors back to appropriate antecedents of work role affect. This dynamic concept of behavior generates numerous interesting theoretical predictions, although these are not considered in this chapter.

Adaptation

Adaptation refers to changes made by living systems in response to their environment. We believe that all individuals in formal organizations adapt to some degree; few of us can hope to find nirvana in any formal organization. Furthermore, there are multiple manifestations of job-related affect, many of which are behaviors enacted to deal with, or adapt to, the organizational environment (Rosse & Miller, 1984). Thus, withdrawal can be said to be a multidimensional construct. Hanisch and Hulin (1990) and Hanisch (1990) present evidence regarding the multidimensional nature of job withdrawal. People change and adapt their behavioral repertoires both to fit the contingencies and constraints in the particular organizational situation and to provide themselves with the maximum possible satisfying outcomes or the fewest dissatisfying outcomes. Further, individual differences likely enter in to determine the rates of change and adaptation. Organizational contingencies also change over time; employees learn, and subsequently adapt to, these new contingencies.

It is not the case that all behaviors enacted in organizations should be considered adaptive. Indeed, many behaviors are enacted solely for the purpose of satisfying responsibilities, completing role-required tasks, meeting deadlines, and avoiding the ire of an unhappy supervisor. These behaviors are stimulated by role demands rather than affect and will not be addressed here. Finally, although all individuals adapt to life in organizations, the most interesting forms of adaptation are likely to occur for individuals with extreme levels of affect toward their jobs—that is, individuals who are highly dissatisfied or satisfied with their work roles. We focus primarily on the dissatisfaction end of the affect continuum.

In conceptualizing the construct of adaptation, it is useful to consider behavioral families. The original notion of behavioral families comes from work in general motivation theory by Atkinson and Birch (1970). According to these theorists, behaviors can be grouped into families by their perceived similarity, their extremity (or severity), and possibly the degree to which the behaviors result in similar valued outcomes for individuals (functional similarity). Our emphasis is on conditional probabilities of behaviors given that another behavior from the same family has been enacted, rather than on unconditional probabilities of behaviors. If an individual selects one behavior from a family, he or she is more likely to select another behavior from that same family before choosing behaviors from a different category. Individuals likely enact behaviors leading to a certain outcome until that outcome becomes less valued relative to different outcomes brought about by other behaviors or changed circumstances.

If an employee is attempting to attain a particular outcome or set of outcomes, he or she is likely to select behaviors from a family of behaviors believed to lead, either directly or indirectly, to that outcome. Thus, one hypothesis about behavioral families is that specific behaviors within families should be nearly equivalent for providing valued outcomes; they should be functionally equivalent.

Individuals may frequently switch from one behavior to another within the same functional family and perhaps only occasionally switch to behaviors in other families. Which specific behavior within a family is selected at any point in time probably cannot be predicted with much accuracy; the relative frequency of behaviors chosen from functionally homogeneous families integrated over a reasonably long period of time, however, should be predictable. Thus, individuals may choose specific behaviors from a family of behaviors perceived as leading to valued job outcomes, and persist in these and related behaviors for some period of time, before changing to another behavioral family with a functionally different set of outcomes. Finally, repetitions of specific behaviors should have negatively accelerated utility curves (Naylor, Pritchard, & Ilgen, 1980), indicating gradually decreasing rates of increasing utility over numerous repetitions.

Further clarification and specification of these ideas in an organizational situation would involve studying behavioral switching due to changes in organizational or other environmental constraints. Some constraints may either block certain behaviors or perhaps block the delivery of the valued outcome subsequent to behavior enactment. Researchers will need to consider these constraints on behavior when studying behavioral adaptation or, at the very least, be aware of the many possible behavior-limiting constraints.

Finally, we should point out that behaviors are considered here from the perspective of the individual employee attempting to adapt to stressful and dissatisfying work situations. The perspective we take for the study of these behaviors is the adaptiveness for the individual in decreasing job stress or increasing job satisfaction. Thus, negative, disruptive behaviors, even those detrimental to the organization or the work group, may be considered adaptive from the employee's point of view. Their rationality or adaptiveness from the perspective of the organization is a matter for another analysis, perhaps an economic one. If an occasional unscheduled day off, for example, is instrumental in decreasing or even temporarily alleviating an employee's job dissatisfaction, then that behavior is adaptive for the purposes for which it was chosen. Even sabotage may be adaptive under some circumstances. The behaviors of modern Luddites may be adaptive for these workers, regardless of organizational managers' perceptions of their behaviors. Ned Lud's followers may regard their behaviors as attempts to regain control over their work; organizations may regard them as saboteurs. A formal analysis of the choice of families of adaptive behaviors or specific behaviors within a family might fruitfully proceed within a valence framework (Naylor, Pritchard, & Ilgen, 1980) or an affect model (Hulin, Roznowski, & Hachiya, 1985). This last point brings us to the discussion of an important conceptual issue regarding explanatory models.

Valence Models

A critical characteristic of the model presented in figure 6–1 is that it provides an affect-based explanation of employee behavior. Job affect is the central construct in the model. However, valence models of job choice and job behaviors (Vroom, 1964; Naylor, Pritchard, & Ilgen, 1980) offer competing explanations of organizational behavior. Such models explain behavior as determined by relative valences of possible alternative behaviors or acts. Valence theorists argue that individuals select acts or behaviors, from among many possible behaviors, that are perceived as generating the greatest positive change in valence. Thus, valence models predict that behavioral choices are guided by individual estimates of future satisfaction, or the anticipation of satisfaction. In valence models, satisfaction is merely an epiphenomenon; it is a byproduct of work role behaviors, but itself has no power to explain behavioral choice.

In contrast, job satisfaction models, such as the one presented in this chapter, implicitly assume job behavior is influenced by current job affect. Dissatisfied individuals behave differently from satisfied individuals, and the choices of behaviors are influenced by satisfaction and dissatisfaction with specific work role inputs and outcomes.

An integrated model of the influences of affect and valence on behavioral choices can be proposed. Such an integration involves incorporating the learning of the utilities of outcomes of past work role behaviors and of perceived contingencies between behaviors and outcomes. It stresses the distinction between impetus to action, a concept not well handled by a strict valence model, and choice or direction of acts.

Through day-to-day experiences, both firsthand and vicarious, individuals become aware of the direct and indirect effects of different work role outcomes on affect levels. For instance, if individuals have experienced money as satisfying because of what can be done with money, they are more likely to commit time and effort to acts that have led to earning more money in their current work roles. Also, if they have found responsibility to be dissatisfying, they are unlikely to commit time and effort today to acts that will lead to increased responsibility tomorrow. Others, because of experienced positive affect resulting from increased responsibility or autonomy, might seek additional responsibility or autonomy through their choice of work behaviors. Examples of such behaviors might include volunteering to do extra work or coming in early or on a holiday, or perhaps making a supervisor aware of responsible, extrarole behaviors.

Current affect levels associated with various job outcomes provide information to job incumbents about expected future outcomes and resultant affect levels if they continue their current behavioral repertoires. Dissatisfied individuals will be expected to change their work role behaviors, or even change their work roles, under the belief that current affect levels are their best personal indicator of future affect; if nothing is done to change the situation, individuals are likely to assume they will continue to be dissatisfied. Likewise, satisfied individuals are expected to make behavioral choices in the future similar to those that led to their current affect levels.

Relative dissatisfaction providing an impetus to action is missing in modern valence models. Many behaviors, particularly those that involve change from the present situation, need a psychological mechanism that stimulates action in addition to the mental calculus and other cognitive activities that generate estimates of valences or future utilities associated with various acts. The stress or discomfort that accompanies job dissatisfaction is such a stimulus. The trigger for these feelings of relative dissatisfaction could be any event, act, or experience in the work environment that generates the perception of relative deprivation (Rosse & Miller, 1984). And, the specific act to which time and effort are committed may be determined in part by anticipated satisfaction with outcomes of the chosen acts. However, knowledge about the anticipated satisfaction (valences of the outcomes of the possible behaviors) comes from satisfaction experienced from similar acts and contingent outcomes in the past and present.

This integration of affect and valence explanations of work role behaviors has the advantage of providing the psychological "trigger" mechanism to behavioral change and offers much more than a cosmetic wording change for the sake of theoretical integration. It also provides a somewhat different interpretation of the roots of individual differences in outcome utility than would be found in a standard need-based theoretic approach. The change we offer avoids an emphasis on unobservable and poorly defined needs that have questionable theoretical bases as explanations for behavior (Campbell & Pritchard, 1976; Ebel, 1974); it also substitutes for needs an emphasis on learning the outcomes of different classes or families of behaviors. We assume individuals are more aware of their satisfaction from outcomes than they are of the links between acts and the satisfaction of abstract needs.

General Behavioral Measures

We have discussed the general usefulness of well-constructed, valid measures of job attitudes and the theoretical basis of an affect-based model of job adaptation. This discussion of the scientific merit of measures of general job attitudes emphasized the variety of organizationally important behavioral responses that general job attitudes have been shown to predict consistently. However, it is important to note that the empirical support for these ideas is not without controversy (see Hackett & Guion, 1985; Hulin, in press; Scott & Taylor, 1985). This apparent problematic support, however, may reflect the research strategies used by researchers in this area as much as it does the underlying relations between job attitudes and job behaviors. The job attitude literature contains many studies in which measures of general job attitudes were related to specific, often low base-rate behaviors. The use of general attitudes as predictors of specific, low base-rate behavioral responses is a strategy with many conceptual and analytic problems (Ajzen & Fishbein, 1977; Doob, 1947; Fishbein & Ajzen, 1974; Thurstone, 1931).

The theoretical looseness involved in expecting significant relations between attitudes and specific behaviors was first discussed by Thurstone (1931) in an early and influential article on the use and measurement of social attitudes. In this article, Thurstone defined attitude as the affect for (or against) an object. He argued that when we identify an individual's attitude toward some object, we have only identified the affective *direction* for or against that object. Nothing about the specific manner in which the person might act can be predicted based on this information. Thurstone (1931) pointed out that it is possible for two individuals to have identical attitudes toward an object but take very different overt actions that have only one thing in common: they are equally favorable (or unfavorable) toward the object.

Thurstone's arguments imply that it is the commonality of behaviors—the overall favorableness or unfavorableness of a set of behaviors relevant to an object, rather than the specific behaviors considered one at a time—that represents the appropriate criterion to be predicted by general attitudes. This argument further implies that using a criterion based on multiple behavioral measures should allow estimates of the overall favorableness of individuals' attitudes. Variation in overall favorableness toward the object represents the common variance among the many manifest behaviors. Such variation defines the underlying behavioral propensity in which we are interested.

In his behavioristic critique of the scientific usefulness of the attitude construct, Doob (1947) noted that most definitions of attitude refer to patterns of overt responses. He argued that any single overt behavior can seldom be predicted from knowledge of the attitude alone; an attitude can mediate a repertoire of overt responses. According to Doob (1947, p. 138), "a favorable attitude toward a social institution, for example, can mediate innumerable responses connected with what is considered to be the welfare of that institution." Which of these innumerable responses an individual chooses is a function of many other acquired tendencies of the individual that presumably reflect past reinforcements for specific behaviors. In the terminology of modern valence theory, past reinforcements should create perceived act-outcome contingencies and result in judgment and behavior tendencies and concordances (Naylor, Pritchard, & Ilgen, 1980).

Hull (1941; also cited in Doob, 1947) similarly argued that attitudes have the property of internal stimuli to which individuals react. These stimuli can evoke other unspecified acts that bring about a reinforcing state of affairs. Which specific acts are evoked again depends on past reinforcements. Campbell's (1963) integration of behavioristic and social psychological interpretations of social attitudes and other acquired behavioral dispositions continues many of the themes enumerated by Thurstone (1931), Doob (1947), and Hull (1941).

On the empirical side of this issue, Wicker (1969) summarized the results of over thirty attitude-behavior studies and concluded that it is unlikely that attitudes will be closely related to specific overt behaviors. We note here that most of the studies reviewed by Wicker (1969) assessed the degree of relationship between general attitudes and specific manifest behaviors rather than between attitudes and the commonality among a series of overt behaviors.

More recently, Fishbein and Ajzen's (1974) and Fishbein's (1980) theoretical developments and empirical reviews applied earlier work by Dulany (1968) and Ryan (1970) to the general attitude-behavior area. Like Thurstone and Doob, Fishbein and Ajzen argued that "a person's attitude toward an object influences the overall pattern of his responses to the object, but [that] it need not predict any given action" (Ajzen & Fishbein, 1977, p. 888). Following Ryan and Dulany, they argued that "a single behavior is determined by the intention to perform the behavior in question" (Ajzen & Fishbein, 1977, p. 888). Following the extensive conceptual developments of Fishbein and Ajzen, the general research strategy used in the study of attitudes and behavior relations changed markedly. Instead of investigations of relations between general attitudes and general behaviors, many researchers began to study attitudes toward a specific act as well as intentions to perform that act as predictors of engaging in that behavior.

The empirical gains from this shift in research strategies have been impressive. Correlations between general attitudes toward an object and any one specific behavior relevant to that object were generally low and often nonsignificant (Wicker, 1969). In contrast, the correlations between specific attitudes and intentions and the occurrence of these specific behaviors are generally significant and often impressively large (Fishbein, 1967; Getman, Goldberg, & Herman, 1976; Hom & Hulin, 1981; Hom, Katerberg, & Hulin, 1979; Mobley, 1977).

However, this shift of research strategies and theoretical orientations, while achieving some impressive correlations between predictors and specific behavioral responses, has been dysfunctional in many ways. In retrospect, the change may have solved the wrong problem. The shift was an excellent solution to the narrowly conceived applied problem of relating attitudes to specific behaviors. However, the solution seems to have ignored the fundamental problem of the relations among theoretical constructs that underlie the specific manifest behavioral responses and the general attitudes. By adhering to behavioral intention models for reasons of high predictability and practical utility, researchers frequently lose sight of important general scientific constructs and instead study specific, typically isolated acts that may be too narrowly conceived for scientific usefulness. Unfortunately, examining any single behavior may preclude learning about constructs and underlying propensities, and consequently limits our ability to generalize to unstudied but related behaviors. As scientific researchers, our focus should be these general constructs that provide a basis for generalizing observed relations to similar problems and behaviors.

The reason for the particular shift of empirical strategies is not obvious. Thurstone, Doob, and Hull argued only for the use of behavioral criteria that represented the commonalities among a series of behaviors related to a social object as criteria to be predicted by general social attitudes. Nothing in their writing suggests the move to a particular attitude-specific behavior strategy.

Similarly, Fishbein and Ajzen (1974) and Ajzen and Fishbein (1977) argued for correspondence between assessed attitudes and behavioral criteria. They discussed and illustrated the benefits of using broad sets of behaviors predicted by general attitudes. They also argued that specific attitudes and intentions should be used to predict single occurrences of specific behaviors. They did not argue for a strategy in which specific behaviors are the criteria of choice. Basic researchers involved in attitude research could have obtained the necessary correspondence between their general attitude measures and their criteria by constructing behavioral measures that reflected the commonality among a heterogeneous series of overt behaviors.

In summary, attitude theorists, starting with Thurstone, have been concerned with the correspondence between attitudes as normally assessed and single behaviors. These theorists have concluded that the lack of correspondence is a serious problem. Later theorists and researchers, beginning with Fishbein and Ajzen (1974), have typically achieved attitude-behavior correspondence by predicting specific behaviors with the use of specific attitudes toward that behavior and behavioral intentions; this particular change in research strategies was by no means required by their theory. The change represents but one way of obtaining the obviously crucial and desirable correspondence between attitude and behavior measures (see Roznowski & Hanisch, 1990). However, it is not necessarily the only scientifically defensible change in research strategies.

Methodological and Measurement Reasons for Congruence

By tailoring attitude measures to match the specificity of behaviors, researchers create both attitude and behavioral variables that are dominated by variance specific to these two variables. In general, the variance of any manifest behavior will be a combination of general construct-relevant variance, specific variance, and error variance. The search for predictors of many of the specific behaviors in which organizational psychologists are interested has led researchers to construct and study series of behavioral intention measures that do one thing very well (predict specific behaviors) but are neither useful nor interesting for other purposes. Relationships that rely on matching the specific variance in the predictor and these criteria may tell us little about antecedents of general behavioral constructs that subsume many important responses. We argue here for developing measures of underlying behavioral constructs that are congruent with the generality of the attitudinal constructs.

In keeping with the intelligence analogy introduced earlier, the thinking described here is similar to research on human intellectual abilities that might attempt to find antecedents and correlates of the knowledge of oxymoron or palindrome or onomatopoeia. Such antecedents and correlates could possibly be found. However, the sci-

entific knowledge gained in the process of identifying these antecedents and correlates—as opposed to the knowledge generated by, say,
the antecedents and correlates of the general construct of verbal ability that might comprise the knowledge of these three terms—is likely
to be scientifically trivial. What is to be gained in a scientific sense
from studies of narrow behaviors, narrow attitudes (intentions), and
narrow abilities?

In addition to the lack of scientific merit in the study of single,
isolated occurrences of specific behaviors, there are serious methodological problems. Such behaviors often have low base rates. Low
base rates of single, binary variables generate decidedly non-normal,
skewed distributions (see Meehl & Rosen, 1955; Wiggins, 1973).
Treating these distributions as if they were normal may create serious statistical problems. Attempting to normalize or otherwise
smooth skewed distributions by aggregating the observations across
longer periods of time or by aggregating from the level of individuals
to groups requires assumptions about organizational time (see Hulin
& Rousseau, 1980; McGrath & Kelly, 1986) and can be only mar-
ginally successful (Harrison & Hulin, 1989) at best. The maximum
correlations between variables with such skewed distributions and
almost any other variable are often less than unity and frequently in
the .20 to .40 range (Wiggins, 1973). If researchers are willing to
make assumptions about the distributions of the latent propensities
underlying manifest single behaviors, then alternative statistical procedures such as log-linear models can be used (Feinberg, 1980; Grizzle, Starmer, & Koch, 1969). Simpler solutions to relations among
low base rate variables and between low base rate variables and continuous variables include biserial and tetrachoric correlations if dis-
tributional assumptions of the underlying behavioral propensities
can be met.

Finally, in addition to the dubious scientific merits, the practical
merits of the study of single occurrences of single behaviors are best
described as illusory. It may ultimately be more useful to study the
antecedents of theoretical constructs that underlie clusters or families of manifest behaviors or verbal responses, even when researchers
are immediately interested in only one of the behaviors in the family.
Such research has the advantage of allowing generalizations to other
unstudied behaviors or verbal or cognitive responses subsumed by
the general constructs. These investigations also have the advantage

of assessing antecedents of common, construct-relevant variance instead of capitalizing on specific variance. With measures containing a small number of items designed to assess the occurrences of a single behavior, specific variance will likely dominate the measure. We are able to build common variance in measures only by carefully designing breadth and trait- or theory-relevant heterogeneity into such an instrument. This property of measures—systematic heterogeneity (see Humphreys, 1985; Roznowski, 1987; Roznowski & Hanisch, 1990)—effectively reduces the impact of trait-irrelevant or "bias" determinants in item responses and increases the contribution of important trait-relevant variance in items, scales, and tests.

Paradoxes of bandwidth-fidelity notwithstanding, Humphreys (1985), Roznowski (1987), and Roznowski and Hanisch (1990) have discussed and demonstrated the benefits of controlled, theory-relevant heterogeneity in items used in the assessments of intellectual abilities and work affect. Such theory-relevant heterogeneity in the behaviors that make up criterion measures in attitude-behavior research should continue to pay equal dividends in the general attitude-behavior research area.

Opposing Forces

There are likely to be many forces opposing the recommendations and ideas in this chapter. For example, directors of blood banks will continue to be interested in the specific practical problems of maintaining volunteer, disease-free blood donations; organizational managers will be interested in predicting and controlling absenteeism and turnover; directors of family planning clinics may be interested in the attitudinal antecedents of the use of birth control methods; ministers may be interested in the correlates of church attendance; and public health officials may be interested in attitudinal correlates of practicing safe sex. However, scientific inquiries would be better directed at identifying the constructs and latent behavioral propensities underlying—in the first example—general prosocial, altruistic behaviors that encompass blood donations. Organizational researchers' interests will likely be better served by knowing both the antecedents of organizational withdrawal propensities and the full range of the manifest behavioral responses comprised by such a behavioral construct. On the purely practical side, ministers might even be better informed about religiosity generally, and their parishioners specifically if they knew the antecedents of a general behavioral construct that subsumed tithing, church attendance, contributing to special church funds, repairing the rectory roof, and serving on the committee to find a new assistant pastor. They might develop better understanding of why some of their flock engage in one behavior but not others and of why, how, and when these different behaviors become functionally equivalent. By knowing and studying the behavioral responses that compose and define the latent behavioral construct underlying important behavioral manifestations, researchers can begin to develop theoretical models that account for behavioral switching among functionally equivalent behaviors and for the structure among seemingly dissimilar organizational behaviors.

Managers as well as organizational researchers might also be better informed about the implications of employee behaviors if they knew what behaviors consistently covary and what behaviors are perceived by employees as substitutable. Likewise, discordances among behavioral manifestations of underlying constructs are frequently as informative as concordances and covariances. Behaviors that are normally part of a functionally similar family but that do not occur with the others in specific organizational or environmental settings may tell us much about the many thresholds, constraints, and perceived contingencies in organizations.

In spite of the scientific merit and empirical advantages of general attitudes as predictors of general behavioral propensities and constructs, we suspect that organizational researchers will continue to focus on the short-term, practical benefits of predicting specific behaviors that are deemed important by organizational managers. This past, and perhaps continued focus, probably reflects a combination of habit, expedience, and belief in the importance of predicting single behaviors—sometimes, any single behavior—and the problematic nature of the evidence about the existence of behavioral families in this area of research. Investigators who pursue research on the antecedents and correlates of general behavioral propensities must first identify the general behavioral construct or behavioral family. They then must generate evidence that the behaviors comprised by the general construct are a sufficiently homogeneous set of responses to be considered a relevant behavioral family. Much past evidence, particularly in the general area of organizational withdrawal, has appeared to raise questions about whether the concept of families of responses is a reliable basis for forming scientifically useful constructs. In the next section we present evidence from a simulation that begins to address these questions.

Expected Relations among Discrete Withdrawal Behaviors

What empirical results might be generated by a simple, single common factor model of withdrawal behaviors? To what extent might we observe correlations between measures of job affect and specific behaviors representing a hypothesized trait or behavioral tendency under the assumptions of (a) reliable and valid measures of work role satisfaction, (b) good measures of the behaviors, and (c) a simple linear model relating affect to the behavioral propensities?

To answer these questions, consider a simple linear model in which three hypothetical behaviors—for instance, absence, lateness, and turnover—are assumed to be manifestations of a single, common underlying trait. Many other behaviors, such as retiring, or leaving work early, or, perhaps, drinking before work, might be chosen as manifestations as well. Each of these behavioral manifestations is assumed to have been generated by thresholds on continuous and normally distributed underlying behavioral propensities. What are the expected correlations among the discrete behaviors? Also, what is the expected Pearson correlation between a continuously distributed measure of work role satisfaction and each of these behavioral manifestations? The data for a simulation using these values as parameters are summarized in table 6–1. Assuming factor loadings of .50, .40, and .60 of the behavioral propensities on the underlying common latent trait, the correlations among the behavioral propensities would be .20, .30, and .24. These values are not overwhelmingly large, but are still theoretically interesting. If thresholds are then imposed on the continuous behavioral propensities that generate discrete absences, latenesses, and resignations and that have distributions consistent with what one might expect given the empirical literature, these correlations drop to .04, .08, and .08 among the discrete manifest behaviors. Attenuating these empirical correlations for the effects of unreliability in the assessments of both variables will reduce the observed correlations even further.

TABLE 6–1
Simulation Results

Factor Loadings

1. Absence	.5
2. Tardiness	.4
3. Turnover	.6
4. satisfaction	−.6

Correlations among Behavioral Propensities

	1	2	3
1. Absence	—	.20	.30
2. Tardiness		—	.24
3. Turnover			—

Correlations among Discrete Behaviors

	1	2	3
1. Absence	—	.04	.08
2. Tardiness		—	.08
3. Turnover		—	

Correlations between Satisfaction and Discrete Behaviors

	Satisfaction
1. Absence	−.12
2. Tardiness	−.22
3. Turnover	−.23

Empirical correlations among such discrete behaviors generated by a single common factor model may provide little information about the hypothetical underlying trait. Of course, the situation is much more complicated than portrayed here. Several different models address relations among different withdrawal behaviors. These models need to be translated into mathematical terms and the implications each has for relations among different discrete behaviors should be examined.

We chose the simple linear model in this illustrative example to demonstrate the severe, downwardly biasing effects of distributions of manifest variables on empirical correlations. A closely related question about the expected Pearson correlations between a continuously distributed measure of work role satisfaction and each of the behavioral manifestations of the assumed latent trait can also be answered with the assumptions of the same model. If work role satisfaction has a loading on the common withdrawal factor of $-.60$, then the expected values of the correlations between this continuously distributed measure and the three discrete behaviors are $-.12$ (absence), $-.22$ (lateness), and $-.23$ (turnover). Again, these correlations have not been attenuated for the effects of unreliability, and they do not tell us the "truth" regarding affect-behavior relations. They do tell us the bounds within which the truth may lie. The similarity of the average Pearson correlations reported in two recent meta-analyses of relations between satisfaction and absenteeism of $-.09$ (Hackett & Guion, 1985) and $-.15$ (Scott & Taylor, 1985) and the correlation of $-.12$ that would be predicted by the proposed theoretical, single factor model is no less than striking.

It is important to note that the average empirical correlation between affect and absenteeism reported in Hackett and Guion's (1985) meta-analysis was used to reject a single common factor model. Empirical correlations, unless corrected for the downwardly biasing effects of distributions and thresholds and discussed within the context of assumed theoretical models, should be interpreted with extreme caution. Based on the consistency of the empirical evidence with the simple, single common factor model, we can only assume that this model represents a useful approximation to reality. The average correlations of $-.09$ and $-.15$ are both within limits of sampling variance of the theoretical value of $-.12$. Nonetheless, the two meta-analyses generated opposite conclusions about the expected relation between affect and absenteeism without addressing questions about the attenuation effects of skewed distributions of manifest variables on observed correlations.

Analyses, meta-analyses, or other reviews of accumulated empirical correlations between satisfaction and dichotomous or polytomous behaviors cannot necessarily be relied upon to estimate population correlations of the continuously distributed underlying behavioral propensities. But it is these underlying general behavioral propensities that permit general statements about job behaviors and that allow generalizations to other conceptually related behaviors.

Pearson correlations involving the behavioral manifestations of the underlying latent traits provide biased estimates of the correlations involving the general constructs.

Behavioral Families

At this point we depart from a general discussion of the usefulness of, and problems with, studying general behavioral constructs to discuss four hypothetical behavioral families that may represent functionally similar, if somewhat heterogeneous, responses to dissatisfaction: (1) attempts to change the work role, (2) attempts to reduce work role inclusion, (3) attempts to decrease work role inputs, and (4) attempts to increase work role outcomes. These four families of responses represent potential behavioral constructs that should be investigated in future research on the employee withdrawal process. We do not claim these four behavioral families are exhaustive, mutually exclusive, or necessarily homogeneous. We think they represent a good first approximation of logical clusters of behaviors in this area.

Attempts to Change the Work Role

For the first behavioral family, we consider formal attempts by individuals to change their work situations. Considerable individual effort and time likely goes into these attempts. Getman, Goldberg, and Herman (1976) analyzed vote intentions and voting patterns in thirty-three union representation elections sponsored by the National Labor Relations Board (NLRB). Job and union attitudes (including general work satisfaction) assessed before the thirty-day election campaign were significantly related to stated voting intentions, to reported votes, and to the outcome of the vote on an election-by-election basis. Employees dissatisfied with characteristics of their work were most likely to vote in favor of union representation. Satisfaction with those elements of the work role likely to be changed by unionization (pay, supervision) was strongly related to stated intentions of voting in favor of union representation. Satisfaction with those elements unlikely to be changed by unionization (work content, coworkers) was less strongly related to union voting.

Similarly, Schriesheim (1978) reported a correlation of −.76 between satisfaction with economic factors of the work role and pro-union voting in one NLRB-sponsored election. The correlation between satisfaction with noneconomic factors and union vote was substantially lower, $r = -.38$.

Hamner and Smith's (1978) empirically developed, cross-validated scale to predict unionization activity (card signing, union organizing drives in potential bargaining units) that precedes NLRB-sanctioned elections contained thirteen items. The content of these items was concentrated in areas of satisfaction with supervision, physical working conditions, and amount of work—all characteristics that unions may be instrumental in changing or controlling.

In a study of an attempt to unionize faculty at a state university, Zalesny (1985) found that the perceived instrumentality of the union for redressing causes of dissatisfaction was an important predictive factor in a model of union voting. The perceived instrumentality of the union for changing economic outcomes was low for faculty members. Financial conditions were dictated by the state legislature; a union would not be expected to have a great deal of influence over this body. The union was perceived as more instrumental in changing other, noneconomic, issues. Hence, satisfaction with economic factors was not strongly related to voting intentions. Faculty members responded as rationally as the blue-collar workers studied by Getman, Goldberg, and Herman (1976). These individuals were selective in terms of how their attitudes toward specific work role characteristics influenced their voting intentions.

Other general areas related to formal work role change, in addition to voting in NLRB elections or precampaign activities, should be considered in the development of measures of behavioral propensities to change work roles in formal ways. Attempts to change or improve enforcement of safety regulations, overtime rules, bonus pay systems, or work assignments should be considered. Another label for these behaviors, one that suggests a slightly different source of commonality among the behaviors, might be "attempts to gain control over the work situation."

Attempts to Reduce Work Role Inclusion

Hypothesized behavioral manifestations of the latent construct of work role change have traditionally included tardiness, absenteeism, and turnover. Because of recent changes in federal laws governing age discrimination in employment, retirement can also be assumed to represent a relevant behavioral manifestation of this underlying propensity (Hanisch & Hulin, 1990). Much empirical research on the correlates of tardiness, absenteeism, and turnover as well as conceptual work on the definition of and structure among the behavioral manifestations of the underlying construct has been published. This substantial literature has generated some controversy, a lack of agreement about the extent to which work role satisfaction is a significant predictor of these behaviors, and even a lack of consensus about the empirical evidence supporting the existence of such a behavioral family or latent trait.

Research on both absenteeism and turnover has been extensive and has been summarized by Goodman and Atkin (1984) and Mowday, Porter, and Steers (1982). As discussed previously, two meta-analyses on the relationship between job satisfaction and absenteeism have been published (Hackett & Guion, 1985; Scott & Taylor, 1985). Much has been written about the assumed structure that exists among the different behaviors composing this family. Writers and researchers such as Baruch (1944), Rice and Trist (1952), March and Simon (1958), Melbin (1961), Porter and Steers (1973), Beehr and Gupta (1978), and Rosse and Miller (1984) have reported relations among different forms of withdrawal and have discussed different conceptual models of these withdrawal behaviors ranging from the independent forms model (March & Simon, 1958) to the progression of withdrawal model (Rosse & Miller, 1984). Unfortunately, these discussions are often without detailed examinations of the effects of the different models and the low base rates of the behaviors on expected statistical relations among the observed withdrawal responses. Most of these articles have done little to provide well-articulated models of withdrawal behaviors that specify in detail the expected relations among manifest behaviors. Thus, we are left with much empirical data that is strongly influenced by the base rates among the behaviors, as well as by the underlying processes that generate individual withdrawal behaviors, and that is problematic in terms of support for any theoretical model.

The simple demonstration reported in the previous section testifies to the strong influence of base rates and skewed distributions on correlations among binary variables (see also Olsson, Drasgow, &

Dorans, 1982; Rosse & Hulin, 1985; Wiggins, 1973). The problems inherent in interpreting empirical correlations among such behaviors as if they reflected theoretical relations among continuously distributed underlying latent constructs must be emphasized. Because of the problems with ceilings on the relations among such behaviors and the lack of well-specified theoretical models of the structures among the manifest behaviors, our interpretation of the available data is that tardiness, absenteeism, turnover, and retirement should be regarded as forming a behavioral family whose manifestations are related to job satisfaction.

To add an additional degree of complexity to the situation, Hanisch and Hulin (1990) and Hanisch (1990) report evidence of multidimensionality among reported withdrawal behaviors in samples of faculty and nonacademic staff members at a major state university. This multidimensionality was accompanied by differential relations between affect measures and the different families or dimensions of withdrawal behavior. Specifically they found two factors were needed to account for the covariances among reported withdrawal behaviors. One factor was labeled "work withdrawal" and was defined by behaviors such as lateness for work or meetings, absenteeism, and a composite scale assessing reported frequencies of engaging in different unfavorable job behaviors. The second factor, labeled "job withdrawal," was defined by turnover, desire to retire, and retirement intentions. Absenteeism loaded on both work and job withdrawal factors, reflecting its position as a more extreme form of work withdrawal than lateness or unfavorable behaviors but less extreme than permanent job withdrawal. These withdrawal factors were both related to hypothesized affect and demographic antecedents in expected directions in well-fitting causal models. The factor analytic results were based on an initial sample of 166 university employees (Hanisch & Hulin, 1990). Both the measurement and structured models were validated on an independent sample of approximately 400 additional university employees (Hanisch, 1990).

Attempts to Reduce Work Role Inputs

We have labeled this hypothesized family "attempts to reduce work role inputs" to maintain its theoretical connections with the overall model of work role satisfaction and job adaptation that was developed in our earlier work (Hulin, Roznowski, & Hachiya, 1985). Another descriptive label might be "psychological job withdrawal" to stress both the distinction between the previous family that involves physical absence or withdrawal from work and the indicators in this family that reflect reductions of effort levels while at work or perhaps reductions in psychological involvement of the individual with the work role. Some of the behaviors in this family might also involve informal and indirect attempts to gain perceived control over the work situation. The label "informal change behaviors" might be used to emphasize those aspects of the behaviors.

This job family was included because of its theoretical role in the model of job affect that stresses the relationship between job inputs, job outcomes, and the feedback loop from the results of job behaviors to these antecedents of work role affect. It also represents a much-needed broadening of the conceptualization of the relevant behaviors that dissatisfied workers may engage in to relieve or reduce their job stress and dissatisfaction.

Development of a construct representing attempts to reduce work role inputs needs to take into consideration a broader array of behaviors than absenteeism and tardiness. We learn little about general psychological principles and behavior by focusing only on absenteeism or tardiness. A more appropriate focus might be on individuals' attempts to withdraw from their organizations or to create psychological distance between themselves and their work organizations. Part-time work, job sharing, and similar acts among those able to engage in full-time work are little studied but deserve attention in the development of this theoretical construct. A logical next step in a scientific investigation of this construct might be learning about other manifestations of employee distancing, such as avoiding certain tasks, leaving early, arguing with coworkers, and missing meetings. Later in the chapter we give empirical results from an attempt at measuring and examining the construct validity of this behavioral family.

Assessments of this construct should stress the heterogeneity of the many possible, often unobserved, behaviors employees enact that represent the range of such psychological withdrawal behaviors. Again, no single behavior should necessarily be the focus of our attention. The assessment of any one behavior is likely to be dominated by unique variance. It is not until we aggregate behaviors and allow covariances among the behaviors to dominate scale variance that we move away from attempting to predict unique variance toward analyses and partitioning of general construct variance.

Attempts to Increase Work Role Outcomes

Little research has been directed toward exploring behaviors in this hypothetical family. Candidates for inclusion as manifestations of this underlying construct might be asking for an off-cycle pay raise, using job equipment for personal benefit, cheating on reported hours worked, stealing, moonlighting, and similarly attempting to increase the rewards associated with a work role without any concomitant increase in job inputs. These behavioral attempts—both informal and formal acts—should reflect individuals' dissatisfaction with their extrinsic job outcomes, not necessarily dissatisfactions with content of their jobs or their intrinsic outcomes. The resultant behaviors may reflect perceived inequity with the work role outcomes and should be related to dissatisfaction with these antecedents.

This is clearly a class of behaviors that would be regarded as maladaptive by most organizations. To the employee, however, this family might reflect a very logical and reasonable way to get a better rate of return for their job investments, contributions, and inputs. Both the existence of this job family and the hypothesized links between job dissatisfaction and the individual behavioral manifestations of this construct remain largely unexplored at this time.

Individual Differences

Thus far in this paper we have discussed approaches individuals might choose in adapting in organizations. A major source of variance in individuals' preferences for different job outcomes may be experience with past outcomes and what they provided in the way of changes in satisfaction and dissatisfaction. Jobs that provide good income may be satisfying to some individuals because of the many desirable things that money can buy; others, with fewer material desires, may not find money particularly satisfying. Jobs that provide status may be satisfying to some because high-status individuals are often treated differently than low-status individuals; others, with less desire for deferential treatment, may find status outcomes a matter of indifference. Jobs with responsibility are dissatisfying to some individuals because of the job stress and other outcomes that may result from responsibility; others may find responsibility a source of positive affect. Challenging jobs may be satisfying to some individuals because of how they feel after completing difficult job assignments; others may find such rewards irrelevant.

Experience as an explanation for individual differences in preferences for job outcomes has the advantage of avoiding reference to needs, values, or related psychological notions with problematical theoretical status. Such an explanation does, however, leave open the question of how individuals come to value differentially material goods, deferential treatment, responsibility, or self-reward. Explanations for acquired preferences for classes of outcomes that depend on social learning and developmental experiences without reference to questionable theoretical constructs may, in the long run, be an advantage. For the organizational researcher, the question can be finessed by assuming the existence of individual differences in preferences for classes of job outcomes and perhaps ignoring the specific sources of the individual differences.

Initial Empirical Results

In this section we depart from summaries of past findings and suggestions for future research and report an ongoing research effort that has been directed toward developing a measure of adaptation to job dissatisfaction that reflects the construct of general work withdrawal. It is an attempt to assess and measure the many things individuals may do while at work, or may do as a direct result of events at work, to increase their psychological distance from their work role ("attempts to reduce work role inputs" from the above discussion) and thereby decrease their dissatisfaction levels.

We have worked with a multi-item (currently fifty-five items) self-report scale. The idea in constructing such a relatively long scale was capturing the multitude of different behaviors enacted on the job (and off the job) as potential responses to affect. It was also necessary to account for the existence of individual differences and organizational and environmental constraints on behavior by incorporating as many different types of behaviors as possible. Work on this measure began with Rosse's (1983) dissertation research on employee withdrawal and adaptation. Most of the items are reflections or manifestations of tendencies to engage in psychological job withdrawal, or more generally, what we have termed adaptation. Occasional neutral items were included to avoid an entire scale of unrelenting questions about negative behaviors that could potentially lead to considerable response bias. In addition, items were included to assess some of the more positive behaviors individuals carry out to contribute to the overall success of the department or the organization or perhaps to improve the work situation. These items were attempts at assessing the other constructs predicted to result from affect. The items have been administered to a number of different samples—staff of a small hospital in central Illinois, blue-collar workers from the municipal operations department of a mid-sized city in Illinois, employees from two large hospitals in Minnesota, workers from two major fast-food chains in Ohio, and faculty and staff at a major state university. Results reported are based on the responses of several thousand employees ($n = 3,694$) from the two Minnesota hospitals. We can report very little resistance from respondents to completing this scale. Of course, we have made it absolutely clear to individuals that their responses are completely confidential and anonymous. The only complaints thus far have been on the length of the scale and the amount of time it takes to complete the items.

A sample of the various items in the scale is presented in table 6–2. Also given are representative means and standard deviations for the behavioral indicants on a six-point scale (with a minimum score of 1, and a maximum of 6) for the hospital sample. As expected, many of the items in this scale have extreme means. Even assuming total honesty in the self-reports, one would expect low means because relatively few employees drink or use drugs regularly before going to work (mean response, 1.1), habitually miss meetings (mean response, 1.7), or frequently wander around looking busy once they get to work (mean response, 2.2). The extreme means probably reflect a combination of reality and self-serving response sets but are well within the limits that would suggest useful and valid data. It is important to note in examining the means and standard deviations for the various items that there is substantial variability in both

TABLE 6-2
Behavior Items and Descriptive Statistics for Hospital Samples

	Mean	Standard Deviation
1. Giving encouragement to new employees	4.3	1.4
2. Daydreaming	3.7	1.8
3. Volunteering to do work you are not required to do	4.7	1.3
4. Being a "clock watcher," working no more than absolutely required	2.8	1.7
5. Working extra hard so that your supervisor will notice your efforts	3.6	1.9
6. Trying to learn more about your job or other jobs so you can transfer	3.0	1.7
7. Refusing to work overtime	2.0	1.4
8. Coming in on your day off to visit patients	1.8	1.0
9. Doing poor quality work	1.7	1.0
10. Taking equipment or supplies home from work	1.4	.8
11. Working extra hard sometimes to make up for periods you may have slacked off	3.1	1.6
12. Being absent when you are not actually sick	1.4	.6
13. Filing a formal grievance about your supervisor or coworkers	1.2	.5
14. Failing to attend scheduled meetings	1.7	.9
15. Arriving at work early to get a start on the day's work	4.2	1.8
16. Accompanying a visitor to their destination rather than just giving directions	3.4	1.4
17. Making frequent or long visits to the restroom	1.9	1.5
18. Discussing ways to improve your job with your supervisor	2.9	1.3
19. Writing personal letters or reading while you are supposed to be working	1.6	1.1
20. Wandering around trying to look busy	2.2	1.4
21. Drinking or getting high after work primarily because of things that occurred at work	1.7	1.2
22. Using illicit drugs before coming to work	1.2	.5
23. Drinking (alcohol) before coming to work	1.1	.5
24. Taking time to explain policies or procedures to new employees	3.8	1.4
25. Volunteering to swap work schedules to help out a coworker	3.2	1.2
26. Letting others do your work for you	1.7	1.0
27. Making excuses to go somewhere to get out of work	1.4	.8

Note: Scale values range from 1 to 6.

means and standard deviations across the items. This result is encouraging in that it provides some preliminary evidence that mere response-response biases and response sets are not largely responsible for the item data.

Measurement is an especially troublesome issue in the area of psychological withdrawal and adaptation. As noted elsewhere in this chapter, behavioral switching likely takes place such that individuals are predicted to enact multiple behaviors; which specific behavior they choose to enact within short time spans may not be easily predictable (Atkinson & Birch, 1970). Instability giving the appearance of unreliability is the obvious result of this switching. Further, individual differences in behavioral choices are likely to be considerable. Organizational or departmental constraints will also limit the stability and frequency of certain behaviors. Thus, we must deal with employee withdrawal behavior from psychometric as well as theoretical perspectives because of the low base rates and potential instability of responses.

We have experimented with several response options for the behavior scale. The one having the most success thus far has been a six-point scale of reported frequencies ranging from "never," "about once a year," and "about once every 6 months" at the low end to "about once a week" and "once or more per day" at the high end. Five of the six options described frequencies of once per week or less in an attempt to provide a scale that covered the expected low frequencies of the behaviors. Options containing specific time-relevant frequencies instead of the standard "sometimes frequently" response stems were found to result in less confusion on the part of the employee, better response distributions, and better psychometric properties of the item responses. We are also now including a "not applicable" (N/A) response option to prevent employees from using "never" when the behavior is simply not applicable to them or their organizational situation. An example might be "leaving notes in the suggestion box" if the organization or department has no suggestion box. We are also now experimenting with an additional stem resulting in a seven-point scale in addition to the N/A option to even out the steps in the frequency metric. Finally, several items are currently under revision to make the stem less extreme and negative sounding. For instance, using the word "taking" instead of "stealing" in items on removing property from the work place for personal use. We believe such painstaking care in item writing will ultimately pay off in terms of better scales and more valid item responses.

In spite of care in response option wording, we continue to obtain highly skewed distributions of item responses for many items. This situation is likely to be unavoidable. Further, attempts to construct scales from this pool of items representing adaptation tendencies have been neither easy nor straightforward. Standard factor analyses can be troublesome. Even with the original multistep response scale, we essentially have binary data for some of the items as well as item distributions that are highly skewed. These two characteristics make estimating the dimensionality of the item pool difficult. We have also factored phi and tetrachoric correlation matrices; we have made content judgments of the items and constructed scales from combinations of items based on these content judgments. None of these procedures has been entirely satisfactory. A combination of methods and procedures will likely be necessary in this research endeavor.

Standard factor analysis (principal factors with squared multiple correlations as communalities) suggests that anywhere from two to four factors are required to explain the variance in the item pool. We are currently exploring a two-factor interpretation of the item pool. One factor (I) is defined by the negative, withdrawal items (regardless of the extremity of the item) and has been labeled job withdrawal. Examples of the indicants of factor I include "being a clock watcher," "making frequent visits to the restroom," and "being absent when you are not really sick." The other dimension (II) was clearly defined by positive items (again with little relation to item extremity) similar to those found in organizational "citizenship" measures, and has been labeled a pro-organization, job commitment factor. Examples include "giving encouragement to new employees" and "taking time to explain policies to new employees." These two factors explained a sufficiently large amount of the variance of the original item responses to make a convincing case that they were reasonable factors.

We are also exploring the adequacy of extracting three and four factors. The last two factors explain considerably less variance of the original item responses than do the first two factors. However, examination of Eigenvalues and a parallel analysis indicated that it might be fruitful to extract these additional factors. Upon extraction and oblique rotation, the third factor (II) seemed to reflect many of the pro-organizational behaviors found in the second factor. However, several relatively pure items loaded primarily on factor III. Examples of these items are "volunteering to work extra projects" and "changing plans to be around when things get busy." Thus, it appears that factor III reflects the more work-oriented behaviors while the items loading on factor II seem to reflect coworker-oriented or social behaviors. The last factor extracted (IV) contained items relating to substance abuse behaviors as well as some of the extreme withdrawal items from the factor I such as "cheating on reported hours worked" and "refusing to do assigned work." These last items crossloaded on both factor I and factor IV. We are currently attempting to determine if these two additional factors are merely artifacts arising from the extreme (low) base rates of several items. Finally, we are finding the correlations among the positive and negative factors to be near-zero, while the similar factors (I and IV, II and III) correlate at about the .20 level. These very low factor correlations are encouraging.

The best items from the two main factors (I and II), in terms of factor loadings, item means, and content, were combined into unit-weighted composites. Standard item analyses suggested the two retained scales were sufficiently internally consistent to be considered further. Coefficient alphas were approximately .78 for both scales. These are reasonable values since we do not expect or want the scales to be highly homogeneous. Discriminant function analyses and analyses of groups (job level, hospital, education, demographic) revealed significant and interpretable differences and suggested that the scales warranted further study.

We do not claim to have established the construct validity of these scales. We believe that the antecedents of the scale responses are not response sets and that the true antecedents make sense psychologically and organizationally. Further research on the items seems justified. Roznowski, Miller, & Rosse (1990) contains a more thorough description of the scales and the various items used.

Some initial results based on the items can be reported. First, the withdrawal composite based on items from factor I was correlated with some well-known indicants of withdrawal tendencies such as intentions and other cognitions about transferring and leaving the organization or being late or absent. The correlations, shown in table 6–3, were all in the expected direction and indicated reasonable

TABLE 6–3

Correlations between Cognitions and the Withdrawal Composite

	Thoughts	Intent	Desire	Ease
Cognitions about being late or absent				
Withdrawal Composite	.37	.25	.33	.18
Cognitions about quitting or transferring				
Withdrawal Composite	.27	.13	.22	.14

Note: All correlations are significant ($p < .001$).

overlap between the withdrawal scale and various cognitions about withdrawal. The largest correlations were observed for cognitions about lateness and absence. This finding likely reflects the severity of quit/transfer cognitions relative to the late/absence cognitions. The withdrawal composite was mostly composed of items much less severe than quitting and transferring. The reasonable patterning of correlations provides an indication that response-response (common method) biases were not largely plaguing these data.

Next, correlations between scores on the JDI facet satisfaction scales, the Faces scale (Kunin, 1955), and the MSQ (Minnesota Satisfaction Questionnaire) (Weiss, Dawis, England, & Lofquist, 1967) and the composites based on the first two factors (withdrawal and pro-organizational) are shown in table 6–4 for the hospital sample. These results are given in the first two rows of table 6–4. In general, the largest correlations occur for JDI work, Faces, and MSQ scales. This reasonable patterning again is encouraging and indicates employees are making valid discriminations in responding to the various items. The more general satisfaction scales (Work, Faces, MSQ) should be more predictive of heterogeneous measures of behavioral tendencies than should the more narrow facets (pay, promotions).

A further attempt to learn about the general withdrawal construct and its relation with affect was carried out. First, a withdrawal cognitions composite was correlated with the satisfaction measures. The withdrawal behavior composite was next combined with this composite consisting of the various cognitions about withdrawing. This scale contained cognitive responses (perceptions, intentions) about the more traditional forms of withdrawal (absenteeism, latenesses, quitting). Correlations between this overall composite and affect are given in the last row of table 6–4.

Correlations for general and overall satisfaction (JDI work, Faces, MSQ) dramatically increase as variance relevant to cognitions about withdrawing are included. Similar results have been found for the other samples studied. We have essentially constructed a very general criterion measure of withdrawal whose breadth closely corresponds to the generality of the attitude measures. As we continue to add small "chunks" of trait-relevant variance to composites, we improve the coverage of the underlying behavioral trait of interest and thereby increase the usefulness of the composite. It is important to note that we are not simply adding parallel items to the composite. Indeed, the various items are decidedly nonparallel. It is also important to realize that the increases in correlations were not merely due to reliability differences in the various components. Trivial differences in reliabilities for the various composites and scales were observed, lending confidence to the interpretation that the broader composites better correspond to the general attitude measures.

TABLE 6–4

Correlations between Attitudes and Behavioral and Cognitive Composites

	JDI Facets						
	Work	Supervision	Coworkers	Promotions	Pay	Faces	MSQ
Pro-Organization	.37	.20	.26	.23	.15	.25	.26
Withdrawal	−.36	−.23	−.23	−.14	−.12	−.27	−.25
Cognitions about withdrawal	−.50	−.42	−.27	−.27	−.28	−.51	−.50
Behaviors and Cognitions about Withdrawal	−.53	−.42	−.29	−.28	−.48	−.54	−.53

Note: All correlations are significant ($p < .001$).

Work is obviously needed to explore further relations between attitudes and these composites reflecting general behavioral tendencies.

Summary

We have argued that scores on well-constructed scales of job satisfaction are the most useful information organizational psychologists or organizational managers could have if they were interested in predicting a variety of behaviors of organizational members. Given past emphases on predicting specific behaviors as responses to job dissatisfaction, the relevance and general usefulness of job satisfaction for predicting these measures is all the more impressive. Systematic attempts to construct and predict more general behavioral response constructs should generate even more impressive evidence about the general utility of job satisfaction measures. This usefulness was suggested in our analyses of relations between job affect and a series of behavioral and cognitive criteria.

References

Ajzen, I., & Fishbein, M. (1977). Attitude-behavior relations: A theoretical analysis and review of empirical literature. *Psychological Bulletin, 84,* 888–918.

Ajzen, I., & Fishbein, M. (1980). *Understanding attitudes and predicting social behavior.* Englewood Cliffs, NJ: Prentice-Hall.

Arvey, R. O., Bouchard, T. J., Segal, N. L., & Abraham, L. M. (1989). Job satisfaction: Environmental and genetic components. *Journal of Applied Psychology, 74,* 187–192.

Atkinson, J. W., & Birch, D. (1970). *The dynamics of action.* New York: Wiley.

Baehr, M. E. (1954). A factorial study of the SRA employee inventory. *Personnel Psychology, 7,* 319–336.

Baehr, M. E. & Renck, R. (1958). The definition and measurement of employee morale. *Administrative Science Quarterly, 3,* 157–184.

Baruch, D. W. (1944). Why they terminate. *Journal of Consulting Psychology, 8,* 35–46.

Bateman, T. S., & Organ, D. W. (1983). Job satisfaction and the good soldier: The relationship between affect and employee "citizenship." *Academy of Management Journal, 26,* 587–595.

Beehr, T. A., & Gupta, N. (1978). A note on the structure of employee withdrawal. *Organizational Behavior and Human Performance, 21,* 73–79.

Campbell, D. T. (1963). Social attitudes and other acquired behavioral predispositions. In S. Koch (Ed.), *Psychology: A study of a science. Vol. 6: Investigations of Man as Socius* (pp. 94–172). New York: McGraw-Hill.

Campbell, J. P., & Pritchard, R. D. (1976). Motivation theory in industrial and organizational psychology. In M. Dunnette (Ed.), *Handbook of industrial and organizational psychooogy.* (pp. 63–130). Chicago: Rand McNally.

Carsten, J. M., & Spector, P. E. (1987). Unemployment, job satisfaction, and employee turnover: A meta-analytic test of the Muchinsky model. *Journal of Applied Psychology, 72,* 374–381.

Doob, L. W. (1947). The behavior of attitudes. *Psychological Review, 54,* 135–156.

Dulany, D. E. (1968). Awareness, rules, and propositional control: A confrontation with behavior S-R theory. In D. Horton & T. Dixon (Eds.), *Verbal behavior and S-R theory* (pp. 340–387). New York: Prentice-Hall.

Ebel, R. L. (1974). And still the dryads linger. *American Psychologist, 29,* 485–492.

Farrell, D. (1983). Exit, voice, loyalty, and neglect as responses to job dissatisfaction: A multidimensional sealing study. *Academy of Management Journal, 26,* 596–607.

Feinberg, S. E. (1980). *The analysis of cross-classified categorical data* (2nd ed). Cambridge, MA: MIT Press.

Fichman, M. (1984). A theoretical approach to understanding employee absence. In P. S. Goodman & R. S. Atkin (Eds.), *Absenteeism: New approaches to understanding, measuring, and managing employee absence* (pp. 1–46). San Francisco: Jossey-Bass.

Fichman, M. (1988). Motivational consequences of absence and attendance: Proportional hazard estimation of a dynamic motivation model. *Journal of Applied Psychology, 73,* 119–134.

Fichman, M. (1989). Attendance makes the heart grow fonder: A hazard rate approach to modeling attendance. *Journal of Applied Psychology, 74,* 325–335.

Fishbein, M. (1967). Attitude and the prediction of behavior. In M. Fishbein (Ed.), *Readings in attitude theory and measurement* (pp. 477–492). New York: Wiley.

Fishbein, M. (1980). A theory of reasoned action: Some applications and implications. In H. Howe & M. M. Page (Eds.), *Nebraska symposium on motivation: Beliefs, attitudes, and values* (pp. 65–116). Lincoln: University of Nebraska Press.

Fishbein, M., & Ajzen, I. (1974). Attitudes towards objects as predictors of single and multiple behavioral criteria. *Psychological Bulletin, 81,* 59–74.

Fishbein, M., & Ajzen, I. (1975). *Beliefs, attitudes, intention and behavior.* Reading, MA: Addison-Wesley.

Fisher, C., & Locke, E. A. (1987). *Job satisfaction and dissatisfaction: Enhancing the prediction of consequences.* Paper presented at a conference entitled Job Satisfaction: Advances in Research and Applications held at Bowling Green State University, October.

Getman, J. G., Goldberg, S. B., & Herman, J. B. (1976). *Union representation elections: Law and reality.* New York: Russell Sage.

Goodman, P. S., & Alkin, R. S. (Eds.). (1984). *Absenteeism: New approaches to understanding, measuring and managing employee absence.* San Francisco: Jossey-Bass.

Grizzle, J. E., Starmer, C. F., & Koch, G. G. (1969). Analysis of categorical data by linear models. *Biometrics, 25,* 489–504.

Gupta, N., & Jenkins, G. D., Jr. (1982). Absenteeism and turnover: Is there a progression? *Journal of Management Studies, 19,* 395–412.

Hackett, R. D., & Guion, R. M. (1985). A reevaluation of the absenteeism-job satisfaction relationship. *Organizational Behavior and Human Decision Processes, 35,* 340–381.

Hackman, J. R., & Oldham, G. R. (1976). Motivation through the design of work: Test of a theory. *Organizational Behavior and Human Performance, 16,* 250–279.

Hamner, W., & Smith, F. (1978). Work attitudes as predictors of unionization activity. *Journal of Applied Psychology, 63,* 415–421.

Hanisch, D. A., & Hulin, C. L. (1990). Job attitudes and organizational withdrawal: An examination of retirement and other voluntary withdrawal behaviors. *Journal of Vocational Behavior, 37,* 60–78.

Hanisch, K. A. (1990). *A causal model of general attitudes, work withdrawal, and job withdrawal, including retirement.* Unpublished doctoral dissertation, University of Illinois at Urbana-Champaign.

Harrison, D., & Hulin, C. L. (1989). Investigations of absenteeism using event history models to study the absence taking process. *Journal of Applied Psychology, 74,* 300–316.

Hom, P. W., & Hulin, C. L. (1981). A competitive test of predictions of reenlistment by several models. *Journal of Applied Psychology, 66,* 23–39.

Hom, P. W., Katerberg, R., Jr., & Hulin, C. L. (1979). Comparative examination of three approaches to the prediction of turnover. *Journal of Applied Psychology, 64,* 280–290.

Hulin, C. L. (1991). Adaptation, persistence, and commitment in organizations. In M. D. Dunnette and L. M. Hough (Eds.), *Handbook of industrial and organizational psychology,* Vol. II (2nd ed., pp. 445–505). Palo Alto, CA: Consulting Psychologists Press.

Hulin, C. L., & Rousseau, D. (1980). Analyzing infrequent events: Once you find them your troubles begin. In K. H. Roberts & L. Burstein (Eds.), *Issues in aggregation: New directions for methodology of social and behavioral science.* Vol. 6. (pp. 39–52). San Francisco, CA: Jossey-Bass.

Hulin, C. L., Roznowski, M., & Hachiya, D. (1985). Alternative opportunities and withdrawal decisions: Empirical and theoretical discrepancies and an integration. *Psychological Bulletin, 97,* 233–250.

Hull, C. L. (1941). *Fractional antedating goal reactions as pure stimulus acts.* Paper delivered to the Institute of Human Relations, October 24.

Humphreys, L. G. (1985). General intelligence: An integration of factor, test, and simplex theory. In B. B. Wolman (Ed.), *Handbook of intelligence: Theories, measurements, and applications.* New York: Wiley.

Judge, T. A. (1990). *Job satisfaction as a reflection of disposition: Investigating the relationship and its effect on employee adaptive behaviors.* Unpublished doctoral dissertation, University of Illinois, Urbana-Champaign.

Kornhauser, A. (1965). *Mental health of the industrial worker: A Detroit study.* New York: Wiley.

Kunin, T. (1955). The construction of a new type of attitude measure. *Personnel Psychology, 8,* 65–78.

Landy, F. J. (1978). An opponent process theory of job satisfaction. *Journal of Applied Psychology, 63,* 533–547.

Lawler, E. E. (1982). Strategies for improving the quality of worklife. *American Psychologist, 37,* 486–493.

March, J. G., & Simon, H. A. (1958). *Organizations.* New York: Wiley.

McGrath, J. E., & Kelly, J. R. (1986). *Time and human interaction: Toward a social psychology of time.* New York: Guilford.

Meehl, P. E., & Rosen, A. (1955). Antecedent probability and the efficacy of psychometric signs, patterns, or cutting scores. *Psychological Bulletin, 52,* 194–216.

Melbin, M. (1961). Organizational practice and individual behavior: Absenteeism among psychiatric aides. *American Sociological Review, 26,* 14–23.

Miller, H. E. (1981). *Withdrawal behaviors among hospital employees.* Unpublished doctoral dissertation, University of Illinois at Urbana-Champaign.

Miller, H. E., Katerberg, R., Jr., & Hulin, C. L. (1979). Evaluation of the Mobley, Horner, and Hollingsworth model of employee turnover. *Journal of Applied Psychology, 64,* 509–517.

Mobley, W. H. (1977). Intermediate linkages in the relationship between job satisfaction and employee turnover. *Journal of Applied Psychology, 62,* 237–240.

Mobley, W. H., Horner, S. O., & Hollingsworth, A. T. (1978). An evaluation of precursors of hospital employee turnover. *Journal of Applied Psychology, 63,* 408–414.

Motowidlo, S. J. (1984). Does job satisfaction lead to consideration and personal sensitivity? *Academy of Management Journal, 27,* 910–915.

Mowday, R. T., Porter, L. W., & Steers, R. M. (1982). *Employee organization linkages: The psychology of commitment, absenteeism, and turnovber.* New York: Academic Press.

Naylor, J. C., Pritchard, R. D., & Ilgen, D. R. (1980). *A theory of behavior in organizations.* New York: Academic Press.

Olsson, U., Drasgow, F., & Dorans, N. J. (1982). The polyserial correlation coefficient. *Psychometrika, 41,* 337–347.

Porter, L. W., & Steers, R. M. (1973). Organizational, work and personal factors in employee turnover and absenteeism. *Psychological Bulletin, 80,* 151–176.

Rice, A. K., & Trist, E. L. (1952). Institutional and subinstitutional determinants of change in labor turnover. *Human Relations, 5,* 347–372.

Rosse, J. G. (1983). *Employee withdrawl and adaptation: An expanded framework.* Unpublished doctoral dissertation, University of Illinois at Urbana-Champaign.

Rosse, J. G., & Hulin, C. L. (1985). Adaptation to work: An analysis of employee health, withdrawal, and change. *Organizational Behavior and Human Decision Processes, 36,* 324–347.

Rosse, J. G., & Miller, H. E. (1984). Relationship between absenteeism and other employee behaviors. In P. S. Goodman & R. S. Atkin (Eds.), *Absenteeism: New approaches to understanding, measuring, and managing employee absence* (pp. 194–228). San Francisco: Jossey-Bass.

Roznowski, M. (1987). The use of narrow information tests manifesting sex differences as measures of intelligence: Implications for measurement bias. *Journal of Applied Psychology, 72,* 480–483.

Roznowski, M. (1988). Review of *Test Validity. Journal of Educational Measurement, 25*(4), 357–361.

Roznowski, M., & Hanisch, K. A. (1990). Building systematic heterogeneity into job attitudes and behavior measures. Journal of Vocational Behavior, 36, 361–375.

Roznowski, M., Rosse, J. G., & Miller, H. E. (1991). The scientific and organizational value of breadth in measuring employee responses: The case for employee adaptation and citizenship. Manuscript in review.

Ryan, T. A. (1970). *Intentional behavior: An approach to human motivation.* New York: Ronald Press.

Salancik, G. R., & Pfeffer, J. (1978). A social information processing approach to job attitudes and task design. *Administrative Science Quarterly, 23,* 224–251.

Schmitt, N., & McCune, J. T. (1981). The relationship between job attitudes and the decision to retire. *Academy of Management Journal, 24*(4), 795–802.

Schriesheim, C. (1978). Job satisfaction, attitudes toward unions, and voting in a union representation election. *Journal of Applied Psychology, 63,* 548–552.

Scott, K. D., & Taylor, G. S. (1985). An examination of conflicting findings on the relationship between job satisfaction and absenteeism: A meta-analysis. *Academy of Management Journal, 28,* 599–612.

Smith, C. A., Organ, D. W., & Near, J. (1983). Organizational citizenship behavior: Its nature and antecedents. *Journal of Applied Psychology, 68,* 653–663.

Smith, F. J. (1977). Work attitudes as predictors of attendance on a specific day. *Journal of Applied Psychology, 62,* 16–19.

Smith, P. C., Kendall, L. M., & Hulin, C. L. (1969). *The measurement of satisfaction in work and retirement: A strategy for the study of attitudes.* Skokie, IL: Rand McNally, 1969.

Staw, B. M., Bell, N. E., & Clausen, J. A. (1986). The dispositional approach to job attitudes: A lifetime longitudinal test. *Administrative Science Quarterly, 31,* 56–77.

Thurstone, L. L. (1931). The measurement of social attitudes. *Journal of Abnormal and Social Psychology, 26,* 249–269.

Vroom, V. (1964). *Work and motivation.* New York: Wiley.

Waters, L. K., & Roach, D. (1971). Relationship between job attitudes and two forms of withdrawal from the work situation. *Journal of Applied Psychology, 55,* 92–94.

Waters, L. K., & Roach, D. (1979). Job satisfaction, behavioral intentions, and absenteeism as predictors of turnover. *Personnel Psychology, 32,* 393–397.

Weiss, D. J., Dawis, R. V., England, G. W., & Lofquist, L. H. (1967). Manual for the Minnesota Satisfaction Questionnaire. *Minnesota Studies in Vocational Rehabilitation,* XVI.

Weitz, J. (1952). A neglected concept in the study of job satisfaction. *Personnel Psychology, 5,* 201–205.

Wicker, A. W. (1969). Attitudes vs. actions: The relationship of verbal and overt behavioral responses to attitude objects. *Journal of Social Issues, 25,* 41–78.

Wiggins, J. S. (1973). *Personality and prediction: Principles of personality assessment.* Reading, MA: Addison-Wesley.

Zalesny, M. P. (1985). Comparison of economic and noneconomic factors in predicting faculty vote preference in a union representation election. *Journal of Applied Psychology, 70,* 243–256.

Zedeck, S. (1987). *Affective responses to work and the quality of family life.* Paper presented at a conference entitled Job Satisfaction: Advances in Research and Applications held at Bowling Green State University, October.

7

The New Look in Job Satisfaction Research and Theory

CYNTHIA D. FISHER

EDWIN A. LOCKE

For the past several decades, job satisfaction research has focused predominantly on two goals: discovering the causes of satisfaction, and looking for the effects of satisfaction and dissatisfaction on specific types of actions such as productivity or turnover. Substantial progress has been made in understanding the causes of job satisfaction (Gruneberg, 1979; Locke, 1976), but progress in understanding its effects has been much slower, despite a huge number of studies. Correlations between job satisfaction and specific behavioral criteria tend to be weak.

For instance, two recent meta-analytic reviews agree that satisfaction-performance correlations average about .17 (Iaffaldano & Muchinsky, 1985; Podsakoff & Williams, 1986). Job satisfaction has also been studied as a correlate of other work behaviors such as turnover, absenteeism, lateness, drug use, and sabotage. Turnover has been the most predictable behavior, but even for this dependent variable correlations have been of moderate magnitude at best.

In 1980, Fisher suggested an explanation for these weak results. Job satisfaction is typically conceptualized as a general attitude toward an object, the job. Behavior is usually measured as a single type of act (output, absenteeism, and so on), assessed over a limited span of time and measured by a single method. Thus, behavior measures are highly specific. Attitude theorists have suggested and convincingly supported the idea that strong attitude-behavior correlations will only occur when there is correspondence between the levels of aggregation represented in the attitude and behavior measures (Ajzen & Fishbein, 1977; Fishbein & Ajzen, 1974). In order to predict a specific act, one should measure attitude toward that act, or even more immediately, behavioral intention. As expected, intention to quit is a better predictor of quitting than is overall attitude toward an object (job satisfaction), which is at best a weak predictor of any single behavior toward that object.

On the other hand, attitude toward an object can be expected to predict the overall favorability of a large set of behaviors toward the object over time. Rushton, Brainerd, and Pressley (1983) have shown that in many areas of psychology prediction is greatly enhanced by using aggregated behavior measures. They remind us that, "The sum of a set of multiple measurements is a more stable and representative estimator than any single measurement" (p. 18), and note that this principle is universally accepted and applied when constructing ability measures but is seldom considered when the problem is measuring behavior. Rushton et al. suggest that aggregating measures over time, over specific behaviors, and/or over judges will result in a more predictable criterion with better reliability and construct validity.

Our interest is in the behavioral manifestations of job satisfaction/dissatisfaction as assessed by an aggregated measure of a variety of acts on the job. This type of measure should be strongly related to the attitude of overall job satisfaction. In addition, such a measure is consistent with Staw's (1984) call for expanding our conceptualizations of outcome variables in organizational behavior, and also consistent with the suggestion of Rusbult, Farrell, Rogers, and Mainous (1988, p. 600) that we look at "behavioral patterns or syndromes representing broader theoretical constructs" rather than single dependent variables. The "new look" in job satisfaction research in the title of this paper refers to this shift to multiact criteria as the outcomes of job affect.

New look research has pursued two kinds of multiact criteria; those focusing primarily on positive behaviors that may flow (in part) from job satisfaction, and those focusing on remedial and/or negative behaviors thought to flow from dissatisfaction. Positive behaviors have variously been called extrarole, prosocial, altruistic, or citizenship behaviors. (Although altruism, in its original sense, denotes self-sacrifice, this is not the meaning intended by other authors using this term. Rather, they refer to helping others, and so we will use the term "helping" in the remainder of this chapter.) Organ (1988) has made a good case for the importance of the totality of such behaviors to the smooth and effective functioning of an organization, even though a single positive behavior emitted once may have minimal impact. Several recent studies of aggregate positive behaviors have verified that job satisfaction is usually a significant predictor of them. Results of these studies are summarized in table 7–1. As expected, most of the correlations are stronger than those typically observed when a single act criterion is the dependent variable. It is noteworthy that the strongest correlation in table 7–1 ($r = .54$) comes from the study (Tsui, Hartwick, & Sheppard, 1985) that employed the most comprehensive measure of behavior and aggregated over the largest number of raters (self, subordinates, and several superiors).

Predictive success has also been obtained for the other side of the citizenship coin. Several studies have assessed aggregate negative or "noncompliant" behaviors and their relationship to job satisfaction. Puffer (1987, p. 615) defined noncompliant behaviors as "non-task behaviors that have negative organizational implications." In a furniture retail chain, noncompliant behaviors by salespeople might include being late to work and taking excessivly long breaks, complaining about the company to others, violating rules, making unrealistic promises to clients, and failing to do one's fair share of noncommissioned sales promotion activity. Staehle (1985) and Henne (1986) explored lists of thirty-six and thirty-nine such behaviors, and found that self-reports of the number and frequency of noncompliant behaviors tended to be negatively and rather strongly related to overall job satisfaction (bottom of table 7–1.)

Thus, it seems that progress is being made in answering the question, "What does general job satisfaction relate to?"—the answer being aggregate measures of many job behaviors. However true this answer may be, it is not very elegant or satisfying from a theoretical point of view. Nor is it terribly helpful to organizations, which may be more interested in predicting and influencing specific classes of behavior such as those associated with withdrawal. Attitude theorists would suggest increasing the specificity of attitude measures in

TABLE 7–1

Correlations of Overall Job Satisfaction with Aggregate Behavior Criteria

	Dependent Variable	Correlations	
Positive Behavior Studies			
Bateman & Organ, 1983	Sum of supervisor's rating of 30 citizenship behaviors	.41	
Smith, Organ & Near, 1983	Sum of supervisor's rating of 6 helping behaviors and 8 compliance behaviors	.31 .21	
Tsui, Hartwick, & Sheppard, 1985	Sum of 27 measures of faculty behavior from multiple sources	.54	
Long, 1987	Sum of self ratings on 40 prosocial behaviors	.35	
Graham, 1986	Self and supervisor ratings of five dimensions of citizenship: obedience, pursuit of excellence, neighborliness, loyalty, civic virtue	<u>Self</u> .37 .42 .19 .54 .35	<u>Supervisor</u> .17 .24 .11 .36 .20
Negative Behavior Studies			
Staehle, 1985	Sum of self ratings of 36 negative job behaviors	−.36	
Henne, 1986	Sum of self ratings of 39 negative job behaviors	−.44	

order to predict more circumscribed criterion sets, and this has been occurring in some new look research.

For instance, Organ (1988) and Organ and Konovsky (1989) have suggested that the cognitive component of job satisfaction rather than the affective component is responsible for premeditated, intentional, and sustained citizenship contributions to the organization. This suggestion is based on the idea of maintaining fairness in the social exchange relationship between the individual and the organization. Organ and Konovsky (1989) found evidence that pay cognitions were the strongest and only unique predictor of helping and compliance behaviors in a sample of hospital employees. However, the separate correlations between components of satisfaction (pay cognitions, job cognitions, positive affect, negative affect) and behavior were weaker (maximum $r = .21$) than those typically observed when overall satisfaction has been used as the predictor of citizenship behaviors.

Another approach to making the attitude measure more specific is to assess facet satisfaction rather than overall satisfaction. Puffer (1987) explored a number of possible correlates of positive and negative job behaviors. Three of these bear similarities to facets of job satisfaction: satisfaction with material rewards, faith in peers, and trust in management. These were related to aggregate citizenship and noncompliant behaviors as expected, with correlations ranging from $-.23$ to $+.23$. Several researchers have made the attitude measure more specific by using the five facets of job satisfaction assessed by the Job Descriptive Index (Smith, Kendall, & Hulin, 1969). Correlations with aggregate negative behaviors ranged from $-.44$ (JDI work) to $-.14$ (JDI pay) for the Staehle study and $-.32$ (JDI supervisor) to $-.12$ (JDI promotions) in the Henne study. In Bateman and Organ's study of citizenship behaviors, JDI supervision and promotions were the strongest predictors, while satisfaction with the work itself was the weakest. Williams, Podsakoff, and Huber (1986) also found that satisfaction with the work itself failed to predict citizenship behaviors, but that supervisor satisfaction was a significant predictor.

The results of these studies appear inconsistent, probably because the attitude and behavior measures still do not match in terms of object or level of aggregation. For instance, satisfaction with peers should lead to prosocial behavior directed toward peers—such as helping a peer who has been ill or who is experiencing a heavy workload or personal problem—but should not necessarily predict helping the supervisor or working extra hours. Dissatisfaction with the work itself might lead to a variety of task-avoidance behaviors (daydreaming, taking long breaks, visiting with peers), some of which might even appear to be prosocial (helping a peer with a personal problem because it is more interesting than doing the work).

Thus, a typology of nontask behaviors and underlying constructs is needed. There has been relatively little work directed toward developing typologies of positive behavioral responses to job satisfaction. Brief and Motowidlo (1986) proposed thirteen types of prosocial behaviors. An empirical analyses of these categories has yet to be made. However, several studies have reported factor analyses of the sixteen citizenship behaviors used by Smith, Organ, and Near (1983). A two- or three-factor solution has been found to adequately describe these items. Two factors, helping and generalized compliance, were originally identified by Smith et al., while subsequent studies have found that the compliance factor breaks down into attendance items and negatively worded items about not wasting work time. Based on political science theory, Graham (1986) developed scales for five dimensions of citizenship (obedience, pursuit of excellence, neighborliness, loyalty, civic virtue). She did not report any factor analyses, but did mention that the scales were highly intercorrelated. Thus, it seems doubtful that five dimensions could be empirically distinguished.

Research on a typology of negative and/or remedial job behaviors that may be responses to dissatisfaction is also relatively rare. Some of the work in this area has involved assessing whether various "withdrawal behaviors" actually form a progression and embody a single construct (see Mobley, 1982; Rosse & Miller, 1984; Wolpin & Burke, 1985). Another approach has been to group responses to dissatisfaction on the basis of logic. Hirschman (1970) suggested that consumer reactions to dissatisfaction with the quality of an organization's product might fall into three categories: exit (switching to another brand), voice (complaining in an attempt to restore product quality), and loyalty (quietly continuing to purchase the product). When Farrell (1983) adapted this typology to the case of job dissatisfaction, he added a class of behaviors called "neglect"— remaining in the organization but minimizing time, effort, and care expended. Farrell (1983) has argued that two dimensions underlie these four categories of behavior: an active/passive dimension, with loyalty and neglect being more passive than exit and voice, and a constructive/destructive dimension, with both loyalty and voice being considered constructive. A multidimensional scaling study provided some support for this idea. Subsequent research has verified that job satisfaction is positively associated with voice and loyalty and negatively associated with exit and neglect (Rusbult, Farrell, Rogers, & Wainous, 1988; Rusbult & Lowery, 1985).

Rosse and Hulin (1985) have suggested four "plausible response families" from which behaviors may be chosen as employees attempt to adjust to or improve a dissatisfying work situation. These include physical withdrawal (lateness, absenteeism, turnover, taking long breaks, leaving early, and so on), psychological withdrawal (daydreaming, using drugs at work), attempts to improve the work situation, and aggression/relation. Henne and Locke (1985) have outlined a similar but more detailed theoretical framework of behavioral and psychological responses to the perception of dissatisfaction. These frameworks are shown in table 7–2. We will now present the results of some further efforts to categorize behavioral responses to job dissatisfaction.

TABLE 7–2
Theoretical Typologies of Behavioral Responses

Hirschman (1970)/Farrell (1983)

    Exit

    Voice

    Loyalty

    Neglect

Rosse and Hulin (1985)

    Physical withdrawal

    Psychological withdrawal

    Attempts to change work situation

    Aggression/retaliation

Henne and Locke (1985)

    Action alternatives

        Changes in job performance/effort

        Persuasive protest

        Aggressive protest

        Physical Withdrawal

    Psychological alternatives

        Change perceptions of the job

        Change values

        Change reactions via defense mechanisms

        Toleration

Exploratory Studies

In this section we will describe several unpublished exploratory studies of behavioral responses to dissatisfaction. These data are by no means conclusive, because all the behavior measures are based on self-reports. On the other hand, self-reported data may be especially useful for the purpose of typology development because they tend to contain less halo than do behavior ratings collected from other rating sources (Thornton, 1980).

The Staehle Study

The first set of data comes from an undergraduate honors thesis by Cindy Staehle (1985). To develop a preliminary list of behaviors for the questionnaire, students in an M.B.A. class and a doctoral seminar on motivation were asked to write down all the things they had done or had seen done or had considered doing in response to being dissatisfied with a job. Some items were added to this list based on the categories specified in Henne and Locke's (1985) theoretical article. The final list consisted of thirty-six behaviors. These items were put into a questionnaire along with the JDI satisfaction scales and two single overall job satisfaction items. For the behavior items, subjects were asked to indicate how frequently they actually engaged in each activity on a six-point scale, ranging from "once per year (or never)" to "daily." They also indicated how often they thought about engaging in each activity.

The questionnaire was distributed to 600 M.B.A. students at the University of Maryland, who were asked to respond anonymously. A total of 178 questionnaires were returned. Staehle began by trying to factor analyze the behavior frequency ratings, but no meaningful factors emerged. Thus, the items were grouped into *a priori* factors, which are shown in table 7–3. Clearly one could argue with these classifications, but we decided to use them as a starting point.

Scores were obtained for each *a priori* factor by summing the responses to the appropriate items. Table 7–4 shows the correlations between satisfaction scales and the *a priori* behavior scales, as well as a summary scale of all behaviors. The highest correlations are for the defensive behaviors scale followed by the expressive behaviors scale.

TABLE 7-3

Staehle a Priori *Categories*

Avoidance Actions

    I take more leave than I am allotted

    I avoid responsibility on the job

    I quit my job

    I do other more interesting activities than my work while on the job

    I ask for a transfer

    I call in sick even when I'm not really sick

    I come to work late

    I leave work early

    I take a longer lunch hour than I am supposed to

Defensive Actions

    I drink on the job

    I use drugs such as marijuana while on the job

    I ignore my feelings about my job

    I do not expect much from my job

    I laugh off or shrug off my work

    I daydream on the job

Passive-Aggressive Actions

    I intentionally miss deadlines for projects

    I do not work as hard as I could

    I coast along, doing as little work as possible

    I play practical jokes on people on the job

    I refuse to do any extra work

Expressive Actions

    I get mad at other people on the job

    I complain to family, friends, or co-workers about my job

    I tell off my boss

Persuasive Actions

    I get others to complain to the supervisor for me

    I confront my supervisor with my problems

    I talk to my supervisor about improving the job situation

(continued)

TABLE 7–3 (continued)

Hostile Actions

    I refuse to do my work

    I join group sick-outs when they are planned

    I try to sue the company in court

    I give the organization a bad name to customers or the public

    I go on strike

    I take things from the company like tools and supplies

    I sabotage machines and / or products

    I vandalize company property

    I purposely mess up a project or assignment

    I deliberately do poor-quality work

The persuasive scale showed the lowest correlations (all were nonsignificant).

In sum, these results showed that (1) people are able to think of multiple action alternatives in the face of dissatisfaction, (2) the JDI subscales are differentially related to the various *a priori* behavior scales, and (3) the behavior items do not form clear factors.

The Henne Study

The next study was undertaken by a doctoral student, Doug Henne (1986), as his dissertation research. It represents a further development and refinement of the basic approach used by Staehle. To develop an item pool, eighty-nine people from one organization and one adult education course were asked to list actions they had taken, had felt like taking, or had thought about taking in response to dissatisfaction. This resulted in a pool of 553 items. This list, after being pared down by removing redundancies, situation-specific behaviors, and overly vague items, is shown in table 7–5. Clearly there is substantial overlap with the items in Staehle's questionnaire.

In a preliminary analysis, a class of M.B.A. students was asked to classify the items into any five or six *a priori* categories they could

TABLE 7-4

Satisfaction Measures Correlated with Six a Priori Behavior Categories

Satisfaction Measure	Defensive	Avoidance	Passive-Aggressive	Expressive	Persuasive	Hostile	Sum of All Behaviors
JDI work	-.59[b]	-.18[a]	-.29[b]	-.39[b]	-.07	-.29[b]	-.44[b]
JDI supervision	-.28[b]	-.09	-.16[a]	-.50[b]	-.14	-.12	-.29[b]
JDI pay	-.18[a]	-.31[b]	-.07	-.18[a]	-.10	-.15[a]	-.14
JDI promotions	-.35[b]	-.08	-.14	-.27[b]	.01	-.09	-.23[b]
JDI coworkers	-.34[b]	-.15[a]	-.23[b]	-.25[b]	-.07	-.21[b]	-.31[b]
Overall satisfaction 1	-.50[b]	-.18[a]	-.24[b]	-.36[b]	-.01	-.23[b]	-.37[b]
Overall satisfaction 2	-.51[b]	-.13	-.19[a]	-.39[b]	-.01	-.28[b]	-.37[b]

Data taken from Staehle (1985).

[a] $p < .05$
[b] $p < .01$

TABLE 7–5

Behaviors on the Job (Henne Questionnaire)

I look for a way to transfer out of my present job

I bend the rules to get a job done

I call in sick even though I'm not really sick

I drink alcohol on the job

I "goof off", or don't work as hard as expected

I complain to my supervisor about the work situation

I take a longer lunch hour than I am supposed to take

I avoid contact with my coworkers

I destroy company property

I bad mouth the company to friends and/or customers

I ignore the explicit instructions of my supervisor

I cry on the job

I steal supplies or merchandise from the company

I verbally abuse my coworkers on the job

I suggest ways to improve the situation to my supervisor

I suppress feelings of dissatisfaction

I go over my supervisor's head to make myself heard

I leave work earlier than I should

I come to work later than I should

think of. The results showed that these subjects could not agree on the classification. Subsequently the items were administered to 153 clerical employees in a small life insurance company using a seven-point frequency scale. The JDI scales and some overall job satisfaction items were included in the questionnaire.

One of the findings was that "never" was the single most frequent response for all except one item on the scale (suggest ways to improve the situation to my supervisor). Various factor solutions were attempted and a seven-factor solution produced some meaningful factors. These are summarized in table 7–6. While these factors do not correspond exactly to those hypothesized theoretically by Henne and Locke (1985), and while they are not as "clear" as they look in table 7–6 when all the item loadings are considered, they do make some sense.

TABLE 7-5 (continued)

I don't share important information with people who need it

I intentionally do the work incorrectly

I actually look for employment in another company

I tell myself "the work doesn't matter," and try to think about something else

I talk back to my supervisor

I complain to coworkers about the work

I suggest to other employees that they form a union

I file grievances

I put projects off until the last minute

I talk to myself on the job

I talk to coworkers to see whether they are dissatisfied

I pray on the job

I seek help from the personnel/human resources office

I seek career or psychological counseling

I get others to complain to the supervisor for me

I do other more interesting activities than my work while on the job

I use drugs such as marijuana while on the job

I do as little work as possible

I fail to do what my supervisor tells me to do

I daydream for a large part of the day

Table 7-7 shows the correlations between the satisfaction scales and the behavior scales. Note that the avoidance factor, which contains the "looking for employment" item, is most consistently related to dissatisfaction, especially for the JDI work scale and for the overall satisfaction measure. Somewhat surprising is the frequency with which the direct aggression and defiance factors correlate with dissatisfaction. These factors produced correlations with overall dissatisfaction exceeded only by avoidance and total behaviors.

We should note that in both the Staehle and Henne studies we measured reported frequencies of thoughts about each of the behaviors as well as reported frequencies of the behaviors themselves. As expected, the mean frequency of thoughts was higher than that of behaviors, indicating that people thought about some things that they did not act on. Corresponding thought and behavior items and

TABLE 7-6

Behavior Factors and Sample Items from the Henne Analysis

Factor I:	Avoidance/toleration (I look for employment in another company; I suppress feelings of dissatisfaction)
Factor II:	Defiance of supervisor (I fail to do what my supervisor tells me to do)
Factor III:	Formal protest (I go over my supervisor's head to make myself heard)
Factor IV:	Indirect aggression (I intentionally do the work incorrectly)
Factor V:	Complaining/suggestion (I complain to my supervisor)
Factor VI:	Direct aggression (I call in sick even though I am not sick; I steal supplies or merchandise from the company)
Factor VII:	Withdrawal (I avoid contact with my coworkers)

factors were usually (although not always) highly correlated. In addition, the factor structure of thought items was similar but not identical to, and not any clearer than, the factor structure of the behavior items. Finally, the magnitude of the correlations between satisfaction and the thought scales was not much stronger than the correlations with the actual behavior scales.

Additional Analyses of the Staehle and Henne Data Sets

As was clear from the items and behavior categories used by both Staehle and Henne, there are many possible responses to dissatisfaction. Further, some of them are probably less aversive or destructive to the organization than others. For instance, praying or seeking counseling may be fairly harmless from the organization's point of view, while sabotage is decidedly not harmless. It seems likely that individuals who are more dissatisfied would not only engage in negative behaviors with greater frequency, but would also tend to choose more strongly negative behaviors. Thus, if behavior frequencies were weighted by the "badness" of each behavior, the resulting composite might be more strongly predicted by job attitudes than the unweighted composite.

In order to test this idea, Fisher collected normative data from 92

TABLE 7-7

Satisfaction Measures Correlated with Behavior Factors

	Avoidance	Defiance	Formal Protest	Indirect Aggression	Complaining Suggesting	Direct Aggression	Psychological Withdrawal	Sum of A Behavio
JDI work	-.51[b]	-.14[a]	-.08	-.02	.00	-.17[a]	-.08	-.26[b]
JDI supervision	-.41[b]	-.20[b]	-.20[b]	-.04	-.11	-.29[b]	-.22[b]	-.32[b]
JDI pay	-.37[b]	.04	-.02	-.08	.10	-.07	-.03	-.14[a]
JDI promotions	-.27[b]	-.10	-.01	.17[a]	.04	-.09	-.10	-.12[a]
JDI coworkers	-.28[b]	.00	-.07	.10	-.17[a]	.00	-.32[b]	-.23[b]
Overall satisfaction	-.50[b]	-.29[b]	-.14[a]	-.08	-.16[a]	-.33[b]	-.17[a]	-.44[b]

Data taken from Henne (1986).

[a] $p < .05$
[b] $p < .01$

employed part-time students regarding the goodness/badness of 200 prosocial and negative behaviors. Respondents were instructed to rate each behavior from the point of view of the organization. Further, half the respondents were asked to rate how good or bad each behavior would be if performed by a blue-collar, hourly-paid clerical employee, and the other half rated the behaviors if performed by a white-collar, professional managerial employee. (It was thought that some prosocial behaviors such as staying late to finish a project or making a suggestion on how to improve the work would be a normal part of the white-collar role, and so would be less outstanding when performed by this type of employee than by a blue-collar employee. Conversely, due to the greater flexibility inherent in many salaried positions, behaviors such as taking a long lunch or leaving early might be perceived as less bad when committed by salaried than by hourly employees.)

Analyses showed that on nearly all behavior items, respondents agreed as to the goodness/badness of the item. Blue- versus white-collar ratings were significantly different on only 9 of 200 items. Seventy five percent of the standard deviations for the combined sample were less than 1.5 on a 9-point scale. It was encouraging to find such high agreement between individuals from many different organizations. While there may be some variations from organization to organization on what is defined by the local norms or culture as bad versus good behavior, these differences seem to be minor. Thus, we felt safe in applying the weights derived from these 92 subjects to the behaviors reported by Staehle's and Henne's respondents.

The average badness ratings corresponding to behaviors appearing in the Staehle and Henne data sets were used to construct weighted total behavior composites, which were then correlated with overall and facet job satisfaction. For both samples, these correlations were virtually identical to those reported in the (unweighted) total behavior columns of tables 7–4 and 7–7. In retrospect, the reason that the weights did not increase the correlations may be the extreme infrequency of really bad behaviors. It appears that dissatisfied individuals more frequently engage in negative behaviors, but confine themselves to relatively less destructive behaviors, perhaps to avoid the severe consequences that accompany the worst behaviors.

The weights would probably be more useful in a study in which both prosocial and negative behaviors were assessed. Rather than using these two types of extrarole behavior as separate dependent variables (as Puffer, 1987, did), they could be weighted into a single composite. No study to date has taken this approach; however, a weighted composite of many positive and negative extrarole behaviors should be very well predicted by job satisfaction. If satisfied individuals tend to engage in positive behaviors, dissatisfied individuals in negative behaviors, and neutral individuals in minimal extrarole behavior of either sort, then the past practice of looking at only positive or only negative behavior may have underestimated the true relationship. This is because both the satisfied and the neutral will largely refrain from negative behaviors, while both the dissatisfied and neutral will eschew positive behaviors. Developing a behavioral criterion with the same range as the predictor will allow the full magnitude of the relationships to emerge.

Locke, Matheny, and Davis Studies

We next decided to make a more systematic attempt to derive meaningful groups of negative behaviors. We started by compiling a list of about 125 negative job behaviors thought to be possible reactions to dissatisfaction. These included the items from Staehle and Henne as well as a number elicited from a separate sample of working students. The latter were asked to list behaviors that an individual might do or think about doing if dissatisfied overall or if dissatisfied with one of five specific facets of a job.

Then we asked ten management professors to sort the behaviors into between five and seven categories and to label the categories. Naturally the faculty members did not all agree on the groupings, but there were substantial similarities in many of the category labels as well as in the items included in each. Locke integrated these ten sortings into a single set of six categories that included 106 of the original items. Note that most of the category labels supplied spontaneously by the faculty members and/or retained by Locke are based on inferred motives for the behaviors. For instance, some behaviors may be undertaken to avoid the work itself, others to change the work situation, and still others to get even with a disliked person. Problems in sorting the behaviors occurred because many behavior statements did not reference a specific motive and could serve any one of several motives. For example, the behavior "complains to the supervisor" could be seen as aggression, resistance to authority, or constructive protest. "Refuses to work overtime" could be motivated by job avoidance, work avoidance, or defiance. A number of such multipurpose items were dropped, while others were rewritten to more clearly indicate the purpose behind the behavior.

In a subsequent study, Chris Matheny (1988) asked thirty-two M.B.A. students to sort the 106 behaviors into one of the six categories. The categories were predefined in a sentence or short paragraph. We retained all items that showed 70 percent or more agreement as to category membership, as well as four items with lower agreement but for which we clarified the wording. The items for each category are shown in table 7–8. Percent agreement and mean badness ratings (from the Fisher data described previously) are also shown. On the whole, constructive protest is the least-bad type of behavior, while defiance and aggression are seen as quite bad from the organization's point of view.

In a final study, Shannon Davis (1988) administered the six behavior scales shown in table 7–8 to thirty-two employees of a landscaping company. Single-item scales were used to measure satisfaction with the usual job facets. We also used the newly developed JDI overall job satisfaction scale. (We are grateful to Patricia Cain Smith for allowing us to use this scale.)

The results are shown in table 7–9. In this sample it was the co-worker scale that related most consistently to the job behavior scales, perhaps reflecting the fact that landscaping work requires extensive cooperation between colleagues. The supervision scale also related significantly to nearly all the behavior scales.

It should be noted that the individual behavior scales showed substantial internal reliability: work avoidance (.75), job avoidance (.77), psychological adjustment (.80), constructive protest (.72), defiance (.65). The alpha for aggression could not be calculated because the means were virtually zero on many of the items.

Discussion

We can conclude that a great many acts may be taken in response to job satisfaction and dissatisfaction—far more than the tired old

TABLE 7-8
New Scales for Negative Behaviors

	Aggreement[a]	Badness[b]
Physical Avoidance or Escape from the Job as a Whole (not from the work as such): Escape may be temporary (short term) or permanent; includes actions that prepare the person for escaping the job. (Escape must be physical, not psychological).		
Avoids job by coming late and/or leaving early	86	7.65
Gets away from job by quitting	86	5.80
Gets away from job by calling in sick when not really sick	69	7.52
Looks for a way to transfer out of a disliked job situation	43[c]	4.14
Looks for employment in another company to avoid disliked job	48[c]	5.41
Avoidance of the Work Itself (not of the job as such): Trying to get out of doing the assigned work or work tasks; may involve passivity; avoidance rather than direct defiance is stressed.		
Avoids undesirable work	91	6.72
Does as little work as possible	88	8.12
Tries to look busy doing nothing	88	6.48
Lets others do the work for him/her	86	7.70
Puts projects off until the last minute	81	7.37
Takes frequent or extra long breaks to avoid doing the work	81	6.92
Writes personal letters, reads, or makes personal calls when supposed to be working	76	7.05
Talks excessively with co-workers when supposed to be working	72	7.59
Makes frequent and/or long trips to water fountain, vending machines, or restroom to avoid work	60[c]	6.73
Psychological Adjustment: The focus is on the internal (mental) rather than the external (the job); may involve healthy or unhealthy mechanisms; may be expressive of feelings (but not hostile attack); may involve getting psychological help.		
Talks to himself/herself on the job	98	5.28

continued

TABLE 7–8 (continued)

	Aggreement[a]	Badness[b]
Lowers aspirations or expectations to make them congruent with a disappointing job	90	6.09
Prays on the job when unhappy	86	5.20
Covers emotion by wearing a mask of impassivity or indifference	83	6.27
Suppresses feeling of dissatisfaction	81	6.17
Refuses to think about job feelings at all	81	—
Seeks psychological or career or job counseling	79	3.55
Uses drugs or alcohol before, during or after work because of work problems	65[c]	8.52

Constructive Protest or Problem Solving: The focus is on attempts to change—that is, improve the present job situation or solve the problem through legal means; the style may be low key or confrontational; direct or indirect; short or long term.

Confronts supervisor with his/her problems to try to work them out	98	3.62
Tries to persuade management to change policies	98	4.17
Discusses problems with supervisor in order to get advice	98	3.94
After discussion with boss, gets more education or training to increase promotability	93	1.70
Files a formal grievance about supervisor or coworkers	91	5.46
Complains to the supervisor about the work situation	85	4.58
Asks for a raise	84	4.46
Suggests to other employees that they all form a union	77	6.56
Uses his/her political influence to try to change things	77	5.38
Talks to coworkers to see whether they will help in a protest	74	4.80
Sees a lawyer regarding his/her job situation	72	6.59

TABLE 7–8 (continued)

	Aggreement[a]	Badness[b]
Defiance, Resistance to Authority: The emphasis here is on the defiance aspect of the action, though it may be direct or indirect, and may be in order to do a better job or in order to do a worse job.		
Deliberately ignores rules or regulations	93	8.37
Fails to follow supervisor's instructions	93	7.76
Refuses to attend scheduled meetings	86	7.73
Openly refuses to do an assignment	86	8.35
Ignores superior and informally works with/or for another boss	84	7.66
Resists influence form others, including the boss	77	6.0
Talks back to supervisor	72	7.17
Aggression, Revenge, Retaliation, Getting Even: May just express anger, may or may not be legal; there is no constructive purpose and no attempt to really change the situation.		
Sells information about company to competitors	95	8.66
Leaks detrimental information about the company to the press	93	8.59
Starts rumors to get revenge	93	8.48
Sabotages the work of coworkers	91	8.61
Uses physical violence against other employees or supervisor(s)	90	8.88
Destroys company property	86	8.65
Steals supplies, tools or merchandise from the company	86	8.47
Purposely interferes with someone else doing their job	82	8.07
Sabotages the work of a superior (tries to make him/her look bad)	79	8.56
Lies in order to get the boss into trouble	74	8.73

[a]Percent of Matheny's 32 respondents sorting the item into this category.

[b]Average goodness-badness of each behavior. Scale: "From the organization's point of view, this behavior is": 1 = extremely good, 2 = good, 3 = somewhat good, 4 = slightly good, 5 = neither good nor bad, 6 = slightly bad, 7 = somewhat bad, 8 = bad, 9 = extremely bad.

[c]Wording has now been changed slightly.

TABLE 7-9

Satisfaction Measures Correlated with New Behavior Scales (Davis Study)

Type of Satisfaction	Job Avoidance	Work Avoidance	Psychological Adjustment	Constructive Protest	Defiance	Aggression	Sum of All Behaviors
Work	−.15	−.13	−.14	.02	.09	16	10
Supervisor	−.33[a]	−.21	−.31[a]	−.32[a]	−.38[a]	−.44[b]	−.45[b]
Pay	.13	.03	−.03	−.03	.17	20	07
Promotion	−.14	.17	−.14	.18	.33[a]	24	10
Coworker	−.59[b]	−.32[a]	−.40[b]	−.36[a]	−.50[b]	−.35[a]	−.61[b]
Job-in-General	−.29[a]	.13	−.43[b]	.21	.18	11	10

Data taken from Davis (1988).

[a] $p < .05$
[b] $p < .01$

troika of performance, turnover, and absenteeism that have been the focus of much past research. Attitude theory suggests that aggregating over multiple acts toward an object will produce a more reliable criterion that is predictable by general attitude toward the object. This has been borne out in new look research in which job satisfaction is often found to be a strong predictor of aggregate measures of positive and negative job behaviors.

Efforts to refine the aggregate behavioral criterion into behavioral dimensions have had mixed results. Empirical approaches using factor analysis (the Staehle and Henne studies) were not particularly successful. Roznowski and Hulin (chapter 6 in this book) have also had difficulty with a factor analytic approach. The failure of behaviors to cluster as expected may be an artifact of the extremely low frequencies of some of the behaviors, may stem from the fact that the same behavior may serve several different purposes, or may flow from aspects of the behavior choice process to be discussed subsequently.

Since empirical approaches seemed fruitless, we turned to efforts to logically group a large set of negative behaviors into dimensions. After several iterations, we came up with six dimensions into which a subset of the behaviors could be reliably sorted. Based on these results, we suggest that Farrell's (1983) four-category model does not adequately represent the complexity of the behavioral repertoire that employees possess and act upon. It is not surprising that Farrell failed to capture this complexity, as he used only twelve behaviors in his study. (Given the data requirements of multidimensional scaling, using the much larger number of behaviors we used would have been impossible with his methodology.) There are similarities in the two typologies—voice (our constructive protest) and exit (our job avoidance) appear to be quite similar. However, Farrell's neglect is multidimensional and includes work avoidance, some aspects of job avoidance, and possibly defiance. Farrell's concept of Loyalty did not appear distinctly in our typology, though some aspects of psychological adjustment seem similar. Finally, Farrell does not include aggression in his typology at all.

For obvious reasons, future new look research should utilize external sources rather than self-ratings of job behavior. Some such studies could even be done in a laboratory setting. There should also be further efforts toward typology development, and research on the

choice process by which particular behaviors are selected as responses to job attitudes. As suggested earlier, another approach to
typology development would be to group behaviors by their target
(that is, the supervisor, the peers, the work itself). Logically, this
type of aggregate behavior measure should be best predicted by the
associated type of facet satisfaction.

A second approach that might be interesting would be to group
behaviors into those that are usually intentional and premeditated
versus those that are spur-of-the-moment. If raters can agree on
which behaviors typically belong in these two categories, then some
interesting hypotheses can be made. For instance, the affective component of job attitudes might predict spur-of-the-moment behaviors
(called "consummatory behaviors" by Millar & Tesser, 1986), while
the cognitive component involving equity/fairness perceptions might
be a better predictor of premeditated, rationally chosen behaviors
(see Organ & Konovsky, 1989).

A third research thrust might explore the choice process among
behavior categories or specific behaviors that are of concern to the
organization. Both Rosse and Miller (1984) and Henne and Locke
(1985) have presented models of the choice process for responding to
job dissatisfaction. We have developed an elaboration on these earlier models, which is presented in figure 7–1. It begins with the job
situation, which is perceived and appraised based on one's personal
values and goals. Appraisal may also include comparing one's situation with that of others, and making attributions about the causes of
the situation. For example, it may be much more dissatisfying to be
singled out for rude treatment by a superior, than to be one of many
subordinates treated brusquely by a superior known to be under an
unusual amount of pressure. Appraisal results in feelings of satisfaction or dissatisfaction (Locke, 1976). We suggest that the prior level
of satisfaction is also important for determining whether the employee will proceed toward action. If one is more satisfied or more
dissatisfied than before, he or she is likely to choose an additional
behavior to reflect the new feelings. Individuals who are chronically
dissatisfied, perhaps due to a dispositional characteristic called negative affectivity (Staw, Bell, & Clausen, 1986; Watson & Clark,
1984), may be unlikely to express these feelings in either destructive
or remedial ways. However, someone who is just as dissatisfied, but
for whom this is a new and uncharacteristic state, may be quite ac-

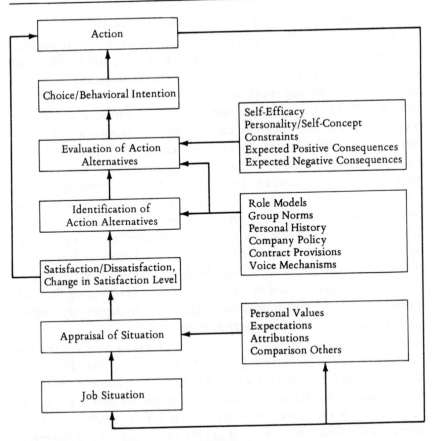

FIGURE 7–1

A Choice Model of Behavioral Responses to Job Satisfaction and Dissatisfaction

tive in trying to change or avoid the job situation. Rosse and Miller (1984) hinted at this idea in the component of their model called "relative dissatisfaction," defined as an awareness that things could be better than they currently are.

The appraisal should trigger a search for action alternatives and an evaluation of these alternatives. Following Rosse and Miller, we agree that one's past experience in the organization, behavior modeled by other organization members, and awareness of group and organizational norms will provide clues to plausible action alternatives. In addition, company- and union-provided mechanisms will supply some action alternatives (formalized "voice" mechanisms, mental health days, and so on). Action alternatives will be evaluated in terms of acceptability to group norms, constraints on implementation, and expected positive consequences in mitigating feelings of dissatisfaction (either by changing the objective situation or by getting even) or fulfilling reciprocity norms in the case of satisfaction (Organ, 1977). In addition, expected negative consequences will be weighed. These might include damage to one's reputation or credibility in the organization, being punished by the organization, or being ostracized by peers. Finally, action alternatives will be compared to the self-concept and personal standards for behavior. A dissatisfied individual may have to decide whether he or she is the type of person who slacks off, screams at the boss, or steals from the employer, no matter how badly provoked. Personality characteristics such as need for achievement (Puffer, 1987) and introversion/extraversion may play a role here. Individuals who have an external locus of control or have learned that they are helpless in changing their job situation may evaluate most contemplated actions negatively and fail to proceed to the choice and action stages.

Expectancy theory would predict that people would choose the action alternative with the highest total expected utility. However, the expectancy model may need revision. For example, Bandura (1986) has shown that self-efficacy (the confidence that one can successfully carry out a course of action) has very powerful effects on choice and action. Self-efficacy is not the same thing as effort-performance expectancy but includes one's assessment of all the personal factors that could affect how well one performs (for example, self-assessed ability, creativity, adaptability, capacity to deal with stress, and so on). Thus it should prove useful to measure not only what consequences a person expects as a result of a given action, but also the individual's confidence in being able to carry it out. Protesting to a supervisor, for example, involves the orchestration of a number of specific skills (formulating the problem, identifying its causes, suggesting remedies, presenting the argument to an authority figure, answering objections, persisting, and so on). Some people feel much more confident than others in carrying out such sequences of actions.

The model suggests the thoughtful choice of one action at a time. If the behavior is successful, subsequent actions will not be necessary. Consistent with this prediction, Spencer (1986) found that when formal voice mechanisms were available and perceived as effective, turnover was lower than when effective mechanisms were not available. If the action chosen is not successful, the model suggests that another action viewed as likely to improve the situation will be selected and implemented. The model allows for learning from experience, and thus may be able to explain why *a priori* response categories do not form clear factors in practice. If an individual uses one or two actions from a response category, such as constructive protest, and they are unsuccessful, he or she may decide that the whole category is ineffective and select from a different or more severe category the next time. Continuing this line of thought, different behaviors from the same category may be equal and interchangeable in their impact, so that there is no need to select more than one from a given category. If one is attempting to resolve an inequity situation resulting in dissatisfaction with pay, either loafing on the job or coming to work late may be equally effective in restoring perceived equity. Thus, factors based on frequency of doing apparently similar behaviors do not emerge. Further, greater sanctions may be associated with the overuse of the same category. Too much voice may get one the reputation of being a complainer and thus weaken the impact of subsequent complaints. Too many work-avoidance behaviors may lead to punishment, even discharge, while distributing one's actions across several categories may be both safer and more effective in producing desired change.

Finally, seemingly similar actions may not cluster together if some are impulsive behaviors and others are planned. The arrow on the left side of figure 7–1 leading from experienced satisfaction/dissatisfaction directly to action allows for such nonpremediated behaviors to occur when a transient opportunity to act occurs in conjunction with a peak or trough of affect. Conventional wisdom suggests that job dissatisfaction may be displaced and expressed in hostility toward the spouse or family dog. That is, the targets of the attitude and the behavior may not always match. Surely some negative behaviors at work may be chosen for their ready availability and cathartic value rather than because they are rationally related to the actual cause of the distress. A rational choice model featuring specific categories of behavior will not be able to predict these actions.

However, a relatively atheoretical aggregate measure of all negative job behaviors will capture these random discharges of negative affect, and as we have shown, will be predicted by overall job satisfaction.

In sum, the new look in job satisfaction research opens up many new opportunities for interesting research. It somewhat rehabilitates the reputation of job satisfaction as an important predictor in organizational research, and it brings attention to the wide variety of positive and negative behaviors that can be displayed by job incumbents. These behaviors have been neglected by traditional organizational research, but in the aggregate, they are crucial to organizational health and success. Finally, new look research partially vindicates the man-in-the-street perception that somehow satisfied workers must be "better" for the organization than dissatisfied workers.

References

Ajzen, I., & Fishbein, M. (1977). Attitude-behavior relations: A theoretical analysis and review of empirical research. *Psychological Bulletin, 84,* 888–918.

Bandura, A. (1986). *Social foundations of thought and action: A social-cognitive view.* Englewood Cliffs, NJ: Prentice Hall.

Bateman, T. S., & Organ, D. W. (1983). Job satisfaction and the good solider: The relationship between affect and employee "citizenship." *Academy of Management Journal, 26,* 587–595.

Brief, A. P., & Motowidlo, S. J. (1986). Prosocial organizational behaviors. *Academy of Management Review, 11,* 710–725.

Davis, S. K. (1988). *Behavioral consequences of dissatisfaction: A field study.* Unpublished paper, College of Business and Management, University of Maryland.

Diener, E., & Larsen, R. J. (1984). Temporal stability and cross-situational consistency of affective, behavioral, and cognitive responses. *Journal of Personality and Social Psychology, 47,* 871–883.

Farrell, D. (1983). Exit, voice, loyalty, and neglect as responses to job dissatisfaction: A multi-dimensional scaling analysis. *Academy of Management Journal, 26,* 596–607.

Fishbein, M., & Ajzen, I. (1974). Attitudes toward objects as predictors of single and multiple behavioral criteria. *Psychological Review, 81,* 59–74.

Fisher, C. D. (1980). On the dubious wisdom of expecting job satisfaction to correlate with performance. *Academy of Management Review, 5,* 607–612.

Graham, J. W. (1986). *Organizational citizenship informed by political theory.* Paper presented at the Annual Meeting of the Academy of Management, Chicago, August.

Gruneberg, M. M. (1979). *Understanding job satisfaction.* New York: Wiley.

Henne, D. L. (1986). *Thoughts and actions as consequences of job dissatisfaction.*

Unpublished doctoral dissertation, College of Business and Management, University of Maryland.

Henne, D. L., & Locke, E. A. (1985). Job dissatisfaction: What are the consequences? *International Journal of Psychology, 20,* 221–240.

Hirschman, A. O. (1970). *Exit, voice and loyalty.* Cambridge, MA: Harvard University Press.

Iaffaldano, M. T., & Muchinsky, P. M. (1985). Job satisfaction and job performance: A meta-analysis. *Psychological Bulletin, 97,* 251–273.

Locke, E. A. (1976). The nature and causes of job satisfaction. In M. D. Dunnette (Ed.), *Handbook of industrial and organizational psychology* (pp. 1297–1349). Chicago: Rand McNally.

Long, R. (1987). Relationship of aggregate positive behavior measure with job satisfaction. Unpublished raw data.

Matheny, C. T. (1988). *Job dissatisfaction and behaviors in the work environment.* Unpublished paper, College of Business and Management, University of Maryland.

Millar, M. G., & Tesser, A. (1986). Effects of affective and cognitive focus on the attitude-behavior relation. *Journal of Personality and Social Psychology,* 270–276.

Mobley, W. H. (1982). *Employee turnover; causes, consequences, and control.* Reading, MA: Addison-Wesley.

Organ, D. W. (1977). A reappraisal and reinterpretation of the satisfaction-causes performance hypothesis. *Academy of Management Review, 2,* 46–53.

Organ, D. W. (1988). *Organizational citizenship behavior: The "good soldier" syndrome.* Lexington, MA: Lexington Books.

Organ, D. W., & Konovsky, M. (1989). Cognitive versus affective determinants of organizational citizenship behavior. *Journal of Applied Psychology, 74,* 157–164.

Podsakoff, P. M., & Williams, L. (1986). The relationship between job performance and job satisfaction. In E. A. Locke (Ed.), *Generalizing from laboratory to field settings* (pp. 207–253). Lexington, MA: Lexington Books.

Puffer, S. M. (1987). Prosocial behavior, noncompliant behavior, and work performance among commission sales people. *Journal of Applied Psychology, 72,* 615–621.

Rosse, J. G., & Hulin, C. L. (1985). Adaptation to work: An analysis of employee health, withdrawal and change. *Organizational Behavior and Human Decision Processes, 36,* 324–347.

Rosse, J. G., & Miller, H. E. (1984). Relationship between absenteeism & other employee behaviors. In P. S. Goodman & R. S. Atkin (Eds.), *Absenteeism* (pp. 194–228). San Francisco: Jossey-Bass.

Rusbult, C. E., Farrell, D., Rogers, G., & Mainous, A. G. (1988). Impact of exchange variables on exit, voice, loyalty, and neglect: An integrative model of responses to declining job satisfaction. *Academy of Management Journal, 31,* 599–627.

Rusbult, C. E., & Lowery D. (1985). When bureaucrats get the blues: Responses to dissatisfaction among federal employees. *Journal of Applied Social Psychology, 15,* 80–103.

Rushton, J. P., Brainerd, C. J., & Pressley, M. (1983). Behavioral development and construct validity: The principle of aggregation. *Psychological Bulletin, 94,* 18–38.

Smith, C. A., Organ, D. W., & Near, J. (1983). Organizational citizenship behavior: Its nature and antecedents. *Journal of Applied Psychology, 68,* 653–663.

Smith, P. C., Kendall, L. M., & Hulin, C. L. (1969). *The measurement of satisfaction in work and retirement.* Chicago: Rand McNally.

Spencer, D. G. (1986). Employee voice and employee retention. *Academy of Management Journal, 29,* 488–502.

Staehle, C. M. (1985). *Job dissatisfaction and action alternatives: A study of the relationship between dissatisfaction and behaviors in work organization.* Unpublished honors thesis, College of Business and Management, University of Maryland.

Staw, B. M. (1984). Organizational behavior: A review and reformulation of the field's outcome variables. *Annual Review of Psychology, 35,* 627–666.

Staw, B. M., Bell, N. E., & Clausen, J. A. (1986). The dispositional approach to job attitudes: A lifetime longitudinal test. *Administrative Science Quarterly, 31,* 56–77.

Steel, R. P., & Ovalle, N. K. (1984). A review and meta-analysis of research on the relationship between behavioral intentions and employee turnover. *Journal of Applied Psychology, 69,* 673–686.

Thornton, G. C. (1980). Psychometric properties of self-appraisals of job performance. *Personnel Psychology, 33,* 263–271.

Tsui, A., Hartwick, J., & Sheppard, B. H. (1985). *Satisfaction-performance revisited: Are happy workers better workers?* Paper presented to the 93rd annual meeting of the American Psychological Association, Washington, D.C.

Watson, D., & Clark, L. A. (1984). Negative affectivity: The disposition to experience aversive emotional states. *Psychological Bulletin, 96,* 465–490.

Williams, L. J., Podsakoff, P. M., & Huber, V. (1986). *Leader behaviors, role stress, and satisfaction as determinants of organizational citizenship behaviors: A structural equation analysis with cross-validation.* Paper presented to the 46th annual meeting of the Academy of Management, Chicago.

Wolpin, J., & Burke, R. J. (1985). Relationship between absenteeism and turnover: A function of the measures? *Personnel Psychology, 38,* 57–75.

8

How Job Satisfaction
and Job Performance Are
and Are Not Linked

RAYMOND A. KATZELL

DONNA E. THOMPSON

RICHARD A. GUZZO

Attention by behavioral scientists to the linkage between workers' job satisfaction (JS) and job performance (JP) goes back at least as far as the Hawthorne studies (Roethlisberger & Dickson, 1939). The review by Brayfield and Crockett (1955) can be credited with raising the consciousness of I-O psychologists and human resource managers to the ambiguity and complexity of that relationship, a realization that in turn helped launch an avalanche of research aimed at clarifying the link. Reviews of the research literature have concluded that, although the two types of variables are usually correlated positively, the variation among correlations is rather large and the central tendency is low (Brayfield & Crockett, 1955; Vroom, 1964; Iaffaldano & Muchinsky, 1985; Podsakoff & Williams, 1986).

Katzell (1957) noted early that differences in the study characteristics appear to have affected the findings, some methodological, some associated with the employees, and others associated with the work situation. In line with that observation, investigators began studying the effects of variables moderating the JS–JP relationship. Schwab and Cummings (1970) reviewed those early studies and reported the occurrence of significant moderator effects. A recent meta-analysis by Iaffaldano and Muchinsky (1985) failed to detect appreciable effects of nine moderator variables. However, their choice of moderator variables was determined by the statistical requirements of their method more than by theoretical cogency. By contrast, a meta-analysis by Podsakoff and Williams (1986) found that a theoretically derived moderator, namely the extent to which rewards are linked to performance, does significantly affect the JS–JP correlations. They reported that the average correlation was .27 in situations where rewards were contingent on performance, but only .17 when not. Incidentally, the difference in the tenor of Iaffaldano and Muchinsky's (1985) conclusion and that of both Schwab and Cummings (1970) and Podsakoff and Williams (1986) nicely illustrates the caveat voiced by Guzzo, Jackson and Katzell (1987) regarding the limitation of meta-analysis for examining theoretical issues when statistical requirements may divert consideration of theoretically important findings.

The recognition of the role of moderators furthered the formulation of theories that account for variations in job satisfaction and job performance in the context of their respective covariates and causes. Efforts to do so were published by Cherrington, Reitz, and Scott (1971), Herzberg (1966), Lawler and Porter (1967), Locke (1970), Organ (1977), and Wofford (1971) among others. Interestingly, none of those theoretical expositions predicted a uniform degree of association between satisfaction and performance—that is, they postulated various contingencies and interactions that affect the relationship. Only one of those theories has been subjected to extensive empirical testing, the two-factor theory of Herzberg, and the results there are generally regarded as ambiguous at best (King, 1970; Pinder, 1984). In short, the issue still remains up in the air.

This chapter presents a newer model that illuminates the conditions that moderate the JS–JP relationship. It differs from previous formulations in two ways. First, it is part of a larger model of work motivation, derived by integrating a number of contemporary motivational theories; in this view, JS and JP are viewed as elements in a more extensive network of motivational constructs (Katzell & Thompson, 1986). Second, the various elements are connected in a path diagram that constitutes a multivariate hypothesis subject to testing via path analysis. After briefly explaining the model, we will report the results of such empirical testing. In a later section, we will review how the model is further supported by studies of organizational intervention that affect JS and JP.

The Model

Our statement of the JS–JP model is diagrammed in figure 8–1, which we will describe in words below. In figure 8–1 the direction of an arrow between two constructs indicates a positive causal relationship between them, although not necessarily a linear one. The hypothetical causal sequence is depicted in the conventional left-to-right direction, with performance at the far right.

As depicted at the right side of figure 8–1, the two factors that most immediately determine a person's performance are the effort that he or she invests in that performance as well as the person's job satisfaction.

Effort is a multifaceted concept, including not only energy expenditure but also its direction and duration (Naylor, Pritchard, & Ilgen, 1980). Effort is determined partly by factors outside the model, such as the person's physical condition and characteristic arousal level (Naylor, Pritchard, & Ilgen, 1980), but in large measure it is a result of the task-specific goals or intentions that the person adopts (Fishbein & Ajzen, 1975; Locke, Shaw, Saari, & Latham, 1981; Ryan, 1970).

Goals that a person adopts for a task are in turn determined by

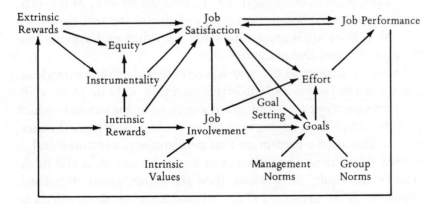

FIGURE 8–1
Path Model of Job Satisfaction and Performance

several factors. Of great importance in work situations are the goal-setting practices and performance norms—that is, goals and standards, set by superiors (Locke, 1974). Also involved are the norms of other significant persons, including peers and role models (Earley & Kanfer, 1985; Moch & Seashore, 1981; Rakestraw & Weiss, 1981). In addition, the individual is a source of self-set goals, as an expression of such personal dispositions as job involvement and intrinsic values (Taylor, Locke, List, & Gist, 1985; Lawler & Hall, 1970).

In addition to goals, a significant determinant of effort is the person's job attitudes, including job involvement and job satisfaction. Although job involvement and satisfaction are related, they are not identical (Cook, Hepworth, Wall & Warr, 1981); together they may be regarded as an attitudinal state of arousal that disposes one to act—that is, to exert effort.

A feedback loop running right-to-left is shown at the bottom of figure 8–1, indicating that performance has certain noteworthy consequences. In addition to its well-known informational function, feedback has an excitation function as well; it is one of the core dimensions characterizing wide-scope, arousing jobs (Hackman & Oldham, 1975). That is, it is a species of intrinsic reward. Other intrinsic rewards that may be generated by the design of one's job include variety or stimulation (Scott, 1966) and a sense of accomplishment or competence (Deci, 1975). Certain extrinsic rewards—that is, those administered by others—also may result from performance, including pay, promotions, social relationships, and so on (for example, Sims & Szilagyi, 1975). In order to serve as rewards, the performance consequences must, of course, be sufficiently valent. Also, there are sources of rewards other than performance, but these are not specified in figure 8–1.

The arousal function of rewards is represented by the arrows leading to job satisfaction and job involvement. In addition to those direct effects, the impact of rewards is mediated by the extent to which they are perceived as having been the result of performance (Lawler, 1977)—that is, the perception that performance is instrumental in reward attainment. The influence of extrinsic rewards is also mediated by the equity with which they are administered (Pritchard, Dunnette, & Jorgenson, 1972). Arrows represent those effects as well.

To the extent that performance may indirectly serve to increase job satisfaction via increased rewards, the model in figure 8–1 posits that performance thereby also increases effort, in turn leading to increased performance. Thus, we find a positive feedback loop, at least until job satisfaction reaches an optimum (not necessarily maximum) level (March & Simon, 1958).

Thus, our model postulates the total effects of job satisfaction on performance to be mainly indirect, involving as many as two intervening variables. Since the indirect effect of one variable on another is equal to the sum of the products of the intervening path coefficients, the impact of job satisfaction on performance may be expected to be quite small. Moreover, as Katzell (1964) pointed out, the same mechanisms that link satisfaction to productive behavior may also link it to nonproductive behavior on the job, thereby further attenuating any positive association between satisfaction and productivity; for example, one way of enhancing equity and hence JS in an underrewarded, noncontingent situation could be to reduce JP (Pritchard, Dunnette, & Jorgenson, 1972).

Since there is evidence that JS may be reciprocally affected by JP (Lawler & Porter, 1967), that path is also represented in the model.

In the following section, we will describe the method that we used to test the model. Later, the results of that test will be reported, followed by a discussion of the fit between the model and data from other studies.

Method

Sample

Research was conducted in four organizations with a total of 1,200 employees from twenty-six departments or organizational subunits participating. The organizations included: the back office division of a securities firm ($n = 316$); exempt personnel in an electrical manufacturing plant ($n = 98$); the sales and service representatives of a medical systems company ($n = 293$); and the controllers division in an industrial organization ($n = 493$).

Procedure

Data were collected by a set of three instruments: a survey of respondents' work attitudes and motivational states; a work group behavior / performance descriptive checklist, completed by first-level supervisors; and an interview conducted with higher-level managers to obtain performance data from existing records that they use to evaluate organizational outcomes, including quantity and quality of work performance. Instructions to subjects insured the confidentiality of individual responses and indicated that participation was voluntary.

These instruments are part of a larger program of research designed to examine the relationships among employee motivation, human resource policies and practices, and performance (Katzell & Thompson, 1986). This research is based on an integrative model that incorporates major theories of work motivation into a theoretical framework that indicates linkages among them. In the present study, the model was trimmed to include those variables considered to be especially relevant to job satisfaction and performance.

Employee Survey

Self-ratings of performance, job satisfaction, and eleven other motivational elements were assessed using scales from the survey (see table 8–1). For many of these scales, we were able to draw upon a number of extant scales from which there was evidence of satisfactory reliability and construct validity. However, because of the large number of constructs involved, it was necessary for practical reasons to reduce the number of items employed for several of the scales. This process was guided by the results of item analyses and / or factor analyses reported by the original authors or from our own pretests of experimental versions of the survey. In some instances we employed the best items from different questionnaires designed to tap the same constructs. It was often necessary to modify the wording or response format of items so that they could be presented in a consistent manner on our questionnaire. In some instances, where existing scales either were not available or provided only partial coverage of our construct, it was necessary to devise new items. The survey has undergone several revisions, and what is reported here is the third version; however, previous versions did not differ substantially. The core constructs remained the same. The scales, together with citations of the principal sources from which each was drawn and a sample item are described below.

Extrinsic rewards. This seven-item scale measured the extent to

TABLE 8–1
Means, Standard Deviations and Internal Consistency Reliabilities

Scale	Mean	Standard Deviation	Number of Items	Internal Consistency Reliability[a]
Extrinsic rewards	29.7	7.9	7	.75
Intrinsic rewards	31.8	7.9	7	.81
Intrinsic values	35.4	4.9	6	.82
Equity	30.8	6.7	7	.79
Instrumentality	31.3	10.1	8	.87
Job satisfaction	21.6	5.3	4	.83
Job involvement	37.0	5.8	7	.60
Production goals	23.8	3.4	4	.63
Goal setting	26.4	5.6	6	.58
Management norms for production	17.1	3.1	3	.70
Group norms for production	17.0	3.3	3	.84
Effort	37.4	6.0	7	.70
Overall performance	37.4	9.0	12	.73

[a]Based on coefficient alpha (Cronbach, 1951)

which respondents felt their jobs provided extrinsic rewards (for example, "The working conditions are good") based on a seven-point range from "Strongly Disagree" to "Strongly Agree." The primary sources of items included the Minnesota Job Description Questionnaire (Borgen, Weiss, Tinsley, Dawis, & Lofquist, 1968), and the Need Satisfaction Questionnaire (Porter, 1961, 1962).

Intrinsic rewards. This seven-item scale assessed the extent to which respondents felt their jobs provided intrinsic rewards based on a seven-point range from "Strongly Disagree" to "Strongly Agree." A sample item is, "Your job gives you the chance to do the kind of work that you do best." The items were derived from the Minnesota Job Description Questionnaire (Borgen, Weiss, Tinsley, Dawis, & Lofquist, 1968), the Need Satisfaction Questionnaire (Porter, 1961, 1962), and the Job Diagnostic Survey (Hackman & Oldham, 1975).

Intrinsic values. This six-item scale assessed how much of various intrinsic features of a work situation respondents would like to have in their jobs. An illustrative item is, "The job involves doing different things from time to time. How much would you like?" Again, subjects ranked their responses according to a seven-point rating, from "A Minimum Amount" to "A Maximum Amount." Sources included the Need Satisfaction Questionnaire (Porter, 1961, 1962) and the Minnesota Importance Questionnaire (Gay, Weiss, Hendel, Dawis, & Lofquist, 1971).

Equity. This seven-item scale assessed participants' evaluations of how fairly the rewards were distributed among employees according to a seven-point rating from "Very Unfairly; I am Treated Badly Compared to Others." to "Very Fairly; My Treatment is Entirely Appropriate Compared to Others." A sample question is, "Compared to other people here, how fairly are you treated?" The Michigan Organizational Assessment Questionnaire (Cammann, Fishman, Jenkins, & Klesh, 1983) was a source of items, but most were specially devised.

Instrumentality. The experienced relationship between performance and reward was evaluated by this eight-item scale. To illustrate, participants were presented with a list of some things that could happen when people do their jobs especially well (for example, more rapid promotion, better work assignments, receive more money) and were asked to rank them on a seven-point scale ranging from "Extremely Unlikely" to "Extremely Likely"). Sources for the items included the Survey of Social and Rehabilitation Service Workers (Katzell, Collins & Levine, 1973), the Michigan Organizational Assessment Questionnaire (Cammann, Fichman, Jenkins, & Klesh, 1983), the Organizational Assessment Instrument (Van de Ven & Ferry, 1980), and Work-Related Expectancies (Sims, Szilagyi, & McKemey, 1976).

Job Satisfaction. This four-item scale assessed overall job satisfaction using a seven-point scale ranging from "Strongly Disagree" to "Strongly Agree." An illustrative item is, "In general, I don't like my job." Items were based on the Michigan Organizational Assessment Questionnaire (Cammann, Fichman, Jenkins, & Klesh, 1983), and Overall Job Satisfaction (Quinn & Staines, 1979).

Job involvement. The extent to which participants felt their jobs and job performance were important to them was evaluated by this seven-item scale. A sample item is, "Most things in life are more important than work." Subjects ranked their responses on a seven-point scale ranging from "Strongly Disagree" to "Strongly Agree." The Internal Work Motivation Scale (Hackman & Oldham, 1975) and the Job Involvement Scale (Lodahl & Kejner, 1965) were sources for the scale items.

Production goals. This four-item scale measured the level of difficulty in the production goals respondents set for themselves (Dachler & Mobley, 1973) according to a seven-point scale ranging from "Strongly Disagree" to "Strongly Agree." For example, "It is important to me to produce as much as I possibly can."

Goal setting. This six-item sale asked respondents to describe attributes of goals set in their organizations, based on the work of Steers (1975). They used a seven-point scale ranging from "Goals Are Entirely Clear" to "Goals Are Vague and Unclear." An illustrative item is, "How clear and specific are the goals and objectives of your job? Do people know exactly what they are supposed to do and what the standards are for a job well done?"

Management norms for production. The standards for production set by management were measured by this three-item scale. Items were based on the work of Litwin and Stringer (1968), Jones and James (1979), and Sims and Szilagyi (1975). A sample item is "How much importance is attached to meeting work schedules by management here in evaluating the performance of a person in your kind of job?" The respondents ranked their answers on a seven-point scale ranging from "Of No Importance" to "Of Utmost Importance."

Group norms for production. The standards set by an employee's work group were measured by this three-item scale, partly based on the work of Jackson (1966) and Jones and James (1979). A sample item is, "How important to co-workers is the quality of work that is produced?" Respondents used a seven-point scale ranging from "Of No Importance" to "Of Utmost Importance."

Effort. This seven-item scale measured how hard the person works. Items were partly based on Lawler, Hall, and Oldham (1974), and Van de Ven and Ferry (1980). For example, "How much effort do you have to exert in order to do the amount of work that you now do?" Subjects used a seven-point scale ranging from

"Not much; I Could Do a Lot More Work if I Tried a Little Harder" to "A Great Deal; I Work as Hard as I Possibly Can."

Overall performance. For 583 employees, the measurement of work performance was based on self-rated performance, plus a rating by an immediate supervisor and/or a department manager.

The twelve-item self-rating scale asked people to rate the quality and quantity of their own work performance, based partly on Dachler and Mobley (1973) and Lawler, Hall, and Oldham (1974). An illustrative item is, "How would you rate the amount of work you get done?" Responses were given according to a seven-point scale ranging from "The Amount of Work Is the Most That Can Be Done by Anyone in This Job" to "The Amount of Work I Do Is Quite a Bit Less Than Can Be Done.")

In addition, each work group supervisor completed a "Supervisor Check List", consisting of thirty-five items relating to group behavior and performance. These items were scored using a seven-point scale, ranging from seven as the most positive to one as the most unfavorable. Only one of the scales, the performance scale, was used in the research reported here. This scale consisted of eleven items concerned with both the quality and the quantity of the work group's performance. The alpha coefficient for this scale was .64.

The final procedure for rating performance was a series of individual meetings with department managers, who were asked to review the objective records of their departmental performance during the past year, including quantity and quality of work. Using a standard rating form, each manager then transformed these records into a scale on which ten represented the best conceivable performance and zero the worst possible that would still enable the department to remain in business. The quality and quantity ratings were combined to produce an overall performance rating.

The average of these last two types of performance scores, which were measured at the group level, were ascribed to the 583 individual members of those groups in calculating individual statistics.

Results

Our model is a multivariate one that hypothesizes a sequential pattern of relationships among a set of variables. An appropriate method for statistically testing that kind of hypothesis is path analysis. Specifically, the LISREL procedure was applied to the intercorrelations among the variables detailed previously, resulting in path coefficients connecting each pair of variables. Those are the numbers that are associated with the arrows in figure 8–2, which is the version of figure 8–1 that emerged after testing by LISREL. Note that the model includes the self-reported and superiors' evaluations of JP described above.

The principal results pertaining to the JS–JP relationship may be itemized as follows:

1. JS is determined substantially by the magnitude of intrinsically rewarding conditions, such as interesting work, challenge, and autonomy. That effect is both direct (path coefficient = .18) and indirect via the perceived instrumentality or linkage of those rewards to performance, as well as via their influence on job involvement.

2. JS is also determined by the magnitude of extrinsic rewards, such as pay and security. The direct effect is small, but statistically significant. Additionally, the indirect effects of extrinsic rewards are appreciable, being mediated by how

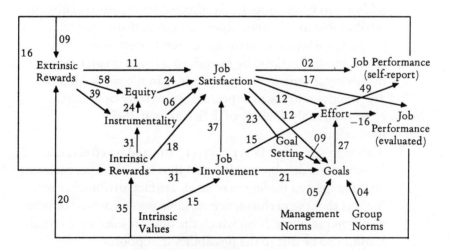

FIGURE 8–2
Path Analysis of Job Satisfaction and Performance
Decimals omitted from coefficients.

they are administered—that is, by their perceived equity and instrumentality.

3. The level of job involvement also positively affects JS, as do aspects of goal-setting practices such as their clarity and specificity.

4. JS has virtually no direct effect on self-rated JP, but does significantly influence JP as evaluated by superiors. The effect is presumably due to the activation/arousal function of a positive attitude that is manifested in greater alertness, more focused attention, and similar facilitating processes other than sheer effort expenditure; given the nature of the measures, a less likely explanation is that superiors were reacting to the more positive feelings of their subordinates.

5. The LISREL's modification indexes did not suggest the relevance of a direct causal path from JP to JS, which is therefore absent from figure 8–2. However, that absence may be due to the need to study that effect longitudinally. Nevertheless, JP is shown here to have an indirect effect on JS via the former's consequences for rewards. Interestingly, the impact of JP on rewards is even greater when JP is evaluated by superiors than when it is self-reported.

6. Effort expenditure is an important factor in self-rated JP. In addition to being moderately affected by JS, effort is directly attributable to job involvement and to performance goal levels. Goal levels, in turn, are directly affected by goal-setting practices, by JS and, to an even greater extent, by job involvement. Norms of others in the work situation are found, contrary to expectations, to have only slight effects, possibly because of deficiencies in their measurement.

7. Although self-rated JP is positively affected by effort, the latter's effect on objectively rated JP is inverse. This curious and unexpected finding may be an artifact attributable to the fact that the performance variable was measured only in a subsample of the N on which the other results were based. It may also be due to the possibility that poorer performance was due partly to a less efficient work system or technology that would also require greater effort on the part of the employees. Measures of such variables were not

employed in this study. Recall that JP measured by either method has a positive indirect effect on JS. Thus, if the latter scenario suggested for the inverse effect of effort on objectively rated JP were correct, one would predict that effort, and therefore JP, would deteriorate over time, a hypothesis that would require longitudinal data for testing.

The goodness-of-fit index is .84, indicating that the data fit the model moderately well. When adjusted for degrees of freedom, the index drops to .70, but that figure could be raised by trimming the model to exclude some insignificant paths, such as those involving norms. The modification indexes suggest that the model's goodness of fit could also be improved by adding certain causal paths, the more theoretically meaningful ones being the reverse causation by job satisfaction of perceptions of both intrinsic and extrinsic reward levels (James & Tetrick, 1986). However, it is not our purpose here to refine or extend the model, because that would not change the basic picture of the JS–JP dynamics, which are our focal concern.

The model shown in figure 8–1, therefore, appears to be a reasonably good representation of what really may be happening as various motivational elements affect each other. In short, it indicates that JS and JP have only a little direct impact on one another. However, they are each overdetermined by a multiplicity of factors, some of which are common to the two, and some of which furnish indirect links between them. This, in turn, suggests that treatments that affect those elements will cause JS and JP to covary. Specifically, the model and the supporting results indicate such roles for valence of intrinsic and extrinsic rewards, for equity, instrumentality, job involvement, and goal setting.

This hypothesis can be further tested by experimental manipulation of variables that operationalize one or more of those constructs. There exist in the literature a number of reports that can be adduced to this purpose. We will discuss such findings in the next section.

Organizational Interventions

This section has two major goals. One is to illustrate the scope of the model in figure 8–1 by relating the model to existing intervention studies of job satisfaction and performance. Intervention studies are those characterized by the systematic evaluation of changes in organizational practices or conditions to enhance performance or satisfaction. The second goal is to discuss the power of the model for guiding future interventions to increase satisfaction and performance. Thus, this section concerns the model as both an integrative device and an applicable guide to the improvement of job attitudes and performance.

Interventions Affecting Satisfaction and Performance

Studies of psychologically based interventions to improve performance and satisfaction have been extensively reviewed (for example, Cummings, 1982; Guzzo, 1988; Guzzo & Bondy, 1983; Katzell, Bienstock, & Faerstein, 1977; Koppelman, 1986). These interventions typically concern changes in the work itself and in human resource management practices, such as those governing the way employees are compensated, trained, hired, and supervised. There is no intent here to catalog exhaustively the studies and their findings. Rather, we intend to use selected examples of intervention studies as well as draw some generalizations about such studies for the purpose of further examining the model of figure 8–1.

Katzell and Guzzo (1983) reviewed 207 studies of the effects of psychologically based interventions on productivity and performance and reported that 87 percent succeeded in raising productivity in at least one measurable aspect. Interestingly, three-quarters of the studies also reported improvements in JS. It now seems clear that interventions designed to affect JP often also affect JS, though these latter effects may have been unintended.

Many examples of interventions that affect both performance and satisfaction exist. One such example is the work of Ivancevich (1977), who examined the effects of goal setting with technicians and maintenance workers in three manufacturing plants. He found that both performance and satisfaction with work increased in response to goal setting. Latham and Yukl (1976) also reported a study in which performance and attitudinal changes followed the implementation of a goal-setting program among typists. In this case, however, JP increased following goal setting, but JS declined. An example of a multifaceted intervention is the work of Pritchard, Jones, Roth, Stuebing, and Ekeberg (1988). Their work successively introduced feedback, goal setting, and incentives in an organization. Following feedback, performance increased 50 percent over baseline. When goal setting was added to the feedback intervention, JP increased to 75 percent over baseline. And when incentives were added to feedback and goal setting, performance increased to 76 percent over baseline. Additionally, JS improved following the interventions.

An understanding of why interventions often affect both satisfaction and performance is provided by the model in figure 8–1, which shows several common determinants of satisfaction and performance. Well-conducted goal setting, for example, has the effect of improving satisfaction. Goal setting also affects performance indirectly through the establishment of goals and resulting goal-directed effort. Thus, the model predicts that goal-setting interventions are likely to have demonstrable effects on both satisfaction and performance. The same is true for interventions that redesign work by increasing the feedback, variety of skills utilized, and importance of one's job. Such interventions enhance the intrinsic rewards of work, which in turn directly influence satisfaction and indirectly influence performance. An organization's change to an instrumental incentive pay system, as shown by the model, is predicted to affect both satisfaction and performance. The model thus provides an explicit rationale for why the majority of interventions that affect performance also affect satisfaction (Katzell & Guzzo, 1983).

While a given intervention may affect both satisfaction and performance at work, the effects are not likely to be equal. As mentioned earlier, the indirect effect of one variable on another is the sum of the products of the path coefficients of each intervening link between the two variables, where path coefficients represent strengths of relationships. Thus, indirect effects are likely to be weaker than direct effects. To illustrate, work redesign interventions should be expected to more strongly influence JS than JP because the design of work's effects on satisfaction are direct, while its effects on performance are indirect, mediated by other variables (see figure 8–1). Indeed, this is consistent with empirical research. Stone (1986) reviewed research on relationships between job scope (analogous to the extent to which the job provides intrinsic rewards) and satisfaction and performance. Job scope was found to be a stronger, more consistent predictor of satisfaction than of performance.

Interventions may not only have unequal effects on JS and JP but also opposite effects. Consider the case in which an organization puts in place new goal-setting procedures without changing compensation. The new goal-setting procedures could raise performance, but the failure to increase pay might create perceptions of inequity that adversely affect JS. Hence, higher performance and lower satisfaction might follow such an intervention, a state of affairs not unheard of (for example, Latham & Yukl, 1976). The possibility of intervention effects being registered on one but not both satisfaction and performance also is permitted by the model in figure 8–1. In summary, organizational interventions affect JS and JP differentially, and the model provides an explanation of why.

Research Methods and the JS–JP Relationship

The methods researchers use to study performance and satisfaction seem to influence the conclusions reached about their interrelationship. More specifically, correlational research tends to show modest relationships, at best, between satisfaction and performance. Intervention research, on the other hand, suggests a stronger relationship between these two variables than that indicated by correlational research.

Correlational studies of the sort reviewed by Vroom (1964) or Iaffaldano and Muchinsky (1985), among others, report small correlations between measures of JS and JP. Vroom (1964) found a median correlation of .14 in empirical literature addressing satisfaction and performance. Iaffaldano and Muchinsky (1985), drawing on a larger sample of empirical reports and summarizing them in a more statistically sophisticated way, report a .17 estimated true population correlation between JS and JP. Based on these research results, typically obtained through static cross-sectional surveys, researchers generally have concluded that changes in performance are not much related to changes in satisfaction.

Intervention studies of the sort reviewed in this chapter, though, imply a stronger link between JS and JP. These are experimental and quasi-experimental studies assessing the effects of some manipulated independent variable, such as a change in pay or supervisory practices. As has been shown, intervention studies that show an impact on performance often show an impact on satisfaction (Katzell & Guzzo, 1983). Based on intervention research, then, a stronger covariance is seen between JS and JP than that suggested by correlational research. Furthermore, closer examination of reviews of correlational studies suggests that even they may have underestimated the JS–JP relationship (Petty, McGee & Cavender, 1984; Podsakoff & Williams, 1986; Wanous, Sullivan, & Malinak, 1989).

The model guiding this chapter addresses this apparent discrepancy between correlational and intervention studies of the JS–JP relationship by explicitly recognizing that each variable is multiply caused. That is, satisfaction and performance are overdetermined. When a simple relationship between satisfaction and performance is computed without controlling for their multiple determinants, their relationship may appear weak and ambiguous. But when mediating and conditional factors are operating and accounted for, the relationship between satisfaction and performance appears clearer.

Additionally, the model's emphasis on the codeterminants (direct and indirect) of performance and satisfaction gives another clue as to why correlational and intervention studies yield different conclusions about the JS–JP relationship. Correlational studies are often done in a way that restricts variance in the determinants of satisfaction and performance, such as by sampling employees at a single time within a single organizational context. Intervention studies, on the other hand, introduce variance in contextual variables and observe the consequences over time. By manipulating one or more of their codeterminants in the organizational context, changes in both satisfaction and performance are more likely to appear.

The model also asserts a causal order involving satisfaction and performance as well as identifying consequences of each. As such, the model may be a useful device for disentangling and reconciling differing results of studies addressing satisfaction and performance when mediating and conditional factors are known.

One other brief comment on the nature of intervention research is in order: Most intervention studies do not go inside the black box of the psychological processes determining performance and satisfaction. Intervention studies usually are very input-output in character, where the input is a change in a pay scheme, for example, and the output is a change in performance or satisfaction. We believe a much stronger collective understanding of the JS–JP relationship would be attained if researchers more often went inside the black box by offering hypotheses about psychological processes that mediate the input-output link and by collecting data bearing on these processes. The model in figure 8–1 is one such multivariate hypothesis of what goes on inside the black box. It is not the only one possible. We offer it in part as a stimulus to other plausible accounts of the processes linking changes in organizational practices or conditions to satisfaction and performance.

Interventions: Single versus Multiple Levers

Each causal variable of the model in figure 8–1 represents an "action lever" for intervening to change performance and satisfaction. Individuals and organizations can choose to act by manipulating these levers one at a time or, conversely, by simultaneously making use of several levers. Implicit in the model, we believe, is the wisdom of multilever interventions. That is, if profound effects on satisfaction and performance are sought, the use of multiple levers will be more successful than interventions that change only one thing at a time.

An essential feature of the model is that redundancies exist in the determination of satisfaction and performance; each is the product of a network of influences. Each variable in the network, though, is an imperfect, incomplete cause of another. Interventions that change only one variable—say, the amount of extrinsic reward available at work—must contend with a considerable amount of uncertainty about whether that change will have an ultimate impact on JS and JP. As pointed out by Raskin (1987), uncertainty about the ultimate effects of an intervention is reduced when that intervention makes several changes at once. When several changes are made—say, in the amount of extrinsic reward, intrinsic reward, and goal setting—the likelihood increases that satisfaction and performance will change. With a three-levered intervention there are more reasons why satisfaction and productivity should change than with a one-lever intervention; hence multifaceted interventions should have a higher success rate than single-faceted interventions. We further expect the strength of multifaceted interventions to be greater, too.

There is some, though sparse, evidence that multifaceted interventions have greater impact than single-faceted interventions (see Guzzo & Gannett, 1988). A meta-analysis of productivity improvement research found that productivity improvements were stronger when multiple rather than single changes were made in organizational practices (Guzzo, Jette, & Katzell, 1985). A meta-analysis of organization development interventions also shows that the strongest favorable changes in JS were obtained when multiple changes rather than a single change were implemented (Neuman, Edwards, & Raju, 1989).

Implications for Organizational Policy

The model reported in this chapter and the discussion of studies of organizational interventions reopen an old issue: the relationship between JS and JP. Contemporary textbook wisdom is that satisfaction and performance are not much related (for example, Muchinsky, 1987, p. 429). This position emerged in the 1950s, when Brayfield and Crockett (1955) reviewed empirical research and concluded that satisfaction bore little appreciable relationship to performance. Associated with this view is the idea that organizations can be managed to promote either of two worthy ends, performance or satisfaction, but that different practices are required for each. As Muchinsky (1987) states, "organizational attempts to enhance both worker satisfaction and performance simultaneously will likely be unsuccessful" (p. 430). We hope this chapter dispels such notions.

Prior to the 1950s, though, the conventional wisdom was that satisfaction and performance were related. Herzberg, Mausner, Peterson, and Capwell's (1957) review of opinion documents this. Herzberg et al. also were quite in agreement with Brayfield and Crockett (1955) in concluding that empirical research (rather than opinion) showed inconsistent relationships between satisfaction and performance. They differed, though, in what to make of this. Herzberg et al. (1957, p. 101) argued that differences in work situations affect the relationship between satisfaction and performance, that in some circumstances a positive relationship exists while in others the relationship is nonexistent or negative.

This chapter makes that old argument new. It does so with an explicit formulation of causes of JS and JP and thus a specification of conditions under which the two relate positively, negatively, or not at all. All other things being equal, the model explains that the two covary as a function of the extent to which certain conditions are met: the work yields intrinsic rewards; valent extrinsic rewards are administered equitably and are linked to performance; job involvement is high; and clear, challenging, and acceptable goals are set. Moreover, this chapter argues that organizations need not manage for one or the other. Provided the organizational context is managed appropriately, high satisfaction and performance are goals that can be met jointly. To achieve these dual objectives would go far to create a good world of work.

References

Borgen, F. H., Weiss, D. J., Tinsley, H. E. A., Dawis, R. V., & Lofquist, L. H. (1968). *The measurement of occupational reinforcer patterns.* Minneapolis: Industrial Relations Center, University of Minnesota.

Brayfield, A. H., & Crockett, W. H. (1955). Employee attitudes and employee performance. *Psychological Bulletin, 52,* 396–424.

Cammann, C., Fichman, M., Jenkins, G. D., Jr., & Klesh, J. R. (1983). Assessing the attitudes of organizational members. In S. E. Seashore, E. E. Lawler, III, P. H. Mirvis & C. Cammann (Eds.), *Assessing organizational change* (pp. 71–138). New York: Wiley.

Cherrington, D. J., Reitz, H. J., & Scott, W. E. (1971). Effects of contingent and non-contingent reward on the relationship between job satisfaction and job performance. *Journal of Applied Psychology, 55,* 531–536.

Cook, J. D., Hepworth, S. J., Wall, T. D., & Warr, P. B. (1981). *The experience of work.* New York: Academic Press.

Cronbach, L. J. (1951). Coefficient alpha and the internal structure of tests. *Psychometrika, 16,* 297–334.

Cummings, L. L. (1982). *Improving human resource effectiveness.* Berea, OH: American Society for Personnel Administration Foundation.

Dachler, H. P., & Mobley, W. H. (1973). Construct validation of an instrumentality-expectancy-task-goal model of work motivation: Some theoretical boundary conditions. *Journal of Applied Psychology, 58,* 397–418.

Deci, E. L. (1975). *Intrinsic motivation.* New York: Plenum.

Earley, P. C., & Kanfer, R. (1985). The influence of component participation and role models on goal acceptance, goal satisfaction, and performance. *Organizational Behavior and Human Decision Processes, 36,* 378–390.

Fishbein, M., & Ajzen, I. (1975). *Belief, attitude, intention, and behavior.* Reading, MA: Addison-Wesley.

Gay, E. G., Weiss, D. J., Hendel, D. D., Dawis, R. V., Lofquist, L. H. (1971). *Manual for the Minnesota Importance Questionnaire.* Minneapolis: Industrial Relations Center, University of Minnesota.

Guzzo, R. A. (1988). Productivity research: Reviewing psychological and economic perspectives. In J. P. Campbell and R. J. Campbell (Eds.), *Productivity in organizations* (pp. 63–81). San Francisco: Jossey-Bass.

Guzzo, R. A., & Bondy, J. S. (1983). *A guide to worker productivity experiments in the United States, 1976–1981.* Elmsford, NY: Pergamon Press, 1983.

Guzzo, R. A., & Gannett, B. A. (1988). The nature of facilitators and inhibitors of effective task performance. In F. D. Schoorman and B. Schneider (Eds.), *Facilitating work effectiveness* (pp. 21–41). Lexington, MA: Lexington Books.

Guzzo, R. A., Jackson, S. E., & Katzell, R. A. (1987). Meta-analysis. In L. L. Cummings & B. M. Staw (Eds.), *Research in organizational behavior.* Vol. 9 (pp. 407–442) Greenwich, CT: JAI Press.

Guzzo, R. A., Jette, R. D., & Katzell, R. A. (1985). The effects of psychologically based intervention programs on worker productivity: A meta-analysis. *Personnel Psychology, 38,* 275–291.

Hackman, J. R., & Oldham, G. R. (1975). The development of the Job Diagnostic Survey. *Journal of Applied Psychology, 60,* 159–170.

Herzberg, F. (1966). *Work and the nature of man.* Cleveland, OH: World Book.

Herzberg, F., Mausner, B., Peterson, R. O., & Capwell, D. F. (1957). *Job attitudes: Review of research and opinion.* Pittsburgh, PA: Psychological Service of Pittsburgh.

Iaffaldano, M. R., & Muchinsky, P. M. (1985). Job satisfaction and job performance: A meta-analysis. *Psychological Bulletin, 97,* 251–273.

Ivancevich, J. M. (1977). Different goal-setting treatments and their effects on performance and job satisfaction. *Academy of Management Journal, 20,* 406–419.

Jackson, J. (1966). A conceptual and measurement model for norms and roles. *Pacific Sociological Review, 9,* 35–47.

James, L. R., & Tetrick, L. E. (1986). Confirmatory analytic tests of three causal models relating job perceptions to job satisfaction. *Journal of Applied Psychology, 71,* 77–82.

Jones, A. P., & James, L. R. (1979). Psychological climate: Dimensions and relationships of individual and aggregated work environment perceptions. *Organizational Behavior and Human Performance, 23,* 201–250.

Katzell, R. A. (1957). Industrial psychology. *Annual Review of Psychology, 8,* 237–268.

Katzell, R. A. (1964). Personal values, job satisfaction, and job performance. In H. Borow (Ed.), *Man in a world of work* (pp. 341–363). Boston: Houghton Mifflin.

Katzell, R. A., Bienstock, P., & Faerstein, P. H. (1977). *A guide to worker productivity experiments in the United States, 1971–75.* New York: New York University Press.

Katzell, R. A., Collins, M. E., & Levine, E. L. (1973). Developing and pre-testing of instruments for national survey of social welfare and rehabilitative workers, work, and organizational contexts. *Technical report of contract SRS, 71–14.* Washington, DC: U. S. Department of Health, Education, and Welfare.

Katzell, R. A., & Guzzo, R. A. (1983). Psychological approaches to productivity improvement. *American Psychologist, 38,* 468–472.

Katzell, R. A., & Thompson, D. E. (1986). *Empirical research on a comprehensive theory of work motivation.* Paper presented at the 21st International Congress of Applied Psychology, Jerusalem, Israel.

King, N. (1970). Clarification and evaluation of the two-factor theory of job satisfaction. *Psychological Bulletin, 74,* 18–31.

Koppelman, R. E. (1986). *Managing productivity in organizations.* New York: McGraw-Hill.

Latham, G. P. & Yukl, G. A. (1976). Effects of assigned and participative goal-setting on performance and job satisfaction. *Journal of Applied Psychology, 61,* 166–171.

Lawler, E. E., III (1977). Reward systems. In J. R. Hackman & J. L. Suttle (Eds.), *Improving life at work* (pp. 163–226). Santa Monica, CA: Goodyear.

Lawler, E. E., III, & Hall, D. T. (1970). Relationship of job characteristics to job involvement, satisfaction, and intrinsic motivation. *Journal of Applied Psychology, 54,* 305–312.

Lawler, E. E., III, Hall, D. T., & Oldham, G. R. (1974). Organizational climate: Relationship to organizational structure, process, and performance. *Organizational Behavior and Human Performance, 11,* 139–155.

Lawler, E. E., III, & Porter, L. W. (1967). The effect of performance on job satisfaction. *Industrial Relations, 7,* 20–28.

Litwin, G. H., & Stringer, R. A. (1968). *Motivation and organizational climate.* Boston: Graduate School of Business Administration, Harvard University.

Locke, E. A. (1970). Job satisfaction and job performance: A theoretical analysis. *Organizational Behavior and Human Performance, 5,* 484–500.

Locke, E. A. (1974). The supervisor as "motivator": His influence on employee performance and satisfaction. In B. M. Bass, R. Cooper, & J. A. Haas (Eds.), *Managing for accomplishment* (pp. 57–67). Lexington, MA: Lexington Books.

Locke, E. A., Shaw, K. N., Saari, L. M., & Latham, G. P. (1981). Goal setting and task performance. *Psychological Bulletin, 90,* 125–152.

Lodahl, T., & Kejner, M. (1965). The definition and measurement of job involvement. *Journal of Applied Psychology, 49,* 24–33.

March, J. G., & Simon, H. A. (1958). *Organizations.* New York: Wiley.

Moch, M., & Seashore, S. E. (1981). How norms affect behaviors in and out of organizations. In C. Nystrom & W. H. Starbuck (Eds.), *Handbook of organizational design.* Vol. 1 (pp. 210–237). New York: Oxford University Press.

Muchinsky, P. M. (1987). *Psychology applied to work* (2nd ed.). Chicago: Dorsey.

Naylor, J. C., Pritchard, R. D., & Ilgen, D. R. (1980). *A theory of behavior in organizations.* New York: Academic Press.

Neuman, G. A., Edwards, J. E., & Raju, N. S. (1989). Organizational development interventions: A meta–analysis of their effects on satisfaction and other attitudes. *Personnel Psychology, 42,* 461–489.

Organ, D. W. (1977). A reappraisal and reinterpretation of the satisfaction-causes-performance hypothesis. *Academy of Management Review, 2,* 46–53.

Petty, M. M., McGee, G. W., & Cavender, J. W. (1984). A meta-analysis of the relationship between individual job satisfaction and individual performance. *Academy of Management Review, 9,* 712–721.

Pinder, C. C. (1984). *Work motivation.* Glenview, IL: Scott Foresman.

Podsakoff, P. M., & Williams, L. J. (1986). The relationship between job performance and job satisfaction. In E. A. Locke (Ed.), *Generalizing from laboratory to field settings* (pp. 207–253). Lexington, MA: Lexington.

Porter, L. W. (1961). A study of perceived need satisfactions in bottom and middle management jobs. *Journal of Applied Psychology, 45,* 1–101.

Porter, L. W. (1962). Job attitudes in management: Perceived deficiencies in need fulfillment as a function of job level. *Journal of Applied Psychology, 46,* 375–384.

Pritchard, R. D., Dunnette, M. D., & Jorgenson, D. O. (1972). Effects of perceptions of equity and inequity on worker satisfaction and performance. *Journal of Applied Psychology, 56,* 75–94.

Pritchard, R. D., Jones, S. D., Roth, P. L., Stuebing, K. K., & Ekeberg, S. E. (1988). Effects of group feedback, goal setting, and incentives on organizational productivity. *Journal of Applied Psychology, 73,* 337–358.

Quinn, R. P., & Staines, G. L. (1979). *The 1977 Quality of Employment Survey.* Ann Arbor, MI: Institute of Social Research, University of Michigan.

Rakestraw, T. L., & Weiss, H. M. (1981). The interaction of social influence and task experience on goals, performance, and performance satisfaction. *Organizational Behavior and Human Performance, 27,* 326–344.

Raskin, M. (1987). *Plato's raft.* Unpublished manuscript.

Roethlisberger, F. J., & Dickson, W. J. (1939). *Management and the worker.* Cambridge, MA: Harvard University Press.

Ryan, T. A. (1970). *Intentional behavior.* New York: Ronald.

Schwab, D. P., & Cummings, L. L. (1970). Theories of performance and satisfaction: A review. *Industrial Relations, 9,* 408–430.

Scott, W. E., Jr. (1966). Activation theory and task design. *Organizational Behavior and Human Performance, 1,* 3–30.

Sims, H. P., & Szilagyi, A. D. (1975). Leader reward behavior and subordinate satisfaction and performance. *Organizational Behavior and Human Performance, 14,* 426–438.

Sims, H. P., Szilagyi, A. D., & McKemey, D. R. (1976). Antecedents of work-related expectancies. *Academy of Management Journal, 19,* 195–212.

Steers, R. M. (1975). Task-goal attributes, n achievement, and supervisory performance. *Organizational Behavior and Human Performance, 13,* 392–403.

Stone, E. F. (1986). Job scope-job satisfaction and job scope-job performance relationships. In E. A. Locke (Ed.), *Generalizing from laboratory to field settings* (pp. 189–206). Lexington, MA: Lexington Books.

Taylor, M. S., Locke, E. A., List, C., & Gist, M. (1985). Type A behavior and faculty research productivity: What are the mechanisms? *Organizational Behavior and Human Performance, 34,* 402–418.

Van de Ven, A. H., & Ferry, D. L. (1980). *Measuring and assessing organizations.* New York: Wiley.

Vroom, V. H. (1964). *Work and motivation.* New York: Wiley.

Wanous, I. P., Sullivan, S. E., & Malinak, J. (1989). The role of judgment calls in meta-analysis. *Journal of Applied Psychology, 74,* 259–264.

Wofford, J. C. (1971). The motivational bases of job satisfaction and job performance. *Personnel Psychology, 24,* 501–518.

9

Job Stress and Health

GAIL H. IRONSON

The relationship between work stress and health outcomes has assumed major importance with mounting health care costs, concerns about absenteeism and lost productivity, and morbidity and mortality at stake. Research in the area has sometimes yielded an array of impressive statistics. One prospective study found that people with high job pressure at two different points in time had a three times higher mortality rate across ten years as compared with those having high job pressure at only one or no time points (House, Strecher, Metzner, & Robbins, 1986). Another study found that psychological stress at work during five years prior to symptoms was associated with a six times greater risk of ischemic heart disease (Orth-Gomer & Ahlbom, 1980). A twenty-seven-month follow-up study of 416 air traffic controllers found 252 percent more injuries and 69 percent greater mortality associated with certain psychological factors such as work change distress, dissatisfaction with management, Type A behavior, and so on (Niemcryk, Jenkins, Rose, & Hurst, 1987). Several retrospective studies have shown that premature heart attack victims were overworked (Liljefors & Rahe, 1970; Russek & Zohman, 1958; Hinkle, 1974); one showed that 90 percent of those having heart attacks were working two jobs or more than sixty hours per week with prolonged emotional strain as compared to 20 percent of controls (Hinkle, 1974). Finally, job satisfaction has been a predictor of longevity over thirteen years (Palmore, 1969a, 1969b) and a strong correlate of coronary heart disease (Sales & House, 1971). This research interest has spread to the popular press as well, with articles on "stress on the job" abounding (Miller, 1988).

Yet despite the preceding findings, the data supporting the view that occupational stress is implicated in the etiology of physical health problems has been referred to as "fragmentary . . . difficult to replicate and subject to multiple etiological interpretations" (Kasl, 1981, p. 682). Much progress has been made during the intervening years in elucidating the various relationships between specific job stressors and particular health patterns. However, as specific and detailed knowledge grows, new questions and complexities arise; the field as a whole remains puzzling.

The purpose of this chapter is to present certain relevant aspects of the relationship between job stress and health. These include a definition of stress, an overview of physiological measures and systems mediating stress, a review of dimensions of job stress and other variables measured in an attempt to understand this relationship, and finally a representative review of studies relating job stress to cardiovascular disease (hypertension and coronary heart disease). It should be noted that investigations of the impact of job stress have included a wide variety of other outcomes such as ulcers, diabetes, poor mental health, suicides, accidents, and so on, which are not included in this review due to space limitations and the vast nature of this literature.

The Definition and Dimensions of Stress

Stress is a term which has been defined and used in many ways (Kasl, 1986). It may sometimes refer to a "stressor" or objective environmental stimulus, a subjective perception, a response or reaction (for example, elevated cortisol may imply stress), or finally, in a relational sense, excess demands beyond an individual's capacity to meet them. Thus, exactly what is meant by stress can often be ambiguous. McCabe and Schneiderman (1985) define stress as change or threat of change demanding adaptation by an organism. A stressor would be the stimulus for change. Adaptation could typically include behavioral or physiochemical (heart rate, norepinephrine) measures. The focus here is largely on a response. A definition which focuses more both on subjective perception and a relational term is that definition offered by Lazarus (1966) where stress is a psychological process defined as the internal state of the individual who perceives threats to his or her physical or psychic well-being.

Physiological Reactions to Stress

Physiological reactions to stress may include (McCabe & Schneider-man, 1985) the "fight or flight" response or defense reaction whereby appropriate coping responses are attempted and the organism prepares for action. This often involves increased flow of blood to the muscles (with accompanying vasodilation) to handle increased muscle activity, increased heart rate, increased cardiac output, and increased blood pressure.

A second response to stress is a "conservation/withdrawal" or immobilizing reaction where active coping does not seem available, and increased vigilance of the situation occurs. In contrast to the fight or flight reaction, this reaction conserves blood flow (that is, constricts blood vessels to muscles) and blood pressure may be increased through increases in vascular resistance. Cardiac output and heart rate, mediated through the vagus, decrease. A person may freeze or feel faint.

Two of the major systems mediating physiological changes during stress are the sympatho-adreno medullary system (SAM) and the hypothalamic, pituitary, adreno- cortical system (HPAC). Briefly, activation of the SAM system involves the release of the catecholamines: norepinephrine from the nerve terminals primarily and epinephrine from the adrenal medulla. Concomitant increases in heart rate, cardiac output, total peripheral resistance, systolic blood pressure, and platelet aggregation are found, together with reduced threshold for ventricular fibrillation. Activation of the HPAC system involves release of corticotropin, releasing factor, adreno- corticotrophic hormone, and finally adreno corticosteroids (such as cortisol). Concomitant elevations of blood pressure, sensitivity to catecholamines, cholesterol level, potassium excretion and platelet mass are found together with a drop in high-density lipoprotein (HDL, or the "good" part of cholesterol). Chronically, these reactions may lead to coronary artery disease; acutely, they may be associated with sudden death (Siltanen, 1987).

The specific pattern of hormonal change during stress may differ depending on the nature of the stress. Factors identified include effort, distress and control. For example, there is some evidence that effort with distress is accompanied by increases in catecholamines and cortisol, whereas effort without distress is accompanied by increases in catecholamines but not cortisol (Frankenhaeuser, 1983). Mason (1975) also found no cortisol increase in the absence of psychological threat. Dimsdale and Moss (1980) noted a relatively greater increase in norepinephrine versus epinephrine in physical stress compared to a relatively greater increase in epinephrine over norepinephrine in psychological stress. Having control (self-paced versus machine-paced work on an assembly line) has been associated with lower output of urinary catecholamines (Frankenhaeuser, 1979). Finally, cortisol and prolactin levels in cerebrospinal fluid have been associated with style of expressing pain emotions (Alaranta, Hurme, Lahtela, & Hyyppa, 1983). All of this evidence suggests that in addition to measuring stress hormones, the specific pattern may be important as well.

Physiological Measures

Thus, as suggested by the preceding discussion, there are a multitude of physiological measures of stress. Cardiovascular measures include: static blood pressure, ambulatory blood pressure, heart rate, cardiac output, peripheral resistance, ejection fraction, ischemia, or heart rhythm irregularities. Other arousal measures include galvanic skin response, respiratory rate, and skin temperature. Stress hormones include, in addition to norepinephrine, epinephrine and cortisol, other neurochemical substances such as dopamine, prolactin, and somatotropin (Hyyppa, 1987). Attention must be paid to the source of measurement as well. For example, 17-OCHS, a steroid derivative, may be measured in blood plasma, urine, and saliva. Other measures include immune markers and functional assays, uric acid, blood sugar, and cholesterol. Further reading on physiological measures of stress may be found in Fried, Rowland, and Ferris (1984) and Baum, Grunberg, and Singer (1982). A word of caution in using these measures is in order. First, the half-life of some substances is quite short (such as epinephrine measured in plasma), so one must decide whether acute or chronic reactions are being investigated. Second, several substances such as cortisol, have a natural diurnal rhythm, so time of day must be controlled for. Third, exogenous substances such as coffee (France & Ditto, 1989), cigarette smoke, or medications may alter physiologic reactivity in stress and thus may be confounds in this type of research. Fourth, physical activity or position such as posture (Gellman et al., 1988) has been shown to influence such measures as blood pressure. So, for example, if one is interested in whether blood pressure is higher at work than at home, one must take into account that people may stand more at certain types of jobs. All of this suggests that if one is to use a physiological measure as an indicator of stress, it must be a complex and careful endeavor.

Dimensions of Job Stress

Many facets of job stress have been suggested in the literature (Holt, 1982; Beehr & Newman, 1978; Cooper, 1985; House, 1974). A representative review combined with experimental observations suggest two broad categories: objectively and subjectively defined. There is obviously some overlap between the two; as for example, pay can be viewed objectively in terms of dollar amounts or subjectively in terms of whether it meets a person's desires for status or material goods.

Some representative objectively defined dimensions include: (1) Physical properties of the job, such as noise, temperature, and hazards. (2) Amount of time working, such as number of hours per week; or, for shift work, whether time is flexible and involves breaks. (3) Workload which may refer to amount, or amount per unit time, such as in machine pacing or in the number of patients needing care during a nursing shift. (4) Rewards, such as pay. (5) Change in job, such as job loss, demotion, or shifts in the promotions ratio.

Representative subjectively defined dimensions include: (1) Workload, which may include having too much to do for the person's resources; having work tasks that are too difficult (overload), or having a boring vigilant monotonous task (underload), or not having enough time to do the work (time pressure). (2) Heavy responsibility for people or large amounts of money—situations in which a small error can lead to large damage (for example, air traffic controllers) or frequent emergencies that must be responded to (for example, rescue workers). (3) Control, which concerns whether the worker can participate in decisions that affect the nature and timing of his or her work. (4) Role ambiguity, in which the worker has unclear work objectives or no understanding of what is expected on the job. (5) Role conflict, such as a perception of incompatible or incongruent demands, or of inadequate facts or resources to do the job. (6) Career development, for example, the provision of adequate preparation, training, opportunities for promotion and growth, and respect. (7) Interpersonal relations, which include relations with supervisors, co-workers, and clients (working with cooperative or uncooperative people, and so on). (8) Job insecurity, such as uncertainty about continued employment with no viable alternative jobs available. (9) Problems and work flow, which includes day-to-day red tape in performing work, smooth coordination of work with others on whom one depends, interruptions, telephone calls, and so on. (10) Perceived equity, in terms of fairness in reward distribution, or in the experience of discrimination on the job because of sex, race, ethnic background, or physical characteristics.

It is important to note that objective and subjective reports of stress do not always agree. LaCroix and Haynes (1987), using a sample from the Framingham heart study, found that when the level of job strain was determined by self-report, the correlation between strain and coronary heart disease (CHD) was higher than when strain was based on job titles. Another example is provided by Aro (1984), who found that perceived discomfort from noise, but not actual noise level, was related to diastolic blood pressure among Finnish workers.

Other Variables Measured

While the preceding account specifically lists work conditions that investigators believe may cause stress, broader conceptual models and other variables have been measured as well. An important issue in the study of stress at work is whether the causative relationship is found within the worker, the workplace, or in the interaction between the two. Other variables measured reflect this etiologic range.

The Person–Environment fit model states that stress results when there is a discrepancy between the needs and abilities of the person and the supplies and demands of the job. For example, Chesney et al. (1981) found that Type A workers who described their work environment as encouraging autonomy had lower blood pressures than those who did not, whereas the reverse was found for Type Bs. Type Bs who described their environment as low in physical comfort had higher systolic blood pressure than those who did not. Thus a better fit resulted in lower blood pressure as a measure of strain.

A major test of the P–E fit model was a study of 2,010 workers in twenty-three occupations. The most important combinations were workload excess, job complexity misfit, underutilization of abilities and unwanted overtime. However, these added only 1.5 percent to 14 percent of the variance in outcome, leading the researchers to conclude that P–E fit supplements but does not replace component measures (Caplan, Cobb, French, Harrison, & Pinneau, 1975; French, Caplan, & Harrison, 1982).

Worker variables have included cognitive, behavioral, and affective measures. A study of dentists revealed that the cognition of seeing oneself as an inflicter of pain rather than a healer was related significantly to diastolic blood pressure (Cooper, Mallinger, & Kahn, 1978). The Type A behavior pattern, composed of excessive competitive drive, impatience, hostility, and pressured speech has been identified as a coronary heart disease risk factor, although more recent evidence reviewed in Krantz, Contrada, Hill, and Friedler (1988) suggests that the lethal component may be hostility. Expression of affect, in particular anger, was identified as a moderator variable in a study by Cottington, Mathews, Talbot, et al. (1986) where the correlations between uncertain job future and hypertension, and dissatisfaction with coworkers and hypertension, were higher for those who suppressed their anger. Another individual difference moderator variable identified in the literature is "hardiness," a view of difficulties mitigated by a sense of challenge, control, and commitment. This variable moderated the correlation between role ambiguity and blood pressure (and triglycerides) in a study done by Howard, Cunningham, and Rechnitzer (1986).

Social Situation and Extrawork Variables

Social situation, both within and outside the job, has been investigated as a stressor or buffer. In a prospective study of air traffic controllers (Niemcryk, Jenkins, Rose, & Hurst, 1987) coworker amicability, a measure of social support was protective; those rarely or never chosen as friends experienced 60 percent more total morbidity and 174 percent more injuries than the often-chosen group. Outside of work, wife's love and support was a protective factor against the development of angina pectoris in a five-year prospective Israeli study, particularly for men who were highly anxious (Medalie & Goldbourt, 1976). The home-work interface has been of increasing interest. Frankenhaeuser, et al. (1987) have been investigating the opportunity to unwind at home after work and have noted that female managers appear to have less of an opportunity for this than male managers (that is, blood pressure and catecholamine levels drop for males after 5 P.M. but not for female managers). Haynes and Feinleib (1980) in the analyses of the Framingham heart study found that working women who had raised three or more children had higher CHD rates. Thus, the interface between home and work may be important to consider in evaluating effects of job stress. Another extrawork variable often considered is commuting stress.

Interaction among Dimensions

One model that has been proposed by Karasek and his colleagues (1981) focuses on two dimensions of job stress simultaneously. According to this theory, highest job strain is present when a job has high demands and low control. Since many of the studies presented in the next section were designed to test this theory, discussion of his model is deferred.

Job Stress and Coronary Heart Disease

Many studies in the area of job stress have investigated which jobs are the most stressful. Other studies have focused on the conditions or dimensions of a job that are associated with a particular ailment. This chapter focuses on the latter. Table 9–1 summarizes representative studies of this type as related to coronary heart disease.

As can be seen from table 9–1, dimensions that have been related to CHD include high job demands such as heavy workload, increased responsibility, lack of control, problems with the boss or coworkers, and work that affords few opportunities for growth or is monotonous. The load appraisal score in the Aro and Hasan (1987) study included several of these, such as pressed working pace, heavy worker responsibility, regret over choice of vocation, and so on.

Much less attention has been paid to individual difference variables that might exacerbate or buffer an effect on CHD in the job context. Anxiety was related to increased risk of angina in the Medalie and Goldbourt study (1976); as noted previously, Type A behavior and the expression of anger have been identified as factors (Krantz et al., 1988) associated with increased coronary risk. Coping style is a variable that may be potentially useful as a moderator of the relationship between job stress and health, but this awaits further research.

As noted, sometimes nonwork factors have been considered in job stress studies. More specifically, with the outcome of interest being CHD, marriage and family (Haynes & Feinleib, 1980) as well as social support (Medalie & Goldbourt, 1976) have been considered. For example, Haynes and Feinleib (1980) identified working women with children (that is, with high family demands) as being more likely to develop CHD, although overall CHD rates were no different between working women and housewives.

Some studies have looked at particular combinations of stressors. A heavy workload combined with low levels of control may be particularly stressful. Frankenhaeuser (1979) found that machine-paced workers (low control) had greater subjective distress and higher urinary catecholamine levels than workers who paced their own activities. The combination of high demand with low control has been referred to by Karasek and colleagues (1981) as a high-strain situation. The ability of this combination to predict or be correlated with cardiovascular morbidity and mortality has been tested in several studies. Cross-sectional analyses of the Swedish working force were done in 1968 and 1974, and a six-year prospective study was done between those years as well. Job demand included the questions "Is your job hectic?" and "Is your job psychologically demanding?" Control was measured by tapping into both intellectual discretion (skill level required and monotony) and personal schedule. In these studies both high demand and low control were independently associated with increased risk of 1.29 and 1.44 odds ratios of CHD symptoms. The association held up even after controlling for age, education, smoking and obesity (Karasek et al. 1981).

Another study related characteristics of 180 U.S. occupations (drawn from the large-scale Health Examination Survey of male workers) to the results of clinical judgments of a panel of four doctors with access to medical history information, EKG, chest X-ray,

TABLE 9-1

Job Stress and Coronary Heart Disease

Investigator	Population	Study Design	Variables Studied	CHD-Related Findings
Theorell, & Floderus-Myrhed, 1977	5,187 building construction workers, Sweden	Prospective, 2 years	Workload, increased responsibility at work	Excess risk of MI
Medalie & Goldbourt, 1976	10,000 men, Israel	Prospective, 5 years	Problems with supervisor, coworkers	Increased risk of angina
			Anxiety buffer—supportive wife	
Haynes & Feinleib, 1980 (Framingham)	350 housewives, 387 working women	Prospective, 8 years	Clerical workers (low job control), nonsupportive boss, and job mobility	More likely to develop CHD
			Working women with children (high family demands)	
Karasek, Bakar, et al., 1981	Several studies: 1,635; 1,915; 1,461 Swedish male workers	Cross-sectional and prospective, 6 years	High demand	Increased risk 1.29 of CHD
				Increased risk 4.00 premature death

Study	Sample	Design	Predictor	Outcome
Karasek, Theorell, et al., 1982	2,159, U.S.A.	Cross-sectional	Low control	Increased risk 1.44 of CHD; Increased risk 6.60 of CHD death
Alfredson et al., 1982	334 cases, 882 controls, Swedish men under 65	Case-control	High job strain, controlling for standard risk factors	Increased risk MI; odds ratio: control 1.99, demands 1.47
Orth-Gomer et al., 1985	55 men who had MI at age < 45 versus 99 controls	Case-control	Hectic work with low decision latitude or few opportunities for growth; Monotonous, shift work	Increased risk MI
House et al., 1986 (Tecumseh)	288 men	Prospective, 9 to 12 years	Monotony at work	Significant predictor of early heart attack
LaCroix & Haynes, 1987	900 men and women	Prospective, 10 years	Moderate to high levels of job pressure at 2 points	Increased risk of dying 3x
Aro & Hasan, 1987	902 white- and blue-collar workers	Prospective 5 &10 year	High strain (job titles and self-report)	Increased risk 1.5x of CHD; Increased risk 3x of CHD women
Reed et al., 1989	8,006 men Japanese	Prospective 18 year	Load appraisal score at baseline or high demand, low control	Predicted angina, chronic illness, not MI, or mortality; no association with CHD

and blood chemistries. Standardized odds ratios are presented in table 9–1. As before, the results are significant and support these job stress factors as related to CHD (Karasek, Theorell, Schwartz, Pieper, & Alfredsson, 1982). These studies however, provide more support for the independent contribution of each factor and so the issue of whether they function additively or interactively or in some other manner is still of interest. In a study of Swedish men, Alfredsson, Karasek, and Theorell (1982) found that hectic work alone was not related to excess risk of myocardial infarction (MI), but in combination with low decision latitude and/or few possibilities for growth it was associated with a significantly increased risk. In a U.S. sample from the Framingham heart study (LaCroix & Haynes, 1987), people in high-strain occupations had 1.5 times the risk of CHD, and it was even higher when the strain was based on self-report.

Finally, a recent paper by Reed, LaCroix, Karasek, Miller, and MacLean (1989) examined the model's ability to predict the incidence of coronary heart disease over eighteen years in a cohort of men of Japanese ancestry living in Hawaii. They found no evidence that CHD can be predicted by a high-strain interaction (combination of high demand and low control), the separate individual elements of high demand, or low control.

Thus, while more results support the model, the situation is far from conclusive. Reasons for the discrepancy are beyond the scope of this chapter, but are covered elsewhere (Reed, LaCroix, Karasek, Miller, & MacLean, 1989; Kasl, 1986).

Job Stress and High Blood Pressure

In general, blood pressure has been found to be higher at work than it is at home (Ironson, Gellman, Spitzer, Llabre, Pasin, Weidler, & Schneiderman, 1989). As with coronary heart disease, some studies relating job stress to high blood pressure have focused on the dimensions of the job that are associated with high blood pressure while others have investigated which jobs are associated with high blood pressure. The classic study of air traffic controllers, which showed them to have a hypertensive rate two to four times that of the general population, is an example of the latter (Cobb & Rose, 1973; see table 9–2).

Further examples of the dimensions approach are provided in table 9–2. Role conflict (receiving ambiguous and conflicting expectations from others at work) and heavy workload were positively related to hypertension among rubber tire workers. Role ambiguity (perhaps related to low control), poor relations with others, and again, heavy workload were associated with higher blood pressure among workers in seventeen companies in the Netherlands. Six stressful work conditions (little opportunity for promotion, low participation in decisions, uncertain job future, unsupportive coworkers, unsupportive foreman, difficulties communicating, and overall job dissatisfaction) were related to elevated diastolic blood pressure (Mathews, Cottington, Talbott, Kuller, & Siegel 1987). There is also evidence that noise (Krantz et al., 1987), perceived discomfort from noise (Aro, 1984), and perceived stress from financial problems (Frommer et al., 1986) are significantly related to blood pressure. Although this evidence does appear to support a link between stressful working conditions and elevated blood pressure, a stronger case could be provided by longitudinal rather than cross-sectional design. Further, some studies have failed to find support for this hypothesis. Frommer et al. (1986) found that differences in systolic blood pressure by occupation could not be explained by differences in perceived work stress (boredom, lack of support, overload, pay, physical working conditions). Idahosa (1987) found that differences in systolic blood pressure between police and civil servants were not due to occupational differences but to the effects of lifestyle and urbanization.

While some studies have focused on the job per se, other studies have sometimes looked at personal characteristics that make individuals more or less susceptible to stress on the job. For example, suppressing feelings at work has been related to diastolic blood pressure (Aro, 1984) whereas ego resilience and social support (Kasl & Cobb, 1970, 1980) played a protective role for blood pressure changes in men undergoing job loss. Other studies (not specifically job-related) have identified individual characteristics such as high John Henryism (believing stressors can be overcome through hard work and a determination to succeed), particularly in combination with low education, to be associated with high blood pressure, suggesting that active coping in an environment where one is not likely to have much control or get ahead is detrimental (James, Hartnett,

TABLE 9–2
Job Stress and Blood Pressure

Investigator	Population	Study Design	Variables Studied	Blood Pressure/Hypertension-Related Findings
Kasl & Cobb, 1970, 1980	150 men	Cross-sectional and prospective, 2 years	Job loss, ego resilience, social support	BP higher during anticipation of job loss, actual job loss, probationary reemployment BP high longer if low on ego resilience Social support protective role
Cobb & Rose, 1973	4,325 air traffic controllers versus 8,435 second-class airmen	Cross-sectional	Prevalence and incidence of hypertension, ulcers, and diabetes in air traffic controllers	Air traffic controllers have 2 to 4 times the hypertensive rate of the general population, higher rate of peptic ulcers
House et al., 1979	1,809 U.S. rubber tire workers	Cross-sectional	12 measures of perceived stress	Perceived stress (role conflict, workload) positively related to hypertension and self-reported angina, ulcers
Aro, 1984	388 Finnish white- and blue-collar workers	Cross-sectional and 5-year	Noise, monotony, self-suppression of opinion	Suppressing feelings at work and perceived

Study	Sample	Design	Factors	Findings
		prospective		discomfort from noise but not actual noise level related to DBP
van Dijkhuizen, 1980	17 companies, Netherlands	Cross-sectional	Job ambiguity, workload	Higher BP significantly associated with workload, poor relations with others, ambiguity of job
Frommer et al., 1986	4,607 Australian government employees	Cross-sectional	A/B typology, company size	
Idahosa, 1987	594 policemen versus 521 civil servants, Nigeria	Cross-sectional	Six adverse job characteristics	Perceived stress from financial problems significantly associated with SBP Differences in SBP by occupation not explained by perceived work stress
Matthews et al., 1987	288 male hourly workers, Pittsburgh, PA	Cross-sectional	Effects of occupation versus lifestyle	Differences in SBP between police and civil servants due to lifestyle/urbanization effects rather than to occupation as such
			15 stressful work conditions	Elevated DBP associated with six stressful work conditions and overall job dissatisfaction

& Kalsbeek, 1983). In agreement with the Aro (1984) study, other studies have found an association between suppressed anger or resentment and high blood pressure elevation (for example, Gentry, Chesney, Kennedy, Gary, & Hall, 1983). Further factors related to blood pressure reactivity such as race, gender, family history, personality, exogenous substances and the nature of tasks are reviewed in Schneiderman, Ironson, and McCabe (1987).

In addition to job and individual characteristics that relate to high blood pressure, social and societal characteristics have been examined in some studies. As noted, Idahosa (1987) found evidence that differences in systolic blood pressure between police and civil servants were due to urbanization rather than to occupation per se. Many other studies, reviewed in James (1987), support a positive relationship between modernization (in developing countries or via migration studies) and elevated blood pressure. Another societal variable of interest is the "unwinding hypothesis" under investigation by Frankenhaeuser and colleagues (1987). According to this hypothesis, women have less chance to unwind when they get home from work; thus their blood pressure remains elevated. Finally, the influence of social context on blood pressure has been investigated by Spitzer et al. (1988), who found that blood pressure is higher when one is with strangers than with friends or family. Finally, aside from specific job, individual and societal characteristics related to blood pressure and job loss (including both the anticipation phase and the actual loss phase) have both been associated with elevated blood pressure (Kasl & Cobb, 1970, 1980).

Conclusion and Summary

As reviewed in this chapter, a fair amount of evidence suggests a relationship between job stress and cardiovascular outcomes. Evidence exists for both particular job dimensions, such as workload, and certain combinations, such as high demand and low control. Current work is not without contradictory studies and limitations. Kasl (1986) reviews some methodological issues such as the rarity of prospective designs and the absence of controls on biomedical risk factors and life stress events. Other methodological weaknesses are inherent in the varying definitions of stress (for which there is not general agreement) and in the measures used. It has been noted that objective and subjective measures do not always agree; what is stressful for one person may not be for another. The use of multiple measures—including self-report, behavioral, performance, psycho-physiological, and neuroendocrine measures—may be most useful. Biochemical measures have for the most part been underutilized, but have the potential for being a more objective measure of subjective stress than is otherwise attainable by the currently popular measures.

The evidence reviewed points to multidetermined health outcomes. Thus, while job stress contributes to adverse outcomes, so do individual and societal variables. These raise a natural question of where intervention efforts should be targeted. Do we try to change the individual? Do we try to change the job? Do we try to direct efforts at predicting which individuals fit which job? If we know a job is very stressful should we try to identify and screen out "hot reactors"? (There is some evidence, for example, that high blood pressure reactivity at work is related to later health consequences).

Finally, an overall paradigm of the process by which job stress is linked to disease outcomes remains to be developed. This would represent a more dynamic approach than has been taken. For example, is the key detrimental factor chronic stress or is it an organism's failure to habituate to it or recover quickly from it? Does continued stress that one cannot adapt to or recover from result, for example, in chronically elevated blood pressure or increased fatty deposits in coronary arteries?

There obviously remain interesting questions to explore. The search for answers is far from over, and this area will likely be one of continued interest.

References

Alaranta, H., Hurme, M., Lahtela, K., & Hyyppa, M. T. (1983). Prolactin and cortisol in cerebrospinal fluid: Sex related associations with clinical and psychological characteristics of patients with low back pain. *Psychoneuroendocrinology, 9,* 333–41.

Alfredsson, L., Karasek, R., & Theorell, T. (1982). Myocardial infarction risk and psychosocial work environment: An analysis of the male Swedish working force. *Social Science Medicine, 16,* 463–467.

Aro, S. (1984). Occupational stress, health-related behavior, and blood pressure: A 5-year follow-up. *Preventive Medicine, 13,* 333–348.

Aro, S., & Hasan, J. (1987). Occupational class, psychosocial stress and morbidity. *Annals of Clinical Research, 19,* 62–68.

Baum, A., Grunberg, N. E., & Singer, J. E. (1982). The use of psychological and neuroendocrinological measurements in the study of stress. *Health Psychology, 3,* 217–236.

Beehr, T. A., & Newman, J. D. (1978). Job stress, employee health, and organizational effectiveness: A facet analysis, model, and literature review. *Personnel Psychology, 31,* 665–699.

Caplan, R. D., Cobb, S., French, J. R. P., Jr., Harrison, R. V., & Pinneau, S. R., Jr. (1975). *Job demands and worker health.* Washington, DC: Department of Health, Education, and Welfare.

Chesney, M. A., Sevelius, G., Black, G. W., Ward, M. M., Swan, G. E., & Rosenman, R. H. (1981). Work environment, Type A behavior, and coronary heart disease risk factors. *Journal of Occupational Medicine, 23*(8), 551–555.

Cobb, S., & Rose, R. M. (1973). Hypertension, peptic ulcer, and diabetes in air traffic controllers. *Journal of Occupational Medicine, 224*(4), 489–492.

Cooper, C. L. (1985). The stress of work: An overview. *Aviation, Space, and Environmental Medicine, 56,* 627–32.

Cooper, C. L., Mallinger, M., & Kahn, R. (1978). Identifying sources of occupational stress among dentists. *Journal of Occupational Psychology, 51,* 227–234.

Cottington, E. M., Mathews, K. A., Talbot, E., et al. (1986). Occupational stress, suppressed anger, and hypertension. *Psychosomatic Medicine, 48,* 249–60.

Dimsdale, J. E., & Moss, J. (1980). Plasma catecholamines in stress and exercise. *Journal of the American Medical Association, 243,* 340.

France, C., & Ditto, B. (1989). Cardiovascular responses to occupational stress and caffeine in telemarketing employees. *Psychosomatic Medicine, 51,* 145–151.

Frankenhaeuser, M. (1979). Psychoneuroendocrine approaches to the study of emotion as related to stress and coping. In H. E. Howe & R. Dienstbier (Eds.), *Nebraska symposium on motivation 1978* (pp. 123–161). Lincoln: University of Nebraska Press.

Frankenhaeuser, M. (1983). The sympathetic-adrenal and pituitary-adrenal response to challenge: Comparison between the sexes. In T. M. Dembroski, T. H. Schmidt, & G. Blumchen (Eds.), *Biobehavioral bases of coronary heart disease* (pp. 91–105). Basel, Switzerland: Karger.

Frankenhaeuser, M., Lundberg, U., Melin, B., Myrsten, A., Hedman, M., Fredrikson, M., Tuomisto, M., Bergman, B., & Wallig, L. (1987). *Stress on and off the job as related to sex and occupational status in white-collar workers.* Stockholm: Department of Psychology, University of Stockholm.

French, J. R. P., Jr., Caplan, R. D., & Harrison, R. V. (1982). *The mechanisms of job stress and strain.* New York: Wiley.

Fried, Y., Rowland, K. M., & Ferris, G. R. (1984). The physiological measurement of work stress: A critique. *Personnel Psychology, 37,* 583–615.

Frommer, M. S., Edye, B. V., Mandryk, J. A., Grammeno, G. L., Berry, G., & Ferguson, D. A. (1986). Systolic blood pressure in relation to occupation and perceived work stress. *Scandanavian Journal of Work and Environmental Health, 12,* 476–485.

Gellman, M., Spitzer, S., Ironson, G., Llabre, M., Pasin, R., Weidler, D., & Schneiderman, N. (1988). *Posture, place and mood effects on ambulatory blood pressure.* Unpublished manuscript.

Gentry, W. D., Chesney, M. A., Kennedy, D., Gary, H. E., Hall, R. P. (1983). The relationship of demographic attributes and habitual anger-coping styles. *Journal of Social Psychology, 121,* 45.

Haynes, S. G., & Feinleib, M. (1980). Women, work and coronary heart disease: Prospective findings from the Framingham Heart Study. *American Journal of Public Health, 70*(2), 133–141.

Hinkle, L. E., Jr. (1974). The effect of exposure to culture change, social change, and changes in interpersonal relationships on health. B. S. Dohrenwend & B. P. Dohrenwend (Ed.), *Stressful life events—their nature and effects* (pp. 9–44). New York: Wiley.

Holt, R. R. (1982). Occupational stress. In L. Goldberger & S. Bresnitz (Eds.), *Handbook of stress* (pp. 419–444). New York: Free Press.

House, J. S. (1974). Occupational stress and coronary heart disease: A review and theoretical integration. *Journal of Health and Social Behavior, 15,* 12–27.

House, J. S., Strecher, V., Metzner, H. L., & Robbins, C. A. (1986). Occupational stress and health among men and women in the Tecumseh Community Health Study. *Journal of Health and Social Behavior, 27,* 62–77.

House, J. S., Wells, J. A., Landerman, L. R., McMichael, A. J., & Kaplan, B. H. (1979). Occupational stress and health among factory workers. *Journal of Health and Social Behavior, 20,* 139–160.

Howard, H. J., Cunningham, D. A., & Rechnitzer, P. A. (1986). Personality (hardiness) as a moderator of job stress and coronary risk in Type A individuals: A longitudinal study. *Journal of Behavioral Medicine, 9,* 229–244.

Hyyppa, M. T. (1987). Psychoendocrine aspects of coping with distress. *Annals of Clinical Research, 19,* 78–82.

Idahosa, P. E. (1987). Hypertension: An ongoing health hazard in Nigerian workers. *American Journal of Epidemiology, 125*(1), 85–91.

Ironson, G. H., Gellman, M. D., Spitzer, S. B., Llabre, M. M., Pasin, R. D., Weidler, D. J., & Schneiderman, N. (1989). Predicting home and work blood pressure measurements from resting baselines and laboratory reactivity in black and white Americans. *Psychophysiology,* 174–184.

James, S. A. (1987). Psychosocial precursors of hypertension: A review of the epidemiologic evidence. *Circulation, 76* (suppl. I), 60–66.

James, S. A., Hartnett, S. A., & Kalsbeek, W. (1983). John Henryism and blood pressure differences among black men. *Journal of Behavioral Medicine, 6,* 259.

Karasek, R. A., Theorell, T. G. T., Schwartz, J., Pieper, C., & Alfredsson, A. (1982). Job, psychological factors and coronary heart disease: Swedish prospective findings and U.S. prevalence findings using a new occupational inference method. *Advanced Cardiology, 29,* 62–67.

Karasek, R. A., Baker, D., Marxer, F., Ahlbom, A., & Theorell, T. (1981). Job decision latitude, job demands, and cardiovascular disease: A prospective study of Swedish men. *American Journal of Public Health, 71*(7), 694–705.

Kasl, S. V., (1981). The challenge of studying the disease effects of stressful work conditions. *American Journal of Health, 71,* 682–684.

Kasl, S. V., (1986). Stress and disease in the workplace: A methodological commentary on the accumulated evidence. In M. F. Cataldo & T. J. Coates (Eds.), *Health and industry* (pp. 52–85). New York: Wiley.

Kasl, S. V., & Cobb, S. C. (1970). Blood pressure changes in men undergoing job loss: A preliminary report. *Psychosomatic Medicine, 32*(1), 19–38.

Kasl, S. V., & Cobb, S. C. (1980). The experience of losing a job: Some effects on cardiovascular functioning. *Psychotherapy and Psychosometrics, 34,* 88–109.

Krantz, D. S., Contrada, R. J., Hill, D. R., & Friedler, E. (1988). Environmental stress and biobehavioral antecedents of coronary heart disease. *Journal of Consulting and Clinical Psychology, 56*(3), 333–341.

Krantz, D. S., DeQuattro, V., Blackburn, H. W., Eaker, E., Haynes, S., James, S. A., Manuck, S. B., Myers, H., Shekelle, R. B., Syme, S. L., Tyroler, H. A., & Wolf, S. (1987). Task Force 1: Psychosocial factors in hypertension. *Circulation, 76* (suppl. I), 84–88.

LaCroix, A. Z., & Haynes, S. G. (1987). Gender differences in the stressfulness of workplace roles: A focus on work and health. In R. Barnett, G. Baruch, & L. Biener (Eds.), *Gender and stress* (pp. 96–121). New York: Free Press.

Lazarus, R. S. (1966). *Psychological stress and the coping process.* New York: McGraw-Hill.

Liljefors, I., & Rahe, R. H. (1970). An identical twin study of psychosocial factors in coronary heart disease in Sweden. *Psychosomatic Medicine, 32,* 523.

Mason, J. W. (1968). A historical view of the stress field. *Psychosomatic Medicine, 30*(5), 6–12.

Mason, J. W. (1975). A historical view of the stress field. *Journal of Human Stress, 1*(2), 22–36.

Mathews, K. A., Cottington, E. M., Talbott, E., Kuller, L. H., & Siegel, J. M. (1987). Stressful work conditions and diastolic blood pressure among blue collar factory workers. *American Journal of Epidemiology, 126*(2), 280–291.

McCabe, P., & Schneiderman, N. (1985). Psychophysiologic reactions to stress. In N. Schneiderman & J. T. Tapp (Eds.), *Behavioral medicine: A biopsychological approach* (pp. 99–131). Hillsdale, NJ: Erlbaum.

Medalie, J. H., & Goldbourt, U. (1976). Angina pectoris among 10,000 men. II. Psychosocial and other risk factors as evidenced by a multivariate analysis of a five year incidence study. *American Journal of Medicine, 60,* 910–921.

Miller, A. (1988). Stress on the job. *Newsweek,* April 25.

Niemcryk, S. J., Jenkins, C. D., Rose, R. M., & Hurst, M. W. (1987). The prospective impact of psychosocial variables on rates of illness and injury in professional employees. *Journal of Occupational Medicine, 29*(8), 645–652.

Orth-Gomer, K., & Ahlbom, A. (1980). Impact of psychological stress on ischemic heart disease when controlling for conventional risk indicators. *Journal of Human Stress, 6,* 7–15.

Palmore, E. B. (1969a). Physical, mental, and social factors in predicting longevity. *Gerontologist, 9*(2), 103–108.

Palmore, E. B. (1969b). Predicting longevity: A follow–up controlling for age. *Gerontologist, 9*(4), 247–250.

Reed, D. M., LaCroix, A., Karasek, R., Miller, D., & MacLean, C. (1989). Occupational strain and the incidence of coronary heart disease. *American Journal of Epidemiology, 130,* 495–502.

Russek, H. I., & Zohman, B. (1958). Relative significance of heredity, diet and occupational stress in coronary heart disease of young adults. *American Journal of Medical Science, 235,* 266–277.

Sales, S. M., & House, J. (1971). Job dissatisfaction as a possible risk factor in coronary heart disease. *Journal of Chronic Diseases, 23,* 861–873.

Schneiderman, N., Ironson, G. H., & McCabe, P. M. (1987). Physiology of behavior and blood pressure regulation in humans. In S. Julius & D. R. Bassett (Eds.), *Behavioral factors in hypertension.* Vol. 9 (pp. 19–42). New York: Elsevier.

Siltanen, P. (1987). Stress, coronary disease and coronary death. *Annals of Clinical Research, 19*(2), 96–103.

Spitzer, S. B., Llabre, M. M., Pasin, R. D., Gellman, M. D., Ironson, G. H., & Schneiderman, N. (1988). *Ambulatory blood pressure in social situations when posture is controlled.* Coral Gables, FL: University of Miami.

Theorell, T. & Floderus-Myrhed, B. (1977). Workload and risk of myocardial-infarction—Prospective psycho–social analysis. *International Journal of Epidemiology, 6,* 17–21.

van Dijkhuizen, N. (1980), *From stressors to strains.* Amsterdam: Swets and Zeitlinger.

10

The Measurement of Job Stress

Development of the Job Stress Index

BONNIE A. SANDMAN

The Job Stress Index (JSI) was developed to enable individuals and organizations to identify sources of stress in the work place. Additionally, use of a reliable set of scales measuring aspects of job stress would permit examination of the relations among perceived stresses on the job and important work attitude and outcome variables such as job satisfaction, turnover, absences, and intention to quit, as well as self-reported physical symptoms of stress. In reviewing the stress literature, it became evident that the content of any measures should be based on worker-identified stressors, should be comprehensive, and should be applicable to a broad spectrum of organizations (for example, manufacturing, service, and research and development) and to a wide range of job levels (production workers, supervision, clerical workers, managers, and so on).

The need for specific or facet measures of job stress became apparent during the development of measures of job satisfaction. A measure of job satisfaction that has been widely used and researched is the Job Descriptive Index (JDI) (Smith, Kendall, & Hulin, 1969), which covers five principal facets—work, pay, promotions, supervision, and coworkers. Recently a general or global measure has been

I gratefully acknowledge the assistance of Dr. Patricia Cain Smith for her comments, editing, and advice on this chapter; and also Dr. Carlla Smith of Bowling Green State University for kindly providing two of the samples for this research.

developed to accompany the JDI, the Job in General scale (JIG) (Ironson, Smith, Brannick, Gibson, & Paul, 1989).

Job stress has often been assumed to be merely one negative aspect of global, overall job satisfaction. This assumption was proved to be incorrect in the initial phases of development of the JIG (Ironson, Smith, Brannick, Gibson, & Paul, 1989). A factor analysis of a large set of adjectives or phrases that had been variously proposed as indicators of job satisfaction indicated that five of these items formed a second principal component, only very moderately correlated with the first. "Stressful," "tense," "nerve-wracking," "hectic," and "pressured" clearly defined a separate stress factor.

Based on these and other general stress items, Ironson and Smith (1987) constructed an eighteen-item Stress in General (SIG) scale to be parallel to the JIG. Coefficient alpha reliabilities for JIG and SIG are, for a heterogeneous sample of 701 employees in manufacturing and service industries, .92 and .91 respectively; for 4,487 employees, semiskilled through executive levels of an engineering and manufacturing firm, .91 and .91 respectively.

The JIG and SIG scales correlated only $-.32$ and $-.30$ in these two samples. This evidence of discriminant validity is particularly impressive when one considers that the items for the two scales had been presented at the same time, on the same page, with the same instructions, in a single intermixed listing, and that both used the same "Yes, No, ?" response format.

The SIG, however, indicates only that people feel stressed, but not why. The facet scales of the JDI have proved very useful in diagnosing the problems that may be reflected in low overall JIG scores. Facet measures seemed to be needed, similarly, to accompany the global SIG measure. Availability of the complete set would permit further clarification of the differences and similarities of job stress and job dissatisfaction.

There is little agreement concerning the facets to be included in such scales. As summarized by Matteson and Ivancevich (1987), "Employees working in an organization are exposed to a wide range of people, events, and situations that are potential stressors. Stressors in the organization have been studied more than any other category" (p. 41). Commonly mentioned and researched organizational stress variables include job design attributes studied by Turner and Lawrence (1965): variety, autonomy, task identity, face-to-face interaction, knowledge, skill, and responsibility. Work overload (both qualitative and quantitative) has been examined by other researchers (Margolis, Kroes, & Quinn, 1974; Sales, 1969; French & Caplan, 1972). Role conflict and ambiguity have been implicated as sources of work stress (Kahn, Wolfe, Snoek, & Rosenthal, 1964). Additionally, lack of feedback about performance has been mentioned as a source of job-related stress (Fisher, 1979). Moreover, Matteson and Ivancevich (1987) in their model, Organizational Stress Framework (p. 27), list the following organizational stressors: insufficient control, red tape, politics, rigid policies, inequitable rewards, inadequate career opportunities, lack of training, poor relationships, and lack of respect.

Several measures of facets of organizational stress currently exist. The Stress Diagnostic Survey (SDS) (Ivancevich & Matteson, 1980) covers the following constructs: politics, human resource development, rewards, participation, underutilization, supervisory style, organization structure, role ambiguity, role conflict, quantitative workload, qualitative workload, career progress, responsibility for people, time pressure, and job scope. Reliabilities range from .58 to .95. The Michigan Stress Assessment (French & Kahn, 1962) is designed to measure stress related to work load, role ambiguity, role conflict, responsibility for persons, responsibility for things, participation, and relations with work group, with reliabilities ranging from .70 to .85. The Stress Evaluation (Adams, 1978) includes categories of items representing work-related and nonwork-related stress of either episodic or chronic nature. Reliabilities are not reported. The Stressors Checklist (McClean, 1979) covers conflict and uncertainty, job pressure, job scope, and rapport with management. No reliability and validity data are published. The Occupational Stress Inventory (OSI) (Osipow & Spokane, 1981, 1983, 1987) concentrates on roles and role adjustment. It provides scores for six occupational roles, four personal strain scales, and four personal resources scales, with scale reliabilities from .71 to .94. Discriminant validity has not yet been clearly established for these scales.

Ivancevich and Matteson (1980) indicated that "there is more agreement about what constitutes an organizational stressor" (p. 41) than any other category. The literature reviewed by Ivancevich and Matteson (1980) and by other reviewers (for example, Quick & Quick, 1984) does not support this generalization. Almost every variable studied in behavioral science, such as group satisfaction, company size, communication flow, and organizational climate has been listed as a potential stressor. Constructs identified as aspects of job satisfaction were also being labeled stressors. Two purposes of the current research were to clarify and explore the distinction between job satisfaction and job stress that had been highlighted in developing JIG and SIG and to determine the dimensionality of job stress as experienced by the worker.

Therefore, the items in the stress scale(s) should be generated, not by psychologists, but by actual workers, and to be descriptive of conditions, circumstances, and situations in the work place they perceived to be stressors. The scales should also be in the same response format as the Job Descriptive Index (Smith, Kendall, & Hulin, 1969). Issues of method variance could then be eliminated as explanations for findings that the stressors were factorially different from the satisfactions.

The Job Stress Index, or JSI, was developed to meet these needs and to avoid these problems. Our ultimate goals in the development of these scales were to help organizations and individuals diagnose areas of occupational stress, to help pinpoint where organizational interventions should be directed, and to study relations among important job-related variables. The steps we took in this process are outlined in the following sections.

Construction of Scales

Initial Item Generation

Workers (non-supervisory, supervisory, managerial, technical, and professional; $n = 97$) at a mental health facility responded to an open-ended, eight-item questionnaire. A sample question is, "What specific situations/happenings/events, and so on, in your present job have caused you to feel upset, tense, stressed, worried, anxious, or uptight? Please give us at least three specific examples." Responses included over 1,000 potential scale items. After duplicates were culled, the items were edited and sorted into *a priori* categories: administrative/organizational demands, demands of the work itself (including overload), role uncertainty (including both conflict- and ambiguity-type items), supervisory actions, physical demands, environmental conditions, working with others, and task completion and goal attainment. Also, the list of items was checked against the literature on stress to see if important areas had been omitted. Five items were added to the list, resulting in 134 items in total. These items accompanied the SIG scale mentioned previously.

Statistical Evaluation of the Items

Several steps were taken before beginning factor analytic work and computation of the reliabilities of the resulting scales. In one sample ($n = 241$; university workers in maintenance, operations, and repair) we included two response formats for each item. Respondents were first to indicate whether the item was present in their job by circling the Y, N, or ? next to the item (as in the JDI and JIG). If they marked Y, they then indicated whether it "bothered" them (again, circling Y, N, or ?). This resulted in a "stress index" for each item— simply the percentage of those endorsing the item as present in their jobs who also indicated that it bothered them. For example, "No sense of accomplishment" bothered 91 percent of those who endorsed it as being present in their jobs. Additionally, each item was correlated with a graphic rating scale of overall job stress (Overall Stress Rating or OSR). For example, "No sense of accomplishment" correlated .58 ($p < .05$) with OSR. Both of these criteria were considered in retaining items to be included in the scales.

To examine the dimensionality of the items, three exploratory factor analyses were completed on three samples: a large grocery store chain ($n = 500$), an astronautics company ($n = 265$), and a heterogeneous sample ($n = 332$).

Table 10–1 shows the comparison of the original a priori factors with the results of the exploratory factor analyses. Consistently no factor or factors that could be labeled role conflict or role ambiguity emerged. The items that had been called, *a priori,* role uncertainty were not distinguishable as a factor or factors. Also of note, supervisory actions and working with others each seem to have two distinct components: competence and interpersonal skills. Feedback, participation, and achievement did load on one factor in the seven-factor solution. Organizations could, however, target interventions toward, and could conceptually distinguish among, these three areas. Also, when more factors were rotated obliquely, these items fell on

TABLE 10–1

Comparison of the A Priori *Factors and Factor Analysis Results*

A Priori	Factors
Organizational demands	Red tape
Work itself	Time pressure and lack of participation
Role uncertainty	Lack of feedback, lack of achievement, lack of participation, and lack of interpersonal skills of supervisor
Supervisory actions	Lack of competence of supervisor and lack of interpersonal skills of supervisor
Physical strain	Physical demands and danger
Environmental conditions	Physical demands and danger
Working with others	Lack of competence of others and lack of interpersonal skills of others
Task completion and goal attainment	Lack of achievement

separate but correlated factors. Consequently, they were separated when the scales were constructed. The eleven resulting scales of the Job Stress Index are labeled: lack of feedback, lack of participation, lack of achievement, lack of competence of supervisor, lack of interpersonal skills of supervisor, lack of competence of others, lack of interpersonal skills of others, red tape, time pressure, job insecurity, and physical demands and danger.

Coefficients alpha were computed on the proposed scales on five samples ranging in size from $N = 265$ to $N = 4,487$. The reliabilities were: lack of feedback, .78 to .85; lack of participation, .72 to .85; lack of achievement, .53 to .78; time pressure, .86 to .91; lack of interpersonal skills of supervisor, .75 to .85; lack of competence of supervisor, .68 to .88; lack of interpersonal skills of others, .76 to .80; lack of competence of others, .57 to .79; red tape, .68 to .79; job insecurity, .57 to .70; and physical demands and danger, .77 to .81. Those scale items that lowered alpha were eliminated.

Unlike the JDI, where some items are favorable and some unfavorable, all the JSI items represent unfavorable or undesirable circumstances on the job. Items were included in the scales only if respondents indicated that the condition, situation, or circumstance the item described "bothered" them. In early administrations of the scales, favorable items such as "friendships at work," "promotion," "recognition for good work" had been included because they had been suggested in the literature, especially in the nonwork domain (for example, Holmes & Rahe, 1967). None of these favorable items was endorsed as being "bothersome," nor did any of them correlate with the overall stress rating. Therefore, they were eliminated from the scales. To avoid response set effects, the JSI items should be mixed with favorable items when used in a questionnaire.

Relation to Other Variables

Two second-order factor analyses were computed to examine the relations among the proposed measures of job stress (JSI and SIG) and job satisfaction as measured by the JDI and the JIG. Table 10–2 shows the results of the second-order factor analysis computed on the heterogeneous manufacturing and service sample (n = 701) mentioned previously. The loadings (varimax rotation) in table 10–2 suggest that some of the JSI scales represent job dissatisfaction. The first factor is clearly job satisfaction-dissatisfaction. The JDI and JIG scales loaded positively. Lack of feedback, lack of participation, and lack of achievement appear with negative signs indicating that deficits in feedback, participation, and achievement are accompanied by reduced job satisfaction. The second factor was named stress. The SIG scale loaded highly on this factor. It is of particular interest that the JSI stress scales that load on this factor are the time pressure, red tape, and job insecurity scales, suggesting that these are the heart of reported job stress. The JSI competence and interpersonal scales concerning coworkers and supervision appear on the corresponding third and fourth factors together with the JDI coworker and supervision scales, respectively. Again, they appear to be measuring the negative aspects of satisfaction in those areas.

It seems, based on these data, that only three of the eleven job stress scales are factorially related to stress in general, while seven scales represent unfavorable aspects of job satisfaction. (The physical demands and danger scale does not load meaningfully on any of these factors.) Red tape, time pressure, and job insecurity share the same underlying dimension as the Stress in General scale, but not as the Job in General scale.

TABLE 10–2
Second Order Factor Analysis (Heterogeneous Sample)

Scale Names	Satisfaction Factor 1	Stress Factor 2	Supervision Factor 3	Coworkers Factor 4
Lack of feedback	−.44		.55	
Lack of participation	−.42		.61	
Lack of achievement	−.54			
Lack of competence of supervisor			.67	
Lack of interpersonal skills of supervisor			.72	
Lack of competence of others				.74
Lack of interpersonal skills of others				.72
Red tape		.57		
Time pressure		.78		
Job insecurity		.35		
Physical demands and danger				
Work	.77			
Pay	.43			
Promotions	.49			
Coworkers	.43			−.58
Supervision	.38		−.71	
Job-in-general satisfaction	.79			
Stress in general	−.34	.74	.12	.15

Loadings of .35 or greater (except stress in general). $n = 701$. Full matrix available upon request.

Another second-order factor analysis including the same items was computed on the large sample ($n = 4,487$) of employees of the engineering and manufacturing company. The results of this second-order factor analysis (table 10–3) show a pattern of factor loadings similar to that described previously in the heterogeneous sample. The questionnaire also included other scales along with the JDI and JSI. The first factor (management) includes several scales addressing

TABLE 10–3

Second-Order Factor Analysis (*Engineering and Manufacturing Company*)

Scales Names	Management and Progress on Keys Factor 1	Supervision Factor 2	Satisfaction and Intent to Quit Factor 3	Stress Factor 4	Coworkers Factor 5	Consolidation and Job Securit Factor 6
Work			.84			
Pay			.50			
Promotions			.57			
Supervision		−.90				
Coworkers					−.85	
Lack of feedback		.68				
Lack of participation		.59				
Lack of achievement			−.72			
Lack of competence of supervisor		.87				
Lack of interpersonal skill of supervisor		−.77				
Lack of competence of others					.78	
Lack of interpersonal skills of others					.81	
Red tape				.47		
Time pressure				.85		
Job insecurity						−.50

continued

TABLE 10–3 (continued)

Scales Names	Management and Progress on Keys Factor 1	Supervision Factor 2	Satisfaction and Intent to Quit Factor 3	Stress Factor 4	Coworkers Factor 5	Consolidation and Job Securi Factor 6
Physical demands and danger						
Corporate climate 1					−.59	
Corporate climate 2	.78					
Corporate climate 3	.44					
Corporate climate 4	.83					
Corporate climate 5						
Corporate climate 6	.77					
Corporate climate 7	.67					
Corporate climate 8	.71					
Corporate climate 9						
Consolidation 1	.49					.71
Consolidation 2						.40
Consolidation 3						.69
Overall stress rating				.85		
Job in general			.77			
Stress in general				.88		
Intent to quit	−.22	−.11	−.68	.18	−.09	.11

Loadings of .40 or greater (except intent to quit). $n = 4,487$. Full matrix available on request.

management attitudes and corporate climate (custom-designed scales on attitudes toward management and managerial issues relevant to the organization). The second (supervision) factor is similar to the supervision factor in the heterogeneous sample. Factor three, satisfaction and intent to quit, includes the JDI work, pay, and promotion scales, the JSI achievement scale, the Job in General scale and intent to quit (a five-item scale adapted from Mobley, Horner, & Hollingsworth, 1978). Job satisfaction predicts intent to quit (r with JDI work = $-.45$, r with JIG = $-.57$,—the higher scores on intent to quit indicating greater desire to leave). The stress factor includes the SIG, OSR (an overall graphic stress rating), and the red tape and time pressure scales. The coworkers factor and the supervision factor here are similar to those found in the factor analysis of the heterogeneous sample described previously. Job insecurity in this analysis loads on a separate factor that also includes custom-designed scales for recent company reorganization. Note that intent to quit does not load highly on the stress factor, but primarily on the satisfaction factor ($r = .18$ and $-.68$, respectively, see Table 10–3). Other lines of evidence indicate that intent to quit is negatively related to satisfaction but not directly to job stress, at least in the short term. Perceived time pressure and red tape are related to overall feelings of job stress ($r = .75$ and $.39$., respectively, n = 4,487) but significantly less related to Job In General satisfaction ($r = -.19$, $-.27$ respectively).

Discussion and Conclusions

In sum, worker-suggested sources of stress used as items in the preliminary JSI instrument factored into eleven interpretable dimensions or scales (see table 10–1). Subsequently, two second-order factor analyses suggested that three of those eleven scales were related to perceived overall stress in these samples. Seven of the other eight scales proved to be more highly correlated with job satisfactions. The physical demands and danger scale of the JSI did not load highly in either second-order factor analysis. The items comprising this scale, however, did form a reliable scale that was relatively independent of the other JSI scales, but apparently was not related to overall stress and overall job satisfaction. These findings help to clarify the distinctions among the various variables that have been called stressors.

JIG and SIG correlated only $-.32$ and $-.30$ in the two samples, despite identical format and simultaneous intermixed presentations. These overall measures of job stress and job satisfaction are not alternate ways of measuring the same thing. Overall feelings of stress on the job are different from overall feelings of job dissatisfaction. Further, the scales that seem to be related to overall job stress are JSI time pressure, red tape, and (to a lesser extent) job insecurity, while the scales related to overall satisfaction are JDI work, pay, promotions, JSI lack of achievement, and Job in General. This separation further bolsters the argument that overall job stress and overall job satisfaction are not the same construct.

The research presented here does not allow identification of which, if any, organizational outcomes are predicted by the JSI scales. One can hypothesize, however, that such variables as time pressure have curvilinear relationships with job behaviors such as turnover, and there is some evidence that in departments in which workers report great time pressure, intent to quit is high despite the workers' high satisfaction scores. It seems likely that the stress measures developed here may prove to be better predictors of longer-term physiological outcomes than of shorter-term outcomes. Furthermore, they may predict these longer-term outcomes better than do satisfaction measures. Also, the JSI scales and their content are more specific than JDI work, the Job in General scale, and the intent to quit scale. Therefore, perhaps the JSI scales would predict more specific outcomes, such as taking longer or more frequent breaks, slowness in following orders, resistance to change, and spreading rumors.

Implications for Organizational Change

Research at this point leads to some suggestions for organizations seeking to reduce costly turnover. Since intent to quit predicts actual quitting, managerial attention should focus on improving job satisfaction. Particularly relevant are sense of achievement in work, the content of the work, and its meaningfulness. Pay and promotion policies should at least be made clear and consistent and rewards increased wherever possible. This is not to say that job stressors should be ignored.

The data presented here suggest that, in the short term at least, improving perceptions of the content of work will have more impact on intent to quit than will reducing stressors such as time pressure, red tape, and job insecurity, as long as these stressors do not reach extremely high levels. Nor does this research address the long-term and/or physiological effects of stressors in the work place. Operationally, increasing feelings of achievement will involve improving supervision in such areas as making tasks clear, giving feedback about task performance, and explaining the meaningfulness of tasks, as well as telling workers how their work fits into the "big picture."

Longitudinal research looking at short-term and long-term consequences of job stress will help to sort out how stress and satisfaction affect workers and organizations over time. Also, the likelihood that extreme levels of stress may lead to severe but infrequent destructive behaviors indicates that organizations should measure the presence of stressors and institute appropriate interventions.

References

Adams, J. D. (1978). Improving stress management: An action-research-based OD intervention. In W. W. Burke (Ed.), *The cutting edge* (pp. 254–261). San Diego, CA: University Associates.

Fisher, C. D. (1979). Transmission of positive and negative feedback to subordinates: A laboratory investigation. *Journal of Applied Psychology, 64*, 533–540.

French, J. R. P., Jr., & Caplan, R. D. (1972). Organizational stress and individual stress. In A. J. Marrow (Ed.), *Failure of success*. New York: AMACOM.

French, J. R. P., Jr., & Kahn, R. L. (1962). A programmatic approach to studying the industrial environment and mental health. *Journal of Social Issues, 18*, 1–47.

Holmes, T. H., & Rahe, R. H. (1967). The social adjustment rating scale. *Journal of Psychosomatic Research, 11*, 213–218.

Ironson, G. H., & Smith, P. C. (1987). *The Job Stress Index (JSI)*. Smith, Sandman, & McCreery.

Ironson, G. H., Smith, P. C., Brannick, M. T., Gibson, W. M., & Paul, K. B. (1989). Construction of a Job in General scale: A comparison of global, composite, and specific measures. *Journal of Applied Psychology, 74*, 193–200.

Ivancevich, J. M., & Matteson, M. T. (1980). *Stress and work*. Glenview, IL: Scott Foresman.

Kahn, R. L., Wolfe, D. M., Snoek, J. E., & Rosenthal, R. A. (1964). *Organizational stress: Studies in role conflict and ambiguity*. New York: Wiley.

Margolis, B. L., Kroes, W. M., & Quinn, R. P. (1974). Job stress: An unlisted occupational hazard. *Journal of Occupational Medicine, 16*, 659–661.

Matteson, J. M., & Ivancevich, M. T. (1987). *Controlling work stress.* San Fransisco, CA: Jossey-Bass.

McClean, A. A. (1979). *Work stress.* Reading, MA: Addison-Wesley.

Mobley, W. H., Horner, S. O., & Hollingsworth, A. T. (1978). An evaluation of precursors of hospital employee turnover. *Journal of Applied Psychology, 63,* 408–414.

Osipow, S. H., & Spokane, A. (1981, 1983, 1987). *Manual for the Occupational Stress Inventory.* Odessa, FL: Psychological Assessment Resources.

Quick, J. C., & Quick, J. D. (1984). *Organizational stress and preventive management.* New York: McGraw-Hill.

Sales, S. M. (1969). Organizational role as a risk factor in coronary disease. *Administrative Science Quarterly, 14,* 325–336.

Smith, P. C., Kendall, L. M., & Hulin, C. L. (1969). *The measurement of satisfaction in work and retirement: A strategy for the study of attitudes.* Chicago, IL: Rand McNally.

Turner, A. N., & Lawrence, P. R. (1965). *Industrial jobs and the worker.* Cambridge, MA: Harvard University Graduate School of Business Administration.

PART FOUR

Job Satisfaction: The Way Forward

11

Agenda for Research and Action

ROBERT M. GUION

I succumb easily to flattery. The suggestion that I might effortlessly pull together loose ends in the presentations at the conference on job satisfaction at Bowling Green State University, and perhaps add something useful, was flattery quickly consumed and enjoyed. As the heroine used to say, "Alas!" By the time the speakers—all leaders in the study of job satisfaction—had put the comments in the proper form for this volume, there were no loose ends. Each of the chapters in this volume is rich in stimuli for research and in implications for management action. As I stared at the blinking cursor on my word processor, I regretted my susceptibility. Clearly, I can be classed as a flattery-abuser, an addict; we addicts hate to lose face. Having agreed to write the chapter, I have to provide an agenda.

Actually, I have not one agenda, but four. The first is a house-cleaning agenda, one of trying to clear away some of the intellectual cobwebs and trash that have accumulated over the years. The idea of going home to a job satisfaction concept of pristine simplicity, yet retaining useful furnishings from accumulated knowledge, is appealing even if hopeless.

The second agenda is an amalgamation of parts 2 and 3 of this book, the antecedents and consequences of job satisfaction. Looking independently at antecedents and consequences is a bit like looking at an art museum brochure's detail of a painting: It's intellectually stimulating and informative, but you miss the grandeur of the artist's complete vision. So the second agenda is for research on the place of job satisfaction in a broader, systematic scheme of the things that happen to and by people at work.

The third agenda is less for research on job satisfaction than for relevant methodological research. Some methodological implications are familiar, but others call for research methods we do not often use—in fact, for some things to do that I, for one, do not know how to do.

The final agenda is for theory and managerial actions. I take perverse pride in putting theory and managerial action together: An academic theory in industrial and organizational psychology with no implication for managerial action is, to me, sterile. On the reverse of the coin, managerial action without some guiding theory or rationale is ad hoc, unpredictable, and dangerous to organizational health. Theory should, of course, be informed by data.

Managers must often take action without collecting immediately relevant data. With all the research that has already been done on job satisfaction, and with the results of further research suggested in and by these chapters, managers have no excuse for using data-free, hot-air, idiosyncratic quasi theories to guide their actions. If research psychologists expect their theories to be adopted as management guides, however, they had better not offer quasi theories managers can justifiably describe as data-free, hot-air, and idiosyncratic.

The Housecleaning Agenda

Articles on job satisfaction have appeared for many years. Some early ideas, and the words used to express them, have either disappeared or been put aside as quaint. Arguments about the right words to use, and about the implications—usually dire—of the wrong verbal choices, have sometimes been heated. Some terms enter the field fleetingly, disappear, and then, Cheshire-cat-like, reappear somewhere else meaning something different. Others, firmly entrenched for years, get banished for one reason or another, and then get replaced with others meaning pretty much the same thing. (It's called progress.) And, of course, we've seen countless arguments about the nature of the beast—even of the number of different beasts—we're talking about.

Some would say, with some justification, that much of the confusion and argument is "merely semantic"—a phrase I hate with a passion. Without semantic clarity we do not have thinking clarity or communication clarity or theoretical clarity; semantic problems are hardly "mere." Where there is semantic confusion, it needs to be clarified. But sometimes we get terribly exercised about semantic distinctions that really don't matter very much, and endless debate over such distinctions may interfere with getting on with more important matters.

Some agenda items call for clarification of terms and of the ideas they represent. Like any attic cleaning, some things will get thrown away, some will be kept for new use, some need repair.

Need Satisfaction, Value Fulfillment, or Whatever

Some terms have atrophied or gone out of style, or have been condemned as wrong or useless or quaint or superfluous. Quaint words include "happy worker" (returning at last in several chapters of this book), "zest" (Hersey, 1955), "maladjusted worker" (Viteles, 1932), "esprit de corps" and, in the sense of the attitude survey, "attitude" (see Campbell, 1948; Vroom, 1964).

Frequently condemned terms include "need" and "trait." (I'll return to "trait" later.) We used to talk, matter of factly, about "need satisfaction" (for example, Guion, 1958; Ross & Zander, 1957; Schaffer, 1953), without much worry about the definition or adamance about the importance of the term. Some people have been mildly annoyed by it. I've often heard Patricia Cain Smith say with benevolent sarcasm that "we don't need needs." In his landmark chapter, Locke (1976, pp. 1303–1307) preferred to speak of values and their fulfillment. Many people wanted to replace needs with desires. If the choice is a matter of personal preference, such words can be used more or less interchangeably.

Some people, however, are more fervent in their efforts to banish the concept of needs and need satisfaction from our thinking about job satisfaction (for example, Salancik & Pfeffer, 1977) or in their defense of the concept (for example, Stone, in chapter 2). Others, such as Dawis (chapter 4), continue to use the term rather matter of factly.

Must the need concept be rigidly defined? When my two-year-old granddaughter says, "I need some applesauce," we all know she means "I want some applesauce." When I say I need a new car, we all know that (a) I mean I want one, (b) that the strength of the want varies with the age and troublesomeness of my old car or the age and beauty of my neighbor's car, and (c) I'm not going to settle just for a car, but for one that offers comfort, prestige, pleasure to the eye, and so on. True, many psychologists have treated prestige (status) as something people need rather than merely want, but only a psychologist would translate that principle into something permanent, immutable, essential, and generalizable to every conceivable situation—the translation that seems implicit in the more rancorous attacks on need as a central concept.

To me, the choice among these terms is much ado about nothing. People at work will use any of them, according to personal preference, to tell us how they feel about their jobs and why. Except for occasional hypotheses detailing differences between things genuinely necessary for an employee's well-being and things that the employee perceives as merely nice to have, our worries about these terms can only take us farther away from the realities of the people we study. Those who believe that the distinctions are real and important bear the burden of proof.

Meaning of Work for the Happy Worker

"The happy worker" is one of those quaint, rather sentimental phrases we rarely hear any more. The chapters of this book are refreshing; there are several references to it, including Smith's title for chapter 1, "In Pursuit of Happiness." She recognizes, even celebrates, the vagueness of the word; giving it more precision is part of her research agenda. But in one of her nine questions, she asked, "Are there more sophisticated personality dimensions that serve better?" I'm sure there are more sophisticated dimensions, but I'm less sure that they serve us better. It seems to me that we sometimes obfuscate reasonably straightforward ideas when we try to be too sophisticated about them. Certainly, as workers, most of us would like to be happy, even if we don't define the term very well.

She divides the happiness continuum into a "happy" part and an "unhappy" part. Maybe it can be divided more finely, with segments carrying such labels as euphoric, happy, contented, accepting, disgruntled, unhappy, depressed, or miserable. Maybe such segments of the continuum could be meaningfully defined and operationalized. Maybe we would even find that such segments are close enough to being discrete that they would not overlap very much.

Maybe. More likely, a serious study of even such a segmented happiness scale would prove it to be continuous, more or less normally distributed except in highly unusual situations, multidimensional, and poorly correlated with itself over time. I don't know, but I think it can be fruitful to consider the things that real people on real jobs mean when they try to define their level of happiness at work.

James and James (chapter 5) have also dusted off this old phrase, but they prefer "well-being." In some respects, so do I. It invokes less sentimentality and euphoria. On the other hand, if it leaves out the euphoric extreme of the continuum, perhaps it is too restrictive a term.

Does it matter? Should both terms be thrown out or go back into our intellectual attics? It depends on whether these relatively out-of-fashion terms imply important things we've been overlooking in our more recent discussions of job satisfaction. The same answer applies to relatively out-of-fashion terms like morale and esprit de corps; in dropping these words from our common vocabularies, have we also dropped ideas that could be important for theory and action relevant to this thing we call job satisfaction? Periodically, I suggest, we should take another look at our discarded language, reexamine its implications in the light of available knowledge and gaps in that knowledge, and incorporate useful implications in both research and theory.

A slightly different kind of verbal obsolescence has returned in at least one of these chapters. James and James (chapter 5) describe their chapter as a continuation of research on the "meaning of work."

The term "meaning of work" is not often encountered in the research literature, but I have a personal interest in it. In the early 1960s, social critics complained that the trouble with modern workers was that work had "lost its meaning." I devised a project to study work motivation as a function of the meaning of work. It required defining meaning of work, both conceptually and operationally. In the literature of the time, I found three concepts of meaning: the personal relevance of the work, which I equated with "need" satisfaction; the structure of the overall work situation, in an information theory sense; and the connotative associations with work, as typically measured by the semantic differential technique. The results, reported by Guion and Landy (1972), were modest. That's not a surprising outcome in a first try, but I've regretted that administrative work cut off opportunities for further tries. More regrettable, the results were so modest that they attracted no attention or follow-up from anyone else. The term disappeared, at least from my reading, until I encountered George England and his international team studying the topic (MOW International Research Team, 1987). And now James and James (chapter 5) write of happiness, well-being, the meaning of work, job satisfaction, and psychological climate as at least interrelated topics.

Job Satisfaction as a Trait

"Trait" is a much abused, much maligned, often condemned word. Some psychologists seem to find it hard to utter the word without a sneer. I guess they think the word implies something permanent, congenital, immutable, and omnifunctional. It doesn't, not in my dictionaries, where it is associated with a characteristic, attribute, property, or personal peculiarity. None of these terms implies permanence, and so on. Nevertheless, some psychologists prefer words with more syllables but less historical baggage, such as "dispositional variable" or "stable individual characteristics" (Staw & Ross, 1985).

The verbal choice is irrelevant; the level of importance of this semantic debate is on par with that concerning need, value, or desire. The important thing is that people who are measured at a given level of satisfaction at one time and place show about the same level at a later time (even if conditions have changed) or in a different job or organization (Staw & Ross, 1985). There is even evidence of a genetic association with measured general job satisfaction (Arvey, Bouchard, Segal, & Abraham, 1989). To some degree, and by whatever name, the level of satisfaction of a person with a job is a function of the person as well as of the job and job situation.

Why? I think some comments in the chapters of this book offer potential answers to the question, and they deserve a place on our research agenda. First, Smith (chapter 1) points out that nonwork satisfactions (for example, home life) tend to be consistent with work-related satisfaction. Second, Schneider, Gunnarson, and

Wheeler (chapter 3) suggest that individual differences in "positive dispositions," stimulus value for others, intuitiveness, and ability might be sources of stable individual differences in affective reactions to work and work settings. In addition, they say, "An individual who is exposed to many opportunities early in life may become more positively disposed to anticipate opportunities in future situations and, therefore, will more actively seek them out." Conversely, maybe such people become especially dissatisfied with settings where such opportunities do not materialize. I've long thought that the idea of critical periods in animal development needs to be explored in work settings. Long-term attitudes may well be influenced by the events of some early period in a person's employment history; for example, consider the impact of early challenge reported by Vicino and Bass (1978).

Finally, Katzell, Thompson, and Guzzo (chapter 8) cite Naylor, Pritchard, and Ilgen (1980) in discussing the role of effort in their (Katzell et al.) path analysis. The Naylor et al. theory led them to suggest that effort is determined in part by things not in their model, such as physical condition and "characteristic arousal level." I suggest that general orientation to work (work ethic?) or work habits could be added as influences on effort. Their model does not call for a reciprocal relation between satisfaction and effort, but it is a plausible speculation, as is the speculation that both are influenced by variables like the characteristic arousal level. "Some people talk, walk, and work faster than others" (Naylor, Pritchard, & Ilgen, 1980, p. 162), and it is reasonable to expect them to have more opportunities for rewarding, satisfying experiences (or frustrating and unpleasant ones) than those who go through life at a slower pace.

General versus Specific Satisfactions

One cobweb to be cleared away is the sometime argument over the relative merits of studying facets or components of job satisfaction versus studying a more general concept. Once upon a time, a rather long time ago, job satisfaction was only a global concept. Then, perhaps under some influence of chemists, we became interested in the elements, but without recognizing that some of our "elements" (usually "factors") were more global than the data from which they were formed. For example, hierarchical factor analyses of the fourteen scale Science Research Associates Employee Inventory (Wherry, 1954) resulted in one general factor and four more specific factors. So, how many factors, elements, or specific satisfactions are there? One? Four? Fourteen? None of the above?

Different measures of job satisfaction purport to measure different numbers of facets, despite conceptual similarities. Different investigators using the same measures claim different numbers of facets. The fact is, however, that the trend in research styles is again toward more generality. We see more on general job satisfaction in this book than I've been accustomed to seeing in recent decades. Examples:

1. Smith (chapter 1) describes her Job in General and Survey of Life Satisfaction scales and their importance in the pursuit of happiness.
2. Schneider, Gunnarson, and Wheeler (chapter 3) suggest that opportunity is a stronger component of general job satisfaction than any of the facet satisfactions.
3. James and James (chapter 5) "confirmed" that four satisfaction (affective) factors are components of a single, general, cognitive "psychological climate" factor. (Impertinently, I must ask whether the general factor might be related to some general predisposition to valuate any work situation in some characteristic level.)
4. The prime example, of course, is the Roznowski and Hulin (chapter 6) argument that a general factor in job satisfaction has a usefulness akin to that of *g* in intelligence.
5. Fisher and Locke (chapter 7), although not adamant about it, look at general satisfaction (more accurately, job dissatisfaction), but they argue for aggregating more specific (less general) descriptions of consequent behavior. However, they also say that grouping behaviors by their "targets" (supervisors, coworkers, work itself) might be predicted better by the corresponding elements of satisfaction.

And that point, I think, is the crux of the matter. How broadly one wants to measure satisfaction depends more on purposes than on theoretical imperative. Smith (1985) pointed out that virtually any

measure can be placed somewhere along a specific-to-global continuum, that measures can be constructed to fit identifiable segments of
the continuum, that a measure at one level of generality is not interchangeable with a measure at another, and that the choice of generality level depends on the level of generality of the variable to be predicted. This seems eminently sensible to me.

The Housecleaning Agenda in Brief

The important agenda for satisfaction research calls for the study of
things people want, things that bother people, and how people feel
about all these things without becoming wedded to specific, restrict-
ing terms. It is proper, of course, for psychologists to develop theories and measures of their theoretical variables. It is also proper to
stop now and then to see if the people we intend to study would offer
different variables for study. If they do, our theories may prosper.
They may even prosper if we reexamine unfashionable terms like
happiness or morale as workers understand them. Are such popular
concepts a mish-mash of unrelated variables, or do they have some
identifiable unity? Do they have peculiar, segmented distributions or
normal ones?

   The agenda, at least as I want it, calls for the study of what work
means to the people who do it. Meaning can be studied on several
fronts and at different levels. Meaningfulness may not be the same as
meaning; if meaning is essentially descriptive, and meaningfulness
affective, we need to know that distinction and account for the
possibility that the same descriptive meaning can vary in meaningfulness for different people.

   The agenda calls for more of us to bring out into the open once-
unpopular ideas about job satisfaction level as a somewhat general
trait. It calls for serious attention to the development of such a trait,
particularly to such influences as characteristic arousal levels or early
work experiences. Perhaps more than any other agenda item, successful attention to this one may influence the way we think about
job satisfaction and the kinds of actions we take to promote it.

   Finally, the agenda calls for clean, articulate thinking leading to
hypotheses formulated carefully enough that the appropriate levels
of generality of measurement are clearly established.

Job Satisfaction in Its Context

The Importance of Opportunity

I was fascinated by the chapter on opportunity (chapter 3). It seems obvious, now that it has been pointed out, that people with great expectations (that is, opportunities) will like their jobs more than those who see no special opportunities.

Surely the concept of opportunity means more now than the traditional opportunity for promotion. For one thing, the chapter makes me consider a good many opportunities associated with chances for promotion. What might a specific promotion opportunity entail for a specific person? In addition to opportunities for pay hikes, challenge, and cooperation from coworkers, I'd add opportunities for prestige or power. In fact, some other opportunities might be seen, some of them negatively: opportunities to take work home every night, opportunities for extended periods of travel, and so on.

Schneider, Gunnarson, & Wheeler correctly point out that demographic variables have not had consistent relationships with job satisfaction, and they suggest that it may be because different demographic groups in different places "may be offered varying opportunities" because of stereotypes or prejudices about the group. It is not clear whether they (the authors) are interested in the actual opportunities offered or in the individual perceptions of those opportunities. Contemporary writings of, for example, black authors vary widely in the degree to which they argue for having more opportunities offered as opposed to finding more opportunities—that is, in the degree to which they attribute the black plight to the racism of nonblacks.[1] If such variability can be found equally among those who are not authors, might it not account for some of the inconsistency in the results of demographic studies?

Another intriguing part of their chapter is "Proposition 2," saying that "people are predisposed to seek opportunity." They go on to specify potential moderators of such seeking: positiveness, intuitiveness, and ability. Confirmation of their proposition, and the further consideration of other psychologically relevant moderators, create a research agenda that will take a long time to cover.

Person–Environment Fit

When Lewin said that behavior is a function of the person and the environment, he did not specify the nature of the function. Both personal and environmental variables may have additive effects. Their interaction may influence behavior. Lewin's topological approach suggested a spatial congruence of person and environment, assessed in more familiar Cartesian terms by some form of profile matching. This is what I usually think of as P–E fit, although Dawis (chapter 4) sees P–E fit as a kind of surrogate for the multiplicative interaction.

The methodological question of how best to consolidate personal and environmental variables is important; chronologically, it comes before theoretical tests of contributions of consolidations. More interesting, I think, is Dawis's statement, "P–E fit is, of course, only one of several possible predictors of job satisfaction. Conversely, job satisfaction is only one of several consequences of P–E fit." The first interesting thing about this quotation is that it places job satisfaction squarely in the role of a dependent variable—the variable to be explained, predicted, and maybe improved. The familiar comment that job satisfaction is worthy of study in its own right usually implies, at least, the humanistic view that (a) people at work deserve to derive some sense of satisfaction from working, and (b) psychological research should lead to ways to change persons or environments, or both, to increase job satisfaction. The second thing that interests me is that this quotation is explicitly multidimensional. It says that the broad picture includes more than a bivariate correlation of a fit measure and a satisfaction measure—that there are multiple effects of fit and that fit is one of the multiple causes of satisfaction. Schneider, Gunnarson, and Wheeler (chapter 3) also identify several correlates of P–E fit, and they indicate that fit measures should include prospective fit (opportunity to fit) as well as a description of presently perceived reality. Perhaps P–E fit, both current and prospective, should have a place in a model like that presented by Katzell, Thompson, and Guzzo (chapter 8).

Fit itself might be a predictable, subjective phenomenon, worthy of study and change in its own right. Both personal and environmental variables can be changed, changing the degree of fit. Human factors engineering, for example, has a long history of "objective" environmental changes to make the environment more "user-friendly" for the person—that is, improving the fit. Changing the subjective view of the environment (presumably what James and James and others mean by "psychological climate") may involve changing the person; for example, realistic job previews, special orientation programs, mentoring, training programs, participative management—all of these are things that can be done in organizations to change people's attitudes, skills, and perceptions. Such changes might improve, or at least modify, subjective P–E fit. The research agenda should call for work on all of these things and more.

The P–E fit concept seems to be treated most often as a global variable; operationally, every one answers the same questions and the answers yield a single numerical score. According to Dawis, the Minnesota work was stimulated by the Schaffer (1953) monograph. If so, then maybe the degree of fit for the one most-important need may be different from a more general matching of a set of needs and reinforcers. This is a line of thinking that seems to have been both started by Schaffer and ended with him. I suggest we reexamine it.

Drawing on the moderating effect of growth-need strength in predictions of job satisfaction, Schneider, Gunnarson, and Wheeler (chapter 3) conclude that P–E fit is an important variable. In contrast, Ironson (chapter 9) mentions that concept without enthusiasm in her discussion of stress. Are these differences due to differences in what pleases the respective authors? Probably not. Does P–E fit have a stronger relationship to job satisfaction than to stress? No clear evidence supports this relationship. Have the methods of investigation cited by these two authors differed enough to account for the different views? We can't say for sure. In any case, the research agenda can include the role of P–E fit in both methodological and substantive components. Is a multiplicative statement, or a congruence measure, the best or only way to identify interactions between personal and environmental variables, or can we get at these interactions in other ways? Does the simple correlation of a fit measure and some other, dependent variable describe the relationship adequately, or is that relationship complex enough to require multivariate analysis? I suspect the latter, and recommend P–E fit for inclusion in structural equation models.

Job Satisfaction as a Predictor

Some data have been described in this book in which job satisfaction has been used in the prediction of performance, stress, or health. In many cases, it would be more accurate to say that dissatisfaction has been examined as a predictor. The implication is that certain behaviors or certain outcomes are more likely to be predicted from the dissatisfaction portion of the scale than from the satisfaction end.

Be that as it may, there are other potential outcomes worth studying, and we should not have our agenda for thinking restricted to the three mentioned here. Neither should it be restricted to the standard view that a specified outcome has some algebraic, functional relationship to satisfaction or dissatisfaction.

CHOICE AND THE SUBSTITUTABILTY OF BEHAVIORS. The most conventional research paradigms call for a single dependent variable and one or more independent variables; the same variables are measured for every subject in the study. This convention is restrictive. It does not allow our research to study systematically what we observe regularly in everyday life. Given a stimulus, the kind that can become an independent variable in research, different people may react quite differently. For example, given warning of a hurricane or tornado or other natural disaster, some people will get as far away as possible as quickly as possible, others will immediately seek more-or-less appropriate shelter, and some will stay out as long as they can to watch it come. If a researcher were to try to predict any one of these behavioral choices from a scale measuring attitudes toward natural disasters, and ignore the other options, the prediction would not be very good. As a generality, when we try to predict a specific behavior from a specific attitude scale, we rarely do very well; the specific behavior we want to predict may not be the behavior of choice for some of the people we study.

The point is made by both Roznowski and Hulin (chapter 6) and Fisher and Locke (chapter 7). Both argue, in somewhat different ways, for the grouping of behaviors into "behavioral families" (the Roznowski and Hulin term) and doing research on the choices people make. Fisher and Locke may be somewhat closer to a traditional paradigm by saying that their "new look" requires a "shift to multiact criteria as the outcomes of job affect"—"an aggregated measure of a variety of acts on the job." By aggregating multiple criteria, one is in effect emphasizing the general factor among them; perhaps a better way to describe it is extracting a common ingredient from them. Fisher and Locke seem to be less insistent on similar generality in the attitude measures than Roznowski and Hulin, but they do seem to call for corresponding levels of generalization on both sides of the prediction equation; for example, the aggregated measure of behaviors with supervisors as targets would, they say, be predicted better by attitude toward supervisor than by some generalized job satisfaction scale. The point is clear, it seems obvious, it has been made before (for example, Smith, 1985), and I wonder why it is necessary—and it is—to repeat it.

I find compelling the Roznowski and Hulin concept of the family of behaviors, from which different people may make different choices. Their notion differs from the aggregation notion in important ways. Their examples suggest that behaviors in a family may be mutually exclusive; choosing one may remove the opportunity for choosing another. If so, they cannot be combined or aggregated. One might, of course, abstract from each behavior in the family the salient ingredient (such as favorability toward an attitude object) and predict that. If the behaviors are not mutually exclusive, if all those in a family can be measured in some way for all subjects in a research study, we might look for a first principal component as the "salient ingredient." Frankly, I have no idea how to go about looking for the salient ingredient among a set of mutually exclusive choices.

The clustering of behaviors into families implies knowledge—or guesses—about such common characteristics, but it does not require that they be scaled or predicted in order to to predict that people at a given attitude level are likely to engage in one or more of the behaviors in the set. This is the concept of substitutability—that one behavior or variable is substitutable for another—which I find compelling.

Almost anyone, reading about the four behavioral families described by Roznowski and Hulin, can quarrel with something, but to what end? Quarrels would be essentially free of data and, moreover, would miss the point that we need to get on with research to identify such families—and that data and theory should go hand in hand in governing such research.

THE PREDICTION OF PERFORMANCE. Katzell, Thompson, and Guzzo (chapter 8) set up a path diagram to suggest, among other things, (a) that job satisfaction mediates the relation of rewards to performance, and (b) that goals and effort mediate the satisfaction-performance relationship. The model is necessarily longitudinal in nature, unlike most bivariate cross-sectional studies of the relation of job satisfaction and performance.

In most respects, their model is supported by the data they reported. One exception is the postulated reciprocal relationship between the two key variables, which was not supported; some findings about self-reported performance were not matched for performance ratings from supervisors. Both of these areas deserve further research. More important, however, is their idea that performance and satisfaction are covarying outcomes of managerial practices (interventions) and that both of these have several determinants.

The research agenda must include the development and testing of other multivariate, longitudinal models. Many kinds of interventions have been promoted by industrial and organizational psychologists. Those of us interested in selection have shown bivariate correlations aplenty between abilities and performance; we've rarely shown such correlations of ability with satisfaction. Would the level of relevant ability have these covarying outcomes if studied in the context of extrinsic and intrinsic rewards, goal achievement, and effort? Would some kinds of training and development, or early work experiences, or realistic job previews, or participative decision making, show stronger relationships to these dual outcomes if studied in such a context? Maybe not—but our understanding of the effects and effectiveness of these activities would surely be enhanced.

THE PREDICTION OF STRESS AND HEALTH. My wife once exclaimed, "No matter what I'm doing, I ought to be doing something else." It was clearly an expression of frustration, it might have been an indication of felt stress, but was it necessarily an expression of her dissatisfaction with the things she was doing? Asked differently, would dissatisfaction and stress be "covarying outcomes"? From the review by Ironson (chapter 9), we must conclude that the evidence that stress or health is predictable from satisfaction measures is slim indeed.

We need to recognize that little of the research reported to date has been as comprehensive as that reported by Katzell, Thompson, and Guzzo in chapter 8. However, the one path analysis I know best didn't support such a relationship. Papper (1983) postulated a path from perceived workload (assumed to be a central component of perceived stress) to satisfaction with the work itself. The path coefficient was not significant, and deleting the path improved the fit of model and data.

One study is like one swallow; neither makes a spring nor springs to a conclusion. Different measures, or slightly different constructs, might lead to different conclusions. Nevertheless, I strongly suspect that further research will show most measures of stress or of satisfaction to be essentially independent. The suspicion was greatly strengthened by the research Sandman (chapter 10) reports. It provided wondrous opportunity for general satisfaction and general stress to correlate highly from common method variance alone—and they didn't.

It does not follow that I also suspect that measure of satisfaction and measures of health are similarly independent. They may, or they may not be. The uncertainty is largely due to methodological problems in measuring both stress and health.

In most of the psychological literature on occupational stress, stress is perceived stress—a subjective experience of being "stressed out"—and the measure is a verbal report of the feeling. Sickness, on the other hand, is physiological. An immune system breaks down, or an organ malfunctions, or a lesion occurs, and the person has a health problem. The existence or degree of sickness (or wellness) can be assessed by verbal report, but it's more likely to be assessed by medical diagnoses.

When it is assessed by verbal report, it generally seems to be assessed by a symptom checklist: the more symptoms one checks, the less healthy one is. I have many problems with this. Response bias aside, such a measure overlooks a substitutability of symptoms much like the substitutability of behaviors already discussed. For example, can peptic ulcers and coronary heart disease be studied as substitutable reactions to perceived stress? If so, counting symptoms in a symptom checklist is a questionable measure of health.

As Ironson points out in a classic understatement, "biochemical measures have for the most part been underutilized." When both stress and health are measured by methods other than self-report, and when both measures are used in multivariate research as possible outcomes of job attitudes, then we may find that they covary.

A Methodological Agenda

Research with Substitutable Variables

Already mentioned, but worth repeating, is that the idea of substitutable behaviors is an excellent idea requiring methodological development. I would place the substitutability problem at the top of my methodological agenda. It would be useful if we have methods allowing us to say, based on the level of a predictor variable, that "this person is predicted to engage in one or more of the following behaviors," or, for someone at a different level, "we predict that this person will not engage in any of the following behaviors." Research allowing such predictions would have many implications beyond the study of job satisfaction.

Nonlinear Functions

Consider these propositions from the preceding chapters:

1. Several chapters, notably Roznowski and Hulin (chapter 6) and Fisher and Locke (chapter 7), suggest that it is job dissatisfaction, not job satisfaction, that has important effects. Unless one goes to the Herzbergian view of two distinguishable dimensions, a most unlikely view for these authors, the inescapable conclusion is that the functional relationship of anything else to the full satisfaction-dissatisfaction scale is asymptotic, not linear.
2. Katzell, Thompson, and Guzzo (chapter 8) say, "we find a positive feedback loop, at least until job satisfaction reaches an optimum (*not necessarily maximum*) level (March & Simon, 1958)" (emphasis mine). The reference here is clearly to Simon's notion of "satisficing," and the idea is not appropriately modeled by linear regression. This may be why they explicitly say that the posited relationships are causal "but not necessarily linear."

3. Explore the Smith's watershed (chapter 1), a metaphor I like better than she does. One of its implications is that it takes years of rain drops before a stream appears; for the moment, let's pass by the implied requirement for longitudinal research and move on. The more difficult research question implied is not so much whether events or practices have an effect but of how many "rain drops" are required for the effect. If satisfaction, or dissatisfaction, is seen as a flood, how many events (rain drops) are needed to cause it—that is, what is the threshold? And, repeating the substitutability question for the independent or predictor variables, is the threshhold level for any given category of event (for a particular tributary) constant, or does it vary with the number of tributaries reaching their own thresholds (constant or interactive) for the effect? Again, the general linear model seems inadequate for testing the threshhold question; a threshold concept implies functional discontinuity.

4. Smith (chapter 1) also says, "Improving the job situation improves satisfaction for the already happy group, while having small or even negative effects on the unhappy group." Suppose that, instead of dividing the continuum into two groups, it is sensible to divide it into the eight groups (the ones ranging from euphoric to miserable) and that they all have different effects; suppose further that the effects do not follow monotonically the order of the eight groups on the happiness scale. Are we prepared to deal with moderators offering nonlinear, nonmonotonic functions? Finding moderators in a straightforward linear, additive equation is hard enough; I think we might need to figure out how to identify them when they have less simple functional relationships.

Linear regression is so easy in the computer age, and linear trends account for so much variance, that searching for best-fitting functions has gone out of style. I'm unimpressed, incidentally, with arguments saying that a linear trend accounts for enough of the total variance that finding the best-fitting function isn't worth the trouble. If we value understanding over simplicity, and if we take these chapters seriously (and I do), our methodological agenda must again include curve fitting.

If there is a threshold function, what is the best way to model it? A graph that is horizontal up to threshold and then monotonically climbing? One that is horizontal up to threshold and at that point jumps to a higher level? If the latter, should the above-threshold function stay horizontal at the new level or increase monotonically? Traditional curve fitting does not handle discontinuities; our agenda should include finding appropriate methods that do.

Longitudinal Questions

Longitudinal questions are answered better by longitudinal than by cross-sectional designs. How long does it take for rain drops in the tributaries to cause a flood in the delta? To what degree are some long-term effects of an event masked by short-term effects (for example, Helmreich, Sawin, & Carsrud, 1986)? I accept and recommend the wisdom of Katzell, Thompson, & Guzzo who regret that static, cross-sectional surveys have little power to convince relative to longitudinal, experimental (or quasi-experimental) intervention studies.

Nomothetic versus Idiographic Designs

Nearly all research reviewed or reported here has been nomothetic; it has described what may be lawfully expected—on the average. Exceptions are treated as error. Many comments in these chapters suggest that idiographic designs should occasionally be used. Maybe classification systems offer compromises such that general principles ("lawful relationships") can be sought within homogeneous types or classifications of people.

Variables now identified as moderators (for example, happiness) might be segmented so that studies of those in a particular region between euphoric and miserable become the homogeneous population of interest. In the Schaffer-like models, a homogeneous group might be people who also share the same "one most important" need (or value or desire). If the "valuation" (James & James, chapter 5) defining the meaning of work is pretty much the same for a subset of workers, that subset can be studied as a homogeneous group. (I'd argue for more idiographic approaches to the study of psychological climate, too.)

If our research designs are purely nomothetic, the individual differences that have colored virtually all of these chapters have importance mainly as error variance. For certain propositions, the preceeding sentence may describe reality quite well; that is, the general, on-the-average generalization may be the only one permitting systematic predictions. However, as long as we assume that individual differences are error, we never get a very clear idea of systematic exceptions. Idiographic research lets us study the odd case, and do so thoroughly, but it doesn't readily yield useful generalizations. It permits generalization only if one finds that the same findings are repeated across many individual cases.

The compromise research more or less controls for individual differences in those variables used as the basis for classification. If these variables are chosen well, and if only slight variation in them is permitted, then repeated similar findings over classifications permits generalization beyond single persons or single kinds of people. Identifying groups for whom the finding is not repeated may also define the limits of generalizability of a proposition. As a research contribution, defining the limits of generalization may be at least as valuable as an on-the-average kind of generalization that ignores the exceptions.

An Agenda for Theory and Management Action

Some Curmudgeonly Thoughts about Theory Building

Roznowski and Hulin (chapter 6) say, "well-developed measures of job satisfaction account for variance in organizationally relevant responses far beyond the demonstrated usefulness of newer and trendier constructs, notions, and variables." Methinks they sigh in the wind. In general, psychologists—and industrial and organizational psychologists maybe more than others—seem to be interested in the new, the different, the trendy or faddish idea, or the new word to describe an old concept because it gives them the appearance of being up to date or, if they can start a trend or usage, innovative.

We may have been too impressed with our own studies of creativity. Mischief may have been the result of defining one component of creative thinking, originality, as a "set to be different" (Guilford & Merrifield, 1960). I think sound theory is less likely to emerge from a deliberate intention merely to do something different (for example, coin a new word for an existing idea) than from a deliberate intention to think thoroughly about all the ramifications of what has been done before.

In fact, I submit that the Sandman (chapter 10) example of the empirical process of building a measuring instrument (the Job Stress Inventory) is a pretty good prototype of theory construction. It's not a great big theory, but it was based on the theoretical notion that stress is somehow different from satisfaction. To test that notion, it was necessary to try to disconfirm it, so the stress measure was designed structurally to match the satisfaction measure as much as possible. Despite the abundance of opportunity for common method variance, the correlation between the two was modest; they confirmed the theoretical notion by failing to disconfirm it.

Her comparison of the *a priori* factor structure and the factors empirically identified is instructive for theory builders. Sitting down and dreaming up a theoretical structure, informed only by a slightly relevant literature and intelligent intuition, is not good theory building. We ought to stop pretending that it is. Good theory building involves logical inferences from solid data, followed by further data to test those inferences. Theory building is gap filling. We have gaps to fill.

Return to Observation

Smith (chapter 1) made me nostalgic in describing her dissertation work. I, too, remember the days when we developed hypotheses by watching people work. I strongly recommend that the agenda for theory building, whether at a scientific or managerial level, include time and opportunity to observe. I know how frustrating it can be when the behavior of interest is internal and not directly observable, but informed observation can pick up useful indirect clues to what is going on. And sometimes, without quite knowing what we have, we can develop insights from direct observation that might take decades of more systematic research to uncover. For example, Thompson, Katzell, and Guzzo (chapter 8) discovered through sophisticated research that goals play a part in performance, at least in self-reported

278 · Job Satisfaction

performance. Nearly fifty years go, by watching people work, Smith found that "production did indeed change during the day, but the changes were related to the person's self-set goals for the day, not to her subjective feelings" (Smith, chapter 1). Or, for a similar example, the authors of these chapters have found several reasons to suspect that we should be studying families of "substitutable behaviors." Smith's observations nearly fifty years ago helped her to learn "once and for all that, although there is no simple relationship between a particular attitude and a particular behavior, people are likely to express attitudes in *some* way," and we can't even guess what behavior follows a given attitude if we don't know the behavioral alternatives available to a person.

Learning and a Cognitive Theory of Affect

Schneider, Gunnarson, and Wheeler (chapter 3) point out that opportunity implies choice. Roznowski and Hulin (chapter 6) say that a combination of valence and affect models of motivation requires a learning theory; people learn the utilities of prior behavior and the contingencies of behavior and outcomes. Their view is that the present affect and the learned understanding of what can be expected to result from certain behavior will jointly influence the choice of behaviors. What they suggest can be called a cognitive theory of the effect of affect. A cognitive theory may have been most explicit in the James and James (chapter 5) demonstration that cognitive appraisals (presumably, the measures of psychological climate) and affective reactions (the satisfaction measures) are reciprocally related.

These are beginnings of what I consider important theoretical developments in our understanding of the place of job satisfaction in that big picture. The action agenda should build on the idea of a relationship between what people think and what they feel on their jobs. Maybe this is not so new. The Job Descriptive Index was, after all, based on the notion that affect can be inferred best from the verbal choices people make in describing their jobs (Smith, Kendall, & Hulin, 1969).

Implications for Management Action

If management believes job satisfaction is important, either in its own right or because of assumed consequences, then management should focus its efforts on the workers who are already satisfied; remember Smith's (chapter 1) observation to the effect that improvements in a job situation improve satisfaction for those already happy but has small or even negative effects for those who are not. We have been shown that satisfaction tends to be somewhat consistent across time and situations. It follows that changes in satisfaction resulting from efforts to effect improvements may increase variance, as Smith suggests, but people are not likely to end up after the effort in a wholly different segment of the overall scale.

Much has been made of the fit of person and environment. Both can be described somewhat objectively or, alternatively, thoroughly subjectively. A similar distinction can be made between the James and Jones (1974) categories of organizational and psychological climates. From the perspective of management action, the objective environment (or "climate") has more immediate value because that is what management might be able to change. From the perspective of scientific understanding, the phenomenological subjective environment may be more interesting. Changing it may also be more fruitful for an organization. The action agenda should include attempts to understand the subjective views of the work environment and the managerial actions that might determine or change their accuracy.

If, subjectively, a worker feels that the environment is pretty bad, and in objective fact it is, will improving the accuracy of the perception improve satisfaction? It seems unlikely. Therefore, the first requirement for management action is likely to be the improvement of the real situation—and then, maybe only then, to find ways to assure that employees have realistic perceptions of it.

The Benediction

Thousands of articles have been published on job satisfaction. Despite that volume, enough questions remain to establish an agenda for more articles. Why?

I think the answer has two dimensions. One is the variety and complexity of the things that we mean when we think about job satisfaction, its components, and its correlates. The other is the confusion in the literature; it is the legacy of the search for little papers. When we have more studies of the scope of the Cornell studies

(Smith, Kendall, & Hulin, 1969) or the Minnesota studies (Dawis & Lofquist, 1984) or of the structural equation models reported in this book (James & James, chapter 5; Katzell, Thompson, & Guzzo, chapter 8), the "little papers" describing small studies will have a hard time competing. I suggest that researchers compete well.

Note

1. Ravitch (1990) wrote of the differences of opinion in education over Eurocentrism versus such orientations as Afrocentrism and other centrisms. Such centrisms teach "children that their identity is determined by their cultural genes.' That something in their blood or their race memory, or their cultural DNA defines who they are and what they may achieve. That the culture in which they live is not their own culture, even though they were born here" (p. 341). She identified Temple University professor Molefi Kete Asante as one who advocates such particularism in cultural analysis and who says that white teachers cannot inspire black students because they are not Africans. In his syndicated column, William Raspberry (1990) took issue with the view, pointing out that few black children in the United States have much African culture to fall back on, that there is no single African culture anyway, and that "the need is not to reach back for some culture we never knew but to lay full claim to the culture in which we exist." Many black writers criticize recent court decisions for removing or reducing the legal imperative for affirmative action in hiring. But Steele (1990, p. 505) said that a self-satisfying "white guilt" had led to "the many forms of preferential treatment that come under the heading of affirmative action—an escapist racial policy, I believe, that offers entitlements rather than development to blacks."

References

Arvey, R. D., Bouchard, T. J., Jr., Segal, N. L., & Abraham, L. M. (1989). Job satisfaction: Environment and genetic components. *Journal of Applied Psychology, 74,* 187–192.

Campbell, J. W. (1948). An attitude survey in a typical manufacturing firm. *Personnel Psychology, 1,* 31–39.

Dawis, R. V., & Lofquist, L. H. (1984). *A psychological theory of work adjustment.* Minneapolis: University of Minnesota Press.

Guilford, J. P., & Merrifield, P. R. (1960). *The structure of intellect model: Its uses and implications.* Report of Psychological Laboratories No. 11. Los Angeles: University of Southern California Press.

Guion, R. M. (1958). Some definitions of morale. *Personnel Psychology, 11,* 59–61.

Guion, R. M., & Landy, F. J. (1972). The meaning of work and the motivation to work. *Organizational Behavior and Human Performance, 7,* 308–339.

Helmreich, R. l., Sawin, L. L. & Carsrud, A. L. (1986). The honeymoon effect in job performance: Temporal increases in the predictive power of achievement motivation. *Journal of Applied Psychology, 71,* 185–188.

Hersey, R. (1955). *Zest for work.* New York: Harper.

James, L. R., & Jones, A P. (1974). Organizational climate: Review of theory and research. *Psychological Bulletin, 81,* 1096–1112.

Locke, E. A (1976). The nature and causes of job satisfaction. In M. D. Dunnette (Ed.), *Handbook of industrial and organizational psychology* (pp. 1297–1349). Chicago: Rand McNally.

MOW International Research Team. (1987). *The meaning of working.* London: Academic Press.

Naylor, J. C., Pritchard, R. D., & Ilgen, D. R. (1980). *A theory of behavior in organizations.* New York: Academic Press.

Papper, E. M. (1983). *Individual and organizational effects of perceived work load.* Doctoral dissertation, Bowling Green State University, Bowling Green, Ohio.

Raspberry, W. (1990). Euro, Afro, and other eccentric 'centrics.' *The Washington Post,* September 10, p. A15.

Ravitch, D. (1990). Multiculturism: E pluribus plures. *The American Scholar, 59,* 337–354.

Ross, I. C., & Zander, A. (1957). Need satisfactions and employee turnover. *Personnel Psychology, 10,* 327–338.

Salancik, G. R., & Pfeffer, J. (1977). An examination of need-satisfaction models of job attitudes. *Administrative Science Quarterly, 2,* 427–456.

Schaffer, R. H. (Ed.). (1953). Job satisfaction as related to need satisfaction in work. *Psychological Monographs, 67*(307).

Smith, P. C. (1985). *Global measures: Do we need them?* Paper presented at the meeting of the American Psychological Association, Los Angeles.

Smith, P. C., Kendall, L. M., & Hulin, C. L. (1969). *The measurement of satisfaction in work and retirement: A strategy for the study of attitudes.* Chicago: Rand McNally.

Staw, B. M., & Ross, J. (1985). Stability in the midst of change: A dispositional approach to job attitudes. *Journal of Applied Psychology, 70,* 469–480.

Steele, S. (1990). White guilt. *The American Scholar, 59,* 497–506.

Vicino, F. L., & Bass, B. M. (1978). Lifespace variables and managerial success. *Journal of Applied Psychology, 63,* 81–88.

Viteles, M. S. (1932). *Industrial psychology.* New York: Norton.

Vroom, V. H. (1964). Employee attitudes. In G. Fisk (Ed.), *The frontiers of management psychology* (pp. 127–143). New York: Harper.

Wherry, R. J. (1954). An orthogonal re-rotation of the Baehr and Ash studies of the SRA Employee Inventory. *Personnel Psychology, 7,* 365–380.

Index

About the
Editors

C. J. Cranny is professor and chair of psychology at Bowling Green State University. He received his B.S. in psychology, and his M.S. and Ph.D. degrees in Industrial psychology in 1962, 1965, and 1967, respectively, from Iowa State University. His research interests are in the area of personnel psychology, including the topics of equal employment opportunity, job analysis, test development and validation, and job attitudes, including job satisfaction.

Dr. Cranny has been a consultant to a number of private and public sector organizations in the United States and Canada on projects concerned with equal employment opportunity, validation of selection procedures, and job attitudes.

Patricia Cain Smith obtained her bachelor's degree at the University of Nebraska and her doctorate at Cornell University. She has taught at Ithaca College, Wells College, Cornell University, and Bowling Green State University. She worked for Aetna Life and Affiliated Companies, developed the Personnel Consulting Division of Kurt Salmon Associates, and headed the consulting firms of Cain-Smith Associates and Bowling Green Industrial Relations Center. Currently she is senior partner of Smith, Sandman, & McCreery and Research Professor Emerita at Bowling Green State University.

She is author or coauthor of 118 journal articles, chapters, and books, including *The Measurement of Satisfaction in Work and Retirement* (Rand McNally, 1969, with L. M. Kendall and C. L. Hulin). In 1984 she received the Distinguished Scientific Contribution Award of the Industrial-Organization Psychology Division of the American Psychological Association.

Her principal interests are in job satisfaction, stress, feedback, performance appraisal, and dysfunctional work behavior.

Eugene F. Stone earned his Ph.D. at the University of California-Irvine in 1974. He is currently professor of psychology and organizational studies and director of the Industrial and Organizational Psychology Program Area at the University at Albany, State University of New York. He is a fellow of the Society for Industrial and Organizational Psychology, The American Psychological Society, and the American Psychological Association. From 1974 to 1984 he served on the editorial board of the *Academy of Management Journal* and is now on the editorial board of the *Journal of Applied Psychology*.

The results of Dr. Stone's research on job satisfaction have been published in such journals as *Organizational Behavior and Human Performance, Journal of Applied Psychology, Journal of Vocational Behavior, Academy of Management Journal,* and *Journal of Management.* He is also the author of a literature review entitled "Job Scope–Job Satisfaction and Job Scope–Job Performance Relationships" that appeared in *Generalizing from Laboratory to Field Settings* (Lexington Books, 1985).

About the Contributors

Rene V. Dawis is professor of psychology and adjunct professor of industrial relations at the University of Minnesota. He did his undergraduate studies in his native Phillipines, and his graduate work at the University of Minnesota, where, in 1956, he obtained a Ph.D. in psychology under Professor Donald G. Patterson. He has taught at the University of the Phillipines and has been teaching at Minnesota since 1962, first in industrial relations and, since 1970, in psychology.

His work has been connected, in one way or another, with the Theory of Work Adjustment. He is the coauthor of three books, author or coauthor of sixteen book chapters, and has published more than fifty refereed publications and forty other nonrefereed publications. He has won a teaching award and four research awards, including the Annual Outstanding Research Award of the American Personnel and Guidance Association (now renamed the American Association of Counseling and Development). He is a fellow of Division 1 of the American Psychological Association, and a member of a number of other professional organizations, including The American Psychological Society and the American Association for the Advancement of Science.

Cynthia D. Fisher received her Ph.D. in industrial-organizational psychology from Purdue University in 1978. She has taught at Texas A&M University, the National University of Singapore, and the University of Baltimore. She is presently associate professor of organisational behaviour at Bond University on the Gold Coast of Queensland, Australia.

Her research interests include organizational entry and new employee socialization, performance appraisal and feedback, job attitudes and behavior, and strategic human resource management.

She has done extensive contract research for the Office of Naval Research and for the Marine Corps. Dr. Fisher is the author of a number of journal articles, serves on the editorial board of the *Journal of Applied Psychology* and *Organizational Behavior and Human Decision Processes,* and is the author of a recent textbook entitled *Human Resource Management.*

Robert M. Guion is Distinguished University Professor Emeritus in the Department of Psychology at Bowling Green State University. He has been on the faculty at Bowling Green since receiving the Ph.D. degree from Purdue University in 1952, and served for five years as department chair. His service at Bowling Green has been punctuated with interruptions, when he acted as visiting faculty at the University of California (Berkeley) and the University of New Mexico and as visiting research scientist at Hawaii's Department of Personnel Services and the Educational Testing Center. He has served as consultant, often as a volunteer, to many federal and local government organizations, including the United States Departments of Labor, State, and Justice and the Congressional Office of Technology Assessment.

Dr. Guion's many honors include election as president of two divisions of the American Psychological Association: the Division of Industrial and Organizational Psychology (now the Society for Industrial and Organizational Psychology, SIOP) and the Division of Evaluation and Measurement. He twice received SIOP's James McKeen Cattell Award for excellence in research design and has also received its Distinguished Scientific Contribution Award. He was editor of the *Journal of Applied Psychology* from 1983 through 1988. His book *Personnel Testing* has been recognized as the dominant textbook in employment testing for a quarter of a century. Dr. Guion has also contributed to the literature in industrial and organizational psychology with a variety of articles and book chapters.

Sarah K. Gunnarson received her B.A. degree in psychology in 1979 from the University of Virginia. She received her M.A. degree in industrial-organizational psychology from the University of Maryland, College Park, where she is currently teaching undergraduates and working toward her Ph.D. Her research interests include managing service organizations and understanding relationships between job satisfaction and work motivation.

Richard A. Guzzo is associate professor of psychology and management at the University of Maryland, College Park. He received his Ph.D. in 1979 from Yale University. In addition to previous work on psychologically based interventions to increase productivity, his primary research concerns the determinants of effective team performance in the work place. His professional activities include current service as a member of three editorial boards.

Charles Hulin received his B.A. with a major in psychology in 1958, his M.A. in labor and industrial relations from Cornell University in 1960, and his Ph.D. in Psychology from Cornell University in 1963. He was Patricia Cain Smith's first Ph.D. student. He has been teaching and conducting research at the University of Illinois since 1962. He spent leaves of absence at the University of California in 1968–69 and the University of Washington in 1975–76. During 1976 he was a member of the Center for Advanced Study at the University of Illinois. Dr. Hulin currently has a joint appointment in the department of psychology and the aviation research laboratory in the Institute of Aviation. His major research interests are establishing causal relations between job attitudes and job behaviors, developing mathematical models of different manifestations of organizational withdrawal, studying the effects of organizational technologies on individuals' responses, and researching crew coordination issues in partially automated technical systems.

Gail H. Ironson is professor of psychology and psychiatry at the University of Miami in Florida, specializing in behavioral medicine. Her rich and varied experience includes industrial psychology (a fellowship and faculty appointment at Bowling Green State University), quantitative psychology (M.S. and Ph.D. from the University of Wisconsin; from assistant to associate professor at the University of South Florida), medicine (M.D. from the University of Miami), and psychiatry (internship, residency training, and fellowship at Stanford University). Her research combines these fields with a focus on how stress and responses to stress affect physiology (especially cardiovascular, endocrine, and immune systems) and health.

Dr. Ironson has published over forty journal articles and book chapters and has received awards for outstanding research (the Norman Poe Award for outstanding cardiovascular research in 1989) and teaching (the Alumni Professor Award, University of South Florida, 1983). Her past experiences include serving as consultant to business and industry, chair of the American Psychological Association's committee on tests and assessments, and former consulting editor for the *Journal of Applied Psychology*. She is currently associate editor of the journal *Health Psychology* and is actively involved in research on the expression of emotions and cardiac disease, stress management and AIDS, and the relationship of work stress to blood pressure, cortisol, and immune function.

Lawrence R. James holds the Pilot Oil Chair of Excellence in Management and Industrial-Organizational Psychology at the University of Tennessee. Dr. James is the author of numerous articles and papers and the coauthor of a book on causal analysis. He is a member of the editorial boards of *Journal of Applied Psychology, Organizational Behavior and Human Decision Processes, Human Performance,* and *Human Resources Management*. He also serves as a consultant to a number of businesses and government agencies.

Dr. James earned his Ph.D. at the University of Utah in 1970, and soon after was awarded a National Research Council Postdoctorate. Following the postdoctorate, he joined the faculty at the Institute of Behavioral Research, Texas Christian University, where he attained the rank of professor and headed the Organizational-Industrial Research Group. In 1980, Dr. James moved to the Georgia Institute of Technology where he was professor of psychology and coordinator of the Industrial-Organizational Psychology Program. He moved to the University of Tennessee in 1988.

As a leading researcher in organizational psychology, Dr. James has been active in studying the effects of organizational environments on individual adaptation, motivation, and productivity. His statistical contributions have been designed to make it possible to test new models in areas such as organizational climate, leadership, and personnel selection.

Lois A. James is a postdoctoral fellow at the Institute of Behavioral Research at the University of Georgia. Her research interests have focused on the processes by which individuals' work-related perceptions and affective responses are generated. She is currently investigating the role of job perceptions and job-related affect as potential predictors of substance abuse in the work place.

Dr. James received her B.S. degree in health science in 1976 from the College of St. Francis, and her M.S. (1986) and Ph.D. (1987) degrees in industrial psychology from the Georgia Institute of Technology.

Raymond A. Katzell has had a distinguished career covering both the academic and the industrial worlds. The latter has included positions with the federal government, a railroad, and a major consulting firm. He has been on the faculties of the University of Tennessee, Syracuse University, and New York University, where he now holds the title of Professor Emeritus of Psychology. Over the years, he has served as consultant to numerous public and private organizations.

Among the offices he has held in professional societies is the presidency of the American Psychological Association's Division of Industrial and Organizational Psychology, from which he recently received the 1988 award for distinguished scientific contributions. Dr. Katzell has authored more than fifty articles and books on worker attitudes and motivation, productivity, leadership, and personnel assessment, evaluation, and development.

Edwin A. Locke is a professor of business and management and of psychology at the University of Maryland. He received his M.A. and Ph.D. degrees from Cornell in 1962 and 1964, respectively. Dr. Locke is the author of *A Guide to Effective Study* (Springer, 1975); "The Nature and Causes of Job Satisfaction" in M. D. Dunnette's *Handbook of Industrial and Organizational Psychology* (Rand McNally, 1976); *Goal Setting: A Motivational Technique That Works* (Prentice Hall, 1984, with G. Latham); *Generalizing from Laboratory to Field Settings* (Lexington Books, 1986), and *A Theory of*

Goal Setting and Task Performance (Prentice Hall, 1990, with G. Latham)

He is an internationally known behavioral scientist whose work is included in leading textbooks and acknowledged in books on the history of management. A recent survey of over one-hundred leading scholars in industrial-organizational psychology and organizational behavior ranked Locke's goal-setting theory as one of the two most valid and useful theories in the field. He has published over 140 books, chapters, and articles in professional journals. His subject areas include work motivation, job satisfaction, incentives, and the philosophy of science. He has also written critiques of proposals for legislation in the behavioral science area (for example, occupational licensing, quality of work life legislation). He is interested in the application of the philosophy of objectivism to the behavioral sciences.

Dr. Locke has been elected a fellow of the American Psychological Association and a fellow of the Academy of Management and is a member of the Society of Organizational Behavior. He is a consulting editor for *Organizational Behavior and Human Decision Processes*. He was named a winner of the Outstanding Teacher-Scholar Award for the College Park campus in 1983–84 and of a Division of Behavioral and Social Sciences Teaching Award in 1985.

Mary Roznowski is an assistant professor of psychology at Ohio State University. She was graduated from the University of Illinois in 1987 with a Ph.D. in Psychology. She received her B.S. and M.A. degrees from Illinois as well. Her training is in industrial-organizational psychology and psychological measurement. Dr. Roznowski's research interests are in the areas of job attitudes and behaviors, measurement issues in applied psychology, quantitative methods, and human abilities.

Bonnie A. Sandman received her M.A. and Ph.D. degrees in industrial and organizational psychology from Bowling Green State University in 1977 and 1978, respectively. She has had consulting and teaching experience in the United States and England and has worked with consulting firms in both countries. Currently she is director of Smith, Sandman, & McCreery, and her practice includes consulting in the areas of performance appraisal, job analysis, attitude measurement, training and development, test development and validation, and program evaluation.

Her domestic and international consulting has been with clients in such diverse fields as automobile manufacturing, defense, steel, telecommunications, retail, utilities, health care, social service, glass manufacturing, and police work.

Dr. Sandman is a member of the American Psychological Association, The American Psychological Society, Houston Area Industrial-Organizational Psychologists, and Sigma Xi Scientific Honorary Society. Dr. Sandman has taught at Central Michigan University, University of Maryland (U.K.), and was an adjunct professor in the Psychology Department at Bowling Green State University. She has authored papers on job satisfaction, job stress, and legal aspects of employment testing.

Benjamin Schneider is currently professor of psychology and of business management at the University of Maryland, College Park where he received his Ph.D. in industrial and social psychology in 1967. He has a B.A. from Alfred University and an M.B.A. from the University of the City of New York (Baruch School). His academic experience includes a position at Yale University, a Fulbright scholarship to Israel, and a chaired professorship at Michigan State University. He has been president of both the Organizational Behavior Division of the Academy of Management and the Society for Industrial and Organizational Psychology. He has consulted on long-term projects with Citicorp, Chase Manhatten Bank, J. C. Penny, AT&T, and GEICO, among others.

Dr. Schneider's work has three main foci: service climate and culture, organizational diagnosis and change, personnel selection, and work facilitation. He has published more than seventy articles and book chapters, as well as five books on these topics. His most recent work has been on the assessment of service climate and culture, the design of human resource systems to enhance service organization effectiveness, and research on "how the people make the place." Dr. Schneider serves on the editorial board of the *Journal of Applied Psychology* and, along with Arthur P. Brief, he edits Lexington Books' Organization and Management Series. He is vice president of Organizational and Personnel Research, Inc., a consulting firm that conducts climate/culture diagnoses of organizational functioning and specializes in service, selection, and implementing change.

Donna E. Thompson is an associate professor in the Department of Psychology at Baruch College, The City University of New York. Prior to this, she was on the faculty at the Graduate School of Management, Rutgers University, and at the Department of Industrial-Organizational Psychology, New York University. She received her Ph.D. degree from Vanderbilt University.

Professor Thompson's research and publications have focused on the relationships among employee motivation, human resource policies, and work performance; the impact of communication style on managerial effectiveness; and the successful advancement of minority managers. Her recent book (with her coauthor Nancy DiTomaso), entitled *Ensuring the Success of Minorities in Corporate Management,* integrates these three research areas. Her current research projects are concerned with individual and situational determinants of motivation and performance; the impact of cultural diversity programs in organizations on employee identity; work attitudes and behavior; and the impact of gender on orientations and reactions to work.

Jill K. Wheeler is a doctoral student in industrial-organizational psychology at the University of Maryland, College Park. She earned her B.A. degree at Wayne State University and her M.A. degree at the University of Maryland, College Park. For her M.A. thesis, she explored the relationship of expectations for future job satisfaction to current satisfaction and work-related behaviors. Her main research interests are in the field of job satisfaction, motivation, and leadership.